ENGLISH POLITICAL THOUGHT
IN THE
NINETEENTH CENTURY

By CRANE BRINTON

HARVARD   UNIVERSITY   PRESS
CAMBRIDGE,   MASSACHUSETTS
1949

PRINTED IN GREAT BRITAIN BY
BISHOP & SONS LTD., EDINBURGH

2.00

Patricia and Richard Falkner

Leslie Stephen, Hist. of Eng. Thought in the 18th c.
The Utilitarians

ENGLISH POLITICAL THOUGHT IN THE NINETEENTH CENTURY

PREFACE

THIS book was undertaken over twenty years ago, at the suggestion of Professor Harold J. Laski, who was then rather under the influence of Acton and Maitland than of Marx and Lenin. It was first published in 1933. I hardly dare confess that I am today in general agreement with myself two decades ago. On going over the text I have indeed been struck with an inevitable series of attacks of *esprit d'escalier*. I think I could say some things now better, more clearly, than I said them then. I should like to revise some snap judgments, notably the one in which I equate Mr. Churchill—the Churchill of the 1920's, it is true—with the unprofitable Brougham. But second thoughts are not always wiser than first thoughts, and they are almost always duller, more cluttered. I do not think I should be justified in trying to alter this book, which is here reprinted in its original form.

No doubt the book shows its age. I cannot claim that it was written with any remarkable prescience. The disasters and the triumphs of the last war are not foreshadowed, nor do the outlines of the great revolution by consent of the nineteen-forties come out clearly in my analysis of the political thought of nineteenth-century Britain. I do not think the semi-socialist Britain of today will appear an unnatural development from the Britain of these pages; but neither do I think it will appear an inevitable development from the political ideas here analysed.

There is, however, no reason why historical writing should be an exercise in either hindsight or foresight. This book is a historical study, a series of critical essays on a group of British *politiques et moralistes* of the last century. From it the reader will at least learn something about the extraordinary rich and diverse currents of thought and feeling on human relations from which our own attitudes have grown; he may even be reconciled to the continued existence of some multanimity in such matters in the second half of the twentieth century.

I have not meant this to be primarily a textbook, nor even an introduction to the subject. Yet I realize that it may well come to the hands of many who wish to use it precisely as an introductory study, as a guide to a hitherto unexplored country. I have done my best to keep the needs of such possible readers in mind, and it is wholly for them that I have introduced bibliographical notes in the text and a brief bibliographical appendix. These bibliographies make no pretence to scholarly completeness. They are intended solely to provide the student with a fairly complete map of the country he has set out to explore.

There has been much detailed work done in this field since my bibliographical suggestions were first made, but no one has yet written the nineteenth-century equivalent of Leslie Stephen's great book on the eighteenth century. Of recent general studies, I should like to recommend especially G. H. Sabine, *A History of Political Theory*, New York and London, 1937, and J. H. Randall, Jr., *The Making of the Modern Mind*, revised edition, Boston, 1940.

CRANE BRINTON

Dunster House,
Harvard University.
April, 1949.

CONTENTS

CHAPTER I

INTRODUCTION

THERE is fortunately no orthodox way of writing the history of political thought. The subject simply will not lend itself to the most objective of formulas. This is, on the whole, a sign of health. For when men agree on anything so fundamental as an historical methodology, they are in danger of a complete and fatal agreement. The nineteenth century, of which we are so obviously the heirs, was particularly insistent upon the value of competition. But, in spite of such pleas for intellectual freedom as Mill's *Essay on Liberty*, it was singularly reluctant to extend the notion of competition to the fundamentals of method. This reluctance we still, in a measure, share. Yet it should be clear that, if men are to differ at all, they must differ in the patterns, in the *order*, which their individual experience of this confusing world suggests to them. If this be really a pluralistic universe, how can we assume that *thought* is one ? And even if logic be somehow exempt from change, must not logic fused with such human and evanescent things as words take on something of the paradoxical quality of personality—an absolute limited by the necessity for struggle ?

This study, then, does not claim to embody the only possible approach to English political thought in the nineteenth century. There are a great many ways of studying political thought, and it is hazardous to condemn any of them. For the purpose of clear exposition, perhaps also for the purpose of constructing one's own system of political philosophy, the best way is to group one's material around some unifying idea or problem. This is the method of ideas rather than men. Brilliant examples of the successful use of this method are Figgis's *Divine Right of Kings* and M. di Ruggiero's *History of European Liberalism*. This is the history of political ideas in the grand manner, and at its best supremely worth doing. The dangers of the method, however, are clear. In the hands of the unskilled or the dogmatic writer, it may result in the barren explanation of

I

"isms" by other "isms." Its clarity may be the false clarity of abstraction. It may explain altogether too much. One need not here resort for examples to professorial manuals built around such simplifications as the rise of democracy or the inevitability of progress. Disraeli's appeal to political history shows the temptations of the method of leading ideas in the hands of a very able and quite unpedantic person. In the *Vindication of the English Constitution*, and in many brilliant passages of the political novels, Disraeli packs a complete political philosophy into his definitions of "Whig" and "Tory." It is an interesting, plausible, to many even a true, philosophy. Yet the Whigs of Disraeli's imagination seem unreal if compared with the Whigs of Mr. Namier's patience. Disraeli's seventeenth and eighteenth centuries are too useful in the nineteenth century to be altogether real.

At the other end of a convenient if not all-including antithesis there is the method of writing the history of political ideas around men rather than currents of thought. Faguet's *Politiques et moralistes du dix-neuvième siècle* is an excellent example of this method. Lord Morley's biographies of eighteenth-century French thinkers are really a history of French thought in that century. Now the use of men rather than movements, the division of chapters into "Mill" and "Maine" rather than into "Utilitarianism" and "The Historical Method," has its disadvantages. The affiliation of ideas, the focusing of ideas and interests of different origins on one point (the Anti-Corn Law agitation, for instance), the almost independent lives of ideas become shibboleths, are all apt to be slighted in the study of individual thinkers, and, indeed, can never be so well brought out as by the method of ideas. Yet the method of men has its virtues. It offers more resistance to the temptation to easy generalization. It gives more room to probe into all the reaches of the subject, and makes resort to mere summarizing less likely. The historian of movements is too apt to fall into cataloguing all thinkers who can be brought under a given rubric, and dismissing each with an epithet or so. Above all, the method of men finds ideas in their natural source, in the living human being.

This last point brings us to a difficulty which any contemporary historian of political thought, whether he seeks unity in men or in ideas, must face. What is the connection between the ideas expressed by political thinkers and the concrete achievements of politics ? Not very long ago Taine could triumphantly point out that because the *philosophes* thought in a certain—and very erroneous—way about politics, France had not only undergone an unnecessarily bloody revolution, but one hundred years later had been humiliated by Prussia. Taine's work has at least served to make the influence of eighteenth-century political thought in France the classical problem of the place of ideas in politics. Champion, Faguet, and Rocquain have insisted that the concrete grievances of the French people, as seen in the *cahiers* and the struggles of the *parlements*, and not the writings of the *philosophes*, produced the movement of 1789. M. Roustan, and in general other writers in the French republican tradition, have cherished and defended the memory of Voltaire, Rousseau, and the *Encyclopédistes* as, to the very limit of the metaphor, Fathers of the Republic. Mr. Kingsley Martin has recently dismissed the sillier part of the quarrel with the sensible remark that ideas and interests would appear to co-exist within human consciousness, and that the real service of the historian of ideas is to trace the complex interplay of thought and desire in action.

Nevertheless, however desirous we may be of abandoning the ultimate solution of this problem to the metaphysician, the modern historian of ideas can hardly avoid a haunting fear that after all he is dealing in unrealities. For one thing, much modern social psychology, from Tarde to Mr. Walter Lippmann, has insisted that ordinary men are immune to the contagion of philosophical ideas. If ideas really do influence the crowd, it is only after they have been transformed into symbols, ritual, stereotypes. The historian of thought cannot afford to content himself with the work of formal thinkers, great or small. He must try and pursue ideas to their ultimate refuge in the mind of the common man. There thus arises still another way of writing the history of political ideas, the history, to adopt Mr. D. C. Somervell's distinction, rather of opinion than of thought. Clearly this sort of writing is very close to the now fashionable social history. Its sources must be whatever reveals the intellectual baggage of the ordinary man—periodical literature, novels, newspapers, even the work of such unprofessional political thinkers as men of letters and scientists. Such sources, rare before the eighteenth century, are abundant in the nineteenth.

Now a complete history of English political thought in the nineteenth century would have to take into account, and partly to employ, all these methods. It would classify movements, it would weigh the personalities of great men, it would trace the impact of desire upon idea and of idea upon desire from the wistful and sometimes disingenuous openmindedness of J. S. Mill down through the relative simplicities of the average Englishman. It would obviously be a many-volumed work, and we may hazard the opinion that the nineteenth century is still too close to us to make the writing of such a work possible. No one, for instance, can generalise adequately about that important part of the subject involved in the phrase " public opinion " until more monographic investigations are carried through. The following study, therefore, adopts the method of men, not as the only, but as one possible, way of writing about nineteenth-century political thought in England. Yet it is to be hoped that the choice of political thinkers has been representative enough to permit some general and tentative conclusions as to the trend of English political thought in the century, and catholic enough to include some part of what went on in the minds of inarticulate Englishmen.

One word as to that principle of choice. The number of nineteenth-century Englishmen who have expressed through the printed word some enduring opinion—enduring in libraries at least—about political principles is very great indeed. Even if one were to limit oneself to men who have published works of formal political philosophy in the narrow sense, such as Bentham's *Principles of Morals and*

INTRODUCTION

Legislation, Coleridge's *Constitution in the Church and State*,
Bagehot's *Physics and Politics*, the number would be considerable. But we cannot nowadays, with our distrust of the
driving force of the intellect, neglect men like Cobbett,
Cobden and Bradlaugh, journalists and agitators who were
always dealing with political ideas, but who never wrote a
formal treatise on political philosophy. Once such men are
included, the field becomes infinite. For the philosophical
Radicals the old dynastic sequence of Bentham, James Mill,
J. S. Mill no longer suffices. Such various persons as Place,
Roebuck, Molesworth, Buller, even men outside the circle,
like Leigh Hunt or Brougham, must be considered. The
most comprehensive of histories must choose some and
reject others.

It would be comforting, at least to some natures, to believe
that this principle of choice must impose itself, like the
metric system, through some objective validity of its own.
In truth, however, the choice exercised would appear to
have inevitably something of the subjectivity of critical
artistic judgment. To pursue the possibly false antithesis of
art and science here to the bitter end would lead us even
farther astray than the problem of the relation between ideas
and interests. But the prestige of the physical and biological
sciences has for over two centuries so influenced all aspects
of what, especially in America, are optimistically called the
social sciences, that we must make clear at the beginning of
this study how far it can claim scientific validity.

Ever since Voltaire found Newton's universe an admirable improvement over Christian polity, writers on man as a
political animal have envied science its success in reducing the
chaos of sense-experience and the varying fables of common
sense to uniformities permitting prediction and therefore control. Ambitious Newtons of politics like Fourier and Buckle,
Darwins like Benjamin Kidd, have arisen, but none have
quite been accepted in their chosen *rôles*. Doubtless this
connection between science and political thought has been
fruitful enough. The natural order which the eighteenth
century borrowed from Newton certainly helped men to a
moral if illogical condemnation of the old *régime* as un-

5

natural, and hence encouraged them to action. The notion of the struggle for life, if it was used by men like Lapouge, von Ammon, and Kidd to justify aggressive nationalism, came in the milder form of a popular theory of evolution to facilitate social changes which the inertia of human nature might otherwise have made very difficult.

Yet a plausible case could be maintained for the statement that the influence of the physical and biological sciences on the study of man in society has been in part evil. At the risk of the reproach of obscurantism, we must go into this matter. Scientists—not all scientists, but certainly the best of them —have always held their laws as at best hypotheses subject to constant modification. Political theorists, and especially political theorists in action, like Robespierre, have tended to hold their conclusions as dogmas. After all, they sought to guide men, and men had always been guided in their social relations by ethical standards sanctioned by religious absolutes. Men have always ultimately sought to please God, and God is not precisely an hypothesis to ordinary men. This tendency to dogmatism was accelerated by the fact that the material with which the political thinker worked was infinitely more complex than the material of the scientist, and by the fact that experimentation, and hence the inductive method, could be but incompletely applied to the study of man. Human parents, for instance, are still reluctant to allow their offspring to be treated like guinea-pigs, a circumstance which has blocked the way to a complete study of human heredity. Uncertainty in the scientific sense had to be complemented by certainty in the sense of faith, if the political thinker was to be satisfyingly sure of himself. Moreover, political thought deals with human beings who are at bottom *evaluating* animals. Now measurement of value stops somewhere short of being mathematical measurement. Scientific measurement, on the contrary, is always mathematical measurement. Science, for instance, can weigh soil and weather conditions, and tell a man whether a given plot of ground will, at a given cost, produce more apples or more beans. It will even be able in terms of calories and vitamins to estimate the extent to which these apples and

6

beans will nourish him. It will even—and this is to date perhaps its greatest achievement over human nature—sometimes persuade him to choose between apples and beans in accordance with the calories and vitamins they contain. But in the last resort a man will choose to eat apples or eat beans because he prefers one to the other, because at that moment he *values* one or the other more highly. Taste, in its widest sense, determines a vast number of the kind of human actions the political thinker must study, and we have as yet no satisfactory calculus of taste—certainly not Bentham's familiar felicific calculus. Mathematics, and therefore science, is simply powerless to choose between Bach and Offenbach, and even, one fears, between Protection and Free Trade.

Now it is quite possible that there are laws of taste, of ethics, of politics. But these laws will be laws arrived at only after patient accumulation of data almost wholly lacking for a study of the past; and they will be laws of average, based on statistical frequencies, and not on a rigid determinism of cause and effect. Contemporary physical science would seem to the layman to have abandoned its determinism, and to admit that its laws are merely statistical probabilities. The social sciences, however, are still modelling themselves on the older physical science. They are apparently aiming at the impossible—the reduction of the actions of human beings to rigid and predictable uniformities. They are going on the assumption that men eat calories and not apples. Naturally enough they have failed.

This is probably the chief reason for the easily observable inferiority complex which most social scientists display. They must maintain at all costs that theirs are the methods of true sciences, that their conclusions are not the tentative and subjective conclusions of the mere critic. Hence the more crudely pragmatic and personal their concrete proposals, the more obviously instinctive their values and aims, the more they envelop themselves with the jargon, and presumably with the prestige, of nineteenth-century science. The worst offenders in this respect are undoubtedly the people known in America as educators, whose science of education has become a serious national danger. But in a sense the difficulty pervades all modern thought in the social sciences. The laudable desire of all sincere thinkers to arrive at truths honestly independent of their likes and dislikes has been distorted into an attempt to deny that human beings put anything inexplicably personal into their judgments of value. The ultimate goal of political investigation, it is tacitly assumed, should be complete agreement. We are all agreed that two plus two equals four: why cannot we agree that Peel and Cobden were right in 1846 and Bentinck and Disraeli wrong?

We cannot agree on this latter point, and we should surely do well to admit it. Whatever the metaphysical problems involved, it is clear that for terrestrial affairs there is a difference between judgment of fact and judgment of value. Common honesty demands from scientist and artist alike a respect for fact. But the business of the political thinker carries him far beyond fact and he is deluding himself and us if he pretends that his judgments of value—his desires—are judgments of fact. The historian of political ideas, too, is dealing with judgments of value. He cannot content himself with mere description. He must choose and must appraise. Choice and appraisal will lose force if he pretends they are determined by something outside him. If only to correct the balance, it may be well to write a history of political thought which deliberately disclaims being scientific, and which aspires to be only another chapter in criticism.

For the critic is really a reputable person, even though his be nothing but an "adventure among the masterpieces." His taste is not necessarily anarchic because it is tentative. His standards may rest on history and a common tradition as well as on personal intuition. What he has to communicate may be as communicable as a mathematical formula, though it spring from an emotion as personal as the formula is impersonal. He is at bottom a moralist in the old and inoffensive sense, one who imaginatively transmutes his private experience—his accumulation of facts, if you like—into something which other men may share. His private experience thus becomes common property, attains an objectivity as apparent as the objectivity of scientific law. He has no more hostility towards the physicist than towards the bricklayer. But he insists that you cannot deal with men in society as you deal with bricks or with an electric current. He will not knowingly refuse help from any source, any more than the architect will refuse help from the engineer. But just as the architect is ultimately aiming at a beauty which no known engineering formula can at present achieve, so the critic is aiming at a moral satisfaction no mere intellectual analysis can at present achieve.

Our standards, then, both for the choice of representative political thinkers, and for our judgments upon them, will be critical rather than scientific. We shall hope to deal with the important rather than with the trivial. But if our importance seem triviality to others, there is no way out of it. We cannot consistently call mathematics to our aid, and browbeat our readers with the prestige of science.

One word more. To study the ideas of a given man involves the student in the whole life of his subject. But not all a man's life is pertinent to his ideas. The greatest danger of what we have called the method of men is that what purports to be a history of thought will degenerate into a collection of more or less picturesque biographical incidents and psychological speculation. Yet the line is a very hard one to draw. What part had Coleridge's opium habit in the composition of the *Constitution in the Church and State*? Less certainly than in that of *Kubla Khan*, and the historian of political thought need dwell upon that personal misfortune less than the historian of literature. Yet even in the *Constitution in the Church and State* there is a noticeable failure to maintain an even power of analysis, and the metaphysical clouds in which it ends may have their source in opium. So, too, Mill's extraordinary notions about his wife afford a difficult problem to his biographer. Certainly they help explain the *Subjection of Women*, and much of the later work. But was Mill's whole political philosophy altered by his estimate of Mrs. Taylor? A doting husband may none the less be a good economist.

Here, too, we can find no rest in a formula. We must ask ourselves whether a given biographical fact seems to enter into the man's political ideas, and if it does not, cast it aside no matter how it may seem to enliven our text. Such matters, however, are imponderable in any scale but that of taste. Taste may be an uncertain thing on which to found a history of political thought, a quicksand and not a rock. But there seems to be no rock available.

CHAPTER II

THE REVOLUTION OF 1832

THERE is hardly a better example of the imprecision of sociological terms than the word revolution. To apply it to the inventions of Watt and Cartwright, to the summoning of the Estates General in 1789, to the first performance of *Hernani*, to the flight of Charles X., and to the latest South American *coup d'état* is almost to deprive it of meaning. In a narrower and purely political sense, it does denote an extra-legal and usually violent change in the existing government. But even here the word revolution, as contrasted with *coup d'état*, implies a change affecting the lives of quite ordinary citizens. Now England underwent in the first third of the nineteenth century industrial and artistic changes which all are agreed in calling revolutionary. A justifiable pride in the fact that the political changes of the time—the repeal of the Test Act, Catholic Emancipation, the Reform Bill of 1832—were achieved without violence, and a less justifiable desire to emphasize that Englishmen are not as Frenchmen are, have prevented our applying the word revolutionary to these political changes. Yet if revolution means in politics, as it does in art, morals, and industry, a real and only comparatively rapid alteration of our fundamental ways of doing things, the term should be used of the transfer of power symbolized in the Act of 1832.

Englishmen of the time were certainly aware of that sense of crisis which is one of the signs of revolutionary change. The ageing Wordsworth declared that, if the Bill were passed, he would retire to a safe and conservative country like Austria. Indeed, the parallel between the French Revolution of 1830 and the Reform Bill crisis is surprisingly close. How real the threat of violence was in England need not be recalled to readers familiar with Mr. Graham Wallas's *Life of Francis Place*. To alter the constituencies and the franchise by what was obviously something close to Rousseau's general will seemed to alter in its fundamen-

tals a constitution certainly as well established as had been
the constitution of Richelieu and Louis XIV. in 1789. To
yield to the demands of men like Cobbett seemed almost
like yielding to Wat Tyler.

The generation of thinkers with whom we are now concerned were quite conscious that a new England was in the
making, and that theirs was the task of seeing that this new
England should be a good one for Englishmen. Some such
notion, indeed, runs through all English political thought
in the nineteenth century, and is as strong as ever to-day. It
is no doubt possible to exaggerate the uniqueness of our
modern acceptance of the fact of change. Even Tennyson's
Cathay was probably less stationary than he liked to think.
But how much we are all inured to discontent and hope in
earthly matters is startlingly evident if one recalls that after
all what Herbert Spencer was trying to do was to construct
a modern *Summa.* How different from the Thomist acquiescence in the will of God is Spencer's petulant dislike for
conditions which could hardly be other than the inevitable
product of his law of evolution! Not even the absolutist
position in metaphysics, as witness the work of T. H. Green,
could in nineteenth-century England accept the highly
logical Leibnitzian best of all possible worlds.

The year 1832 is then at best a mere halting-place for
convenience in a century which was always seeking to remake itself according to a better pattern. The generation
which fought the struggle over the Reform Bill has, however, a certain unity. In the first place, as the text-books
unfailingly point out, the French Revolution and the war
with Napoleon did put a stop to any kind of political agitation, even to any kind of political thinking. Godwin's
Political Justice ends rather than begins a period of fruitful
discussion. For nearly twenty years, until the publication
of Wordsworth's *Tract on the Convention of Cintra* in 1809
(a pamphlet, moreover, which was hardly noticed at the
time) there was produced but one work of importance in
the history of English political thought. And even Malthus's
great work was the product of a closet philosopher, and
at first taken to be the best possible bulwark of the old

order. The mature Bentham, Brougham, Owen, Cobbett, Coleridge and the rest were starting afresh.

In the second place, the long tenure of the Liverpool Cabinet and its patent failure to produce even a policy, let alone a programme, led to a situation curiously like that of France under Louis XVI., where the intellect was definitely in opposition. You cannot find a competent apologist for things as they are in the England of the time. The ablest political minds—Canning, Huskisson—on the Government side are all boring from within in the direction of reform. What may be called eternally Conservative ideas and temperaments indeed there are—a Cobbett or a Coleridge—but they are not on the side of the Government. To study the ideas of the complete standpatter between 1800 and 1832 would be to study the ideas of Eldon or Croker, to study the *Quarterly Review*—not, on the whole, a profitable proceeding.

Finally, there is the commonplace that 1832 marks the accession of the middle class to political power. The phrase " middle class " had complete currency at the time, and, if it hardly received rigorous definition, it was pretty generally understood to correspond to a political and economic reality. This is not the place to inquire too deeply into the question as to where to draw the lines between upper, middle, and working classes. From Defoe onwards the English trading people, from " City " bankers to small retailers, had been growing aware of the fact that they had virtues and tastes not shared by the nobility. From the beginnings of the commercial revolution they had been gaining in wealth and numbers. From the industrial revolution on they had been reminded, often forcibly, that their new wealth had created (some indeed suspected had in a measure been created by) an altogether new urban proletariat. This proletariat, it was clear, was not adequately cared for under existing conditions. Lancashire, within the memory of man, had changed so much, done so much, and Dorset had done so little! Was it unreasonable to suppose that the men who made such excellent and such abundant cotton cloth could

also make an excellent England ? Into the passing of the
Reform Bill there went many and conflicting desires, as we
shall see, but chiefly there went the confidence of the
children of the industrial revolution that theirs was a better
world in the making.

I. BENTHAM[1]

Few generalizations are more firmly rooted in the popular
mind than the proposition that the Englishman will never
let himself speculate in the abstract about politics, that he
views with half distrust and half amusement the spectacle
of the closet philosopher dabbling in matters properly
reserved for the decently practical man of affairs. At the
very end of the eighteenth century, the fulminations of
Burke against French political metaphysicians strengthened
with the prestige of genius this national assurance. Yet
scarcely an English thinker has left more definite trace upon
English legislation than Jeremy Bentham; and scarcely an
English thinker, save perhaps Godwin, fulfils more completely what might be called the music-hall notion of a
philosopher. From the almost legendary infant who read
Rapin's *History of England* at the age of three to the old man
at his " ante-prandial circumgyration " he was all that the

---

[1] Bentham's political writings are innumerable. For an account of them
see Leslie Stephen's " Note on Bentham's Writings " in *The English Utilitarians* (1900), vol. i., pp. 319-326. Bentham's collected *Works* (ed.
Bowring, 11 vols., 1838-1843), though not wholly complete, certainly contain enough to judge him by. The reader who wishes to form an opinion from
the writings of Bentham himself will find the following most useful : *Fragment
on Government* (1776) ; *Introduction to the Principles of Morals and Legislation* (1789) ; and Dumont's famous redactions (later translated into English
and included in Bowring's edition of the *Works*), especially the *Traités de
Législation civile et pénale* (1802) ; *Théorie des Peines et Récompenses* (1811,
1818, 1825) ; *Tactiques des Assemblées législatives suivi d'un Traité des
Sophismes politiques* (1816). Critical writing on Bentham is so complete and
so able as to discourage an attempt to say something new about him. See
especially Stephen, L., *The English Utilitarians* (1900), vol. i. ; Halévy,
E., *La Formation du Radicalisme philosophique*, 3 vols. (1901-1904) ;
" Bentham " in Mill, J. S., *Dissertations* (1874), vol. i.

caricaturist might wish a philosopher to be. Nor did these eccentricities conceal, as one might hope, a sturdily common-sense thinker of the true British pattern. Southey, who certainly tried hard enough to conform to that pattern, was justified in calling Bentham a " metaphysico-critico-politico-patriotico-phoolo-philosopher." Bentham was indeed, if not a philosopher, at least a *philosophe*. His true affiliations are all with that school of eighteenth-century French thinkers whose abstractions are still a part of our political inheritance. Through Bentham, those revolutionary principles against which Burke fought so hard entered into English politics.

It is true that Bentham himself attacked the ideology of the French Revolution, and that he consistently repudiated the notion of " natural rights."[1] That he should feel called upon to do this is in part a touching tribute to his desire to live up to the English tradition of hard-headedness, in part a mere consequence, as we shall see, of his faith that one set of abstractions is better than another. What he really distrusted in the work of the French National Assembly—and distrusted all the more because he shared it a bit himself—was the sentimental faith in human goodness which seemed to him to becloud the Declaration of the Rights of Man. But in the proper paramountcy of Right Reason he had as little doubt as any man. For what passes as the " wisdom of our ancestors," for all the devotion to the consoling adequacy of what has long endured that inspired Burke, he had no respect whatever.[2]

Perhaps the psychological roots of Bentham's ideas lie in this, that he was a sensitive but unimaginative man. Benevolence was fashionable enough in his time, but Bentham was really benevolent. He hated suffering and injustice, though he characteristically declared justice to be " an imaginary personage, feigned for the convenience of discourse, whose dictates are the dictates of utility, applied to certain particular

---

[1] See the *Tactiques des Assemblées législatives suivi d'un Traité des Sophismes politiques* (1822) in Dumont's redaction. The latter part, a criticism of the Declaration of the Rights of Man, appeared in English as *Anarchical Fallacies*.

[2] " Nos ancêtres nous ont été inférieurs en probité comme en tout le reste." *Tactiques des Assemblées législatives*, vol. ii., p. 33.

cases."[1] He was moved by the sight of human unhappiness
—indeed by the sight of unhappiness in any living creature
—to wish to remedy it. But he had a curious incapacity to
enter into the feelings of others. At bottom he identified
suffering with disorder, irregularity, uncertainty. That some
men like disorder, that some men find happiness in a trans-
cendental order imaginatively constructed out of disorder,
that there are in the human soul depths where cruelty feeds
upon itself, could never occur to him. The world of St.
Francis was for him as non-existent as the world of Freud.
He had, indeed, a true intellectual distrust for over-simplifi-
cation. He never really thought that man could so live that
there would be no obstruction to his will. But he did think
that men will pretty much the same things, and that
under a proper system of government and morals the satisfactions willed could be fairly evenly distributed. He was
thus driven into a rough egalitarianism, partly indeed by the
exigencies of his method of thought, but also by his fundamental incapacity to get under the skins of his fellow men,
and to realize that their desires even though " self-regarding," are capable of being submerged and vicariously sated
in a group-whole.

For even more fundamental to an understanding of
Bentham than the famous principle of utility is the rigorously
atomistic metaphysics with which he starts out. (We need
not be unduly troubled by the reflection that he himself
would have denied that he ever entertained a metaphysics.)
It may seem no small violence to Bentham's memory to
describe him in a term drawn from those Middle Ages he so
disliked, but he really is the perfect nominalist. The
individual, John Doe, is for him an ultimate reality. All
universals are mere fictions, usually harmful fictions.
Thought can but perform arithmetical calculations with
individual units. " The community is a fictitious *body*, composed of the individual persons who are considered as
constituting as it were its *members*. The interest of the community then is what ?—the sum of the interests of the

---

[1] *Principles of Morals and Legislation* (Oxford, 1879), p. 125 note.

several members who compose it."[1] As an ultimate meta-physical principle this is perhaps as defensible as any other. But as an analysis of the way men *feel* towards the state or towards any group of which they are members, it is quite wrong. This failure to grasp the support men's emotions find in something—fictitious, perhaps, to the intellect—outside themselves and *superior to their wills* is the failure of Bentham's imagination. In it lies the source of that difficulty with which he was continually struggling, and which M. Halévy has termed the problem of identity of interests.

Let us, then, with Bentham, conceive a world composed of men equipped with the five senses and a desire—we shall probably have to say a reasoned desire—to secure the gratification of these senses. Obviously each man will seek pleasure and avoid pain. Now if we have a dozen empty buckets and a certain fixed quantity of water in a reservoir, we can easily distribute the water equally among the buckets. All we need is a measure of quantity. Bentham's method is not quite so simple as this, but if we regard a human being as a receptacle to be filled with satisfaction, and left to a minimum degree empty from mere dissatisfaction, we are not doing him a grave injustice. The world is full of a certain amount of pleasure and apparently, too, of a certain amount of pain. If all men have as much pleasure and as little pain as possible, this world will be at its best for men. Logic solved the simple problem of the buckets. Is there not some " logic of the will," to use Bentham's phrase,[2] whereby we can also apportion pleasure and pain ? There is indeed. It is the principle of utility. This logic of the will must take as axiomatic, first, that " les sensations des hommes sont assez régulières pour devenir l'objet d'une science et d'un art."[3] That is to say, it must be assumed that a given experience will cause the same *quantity* of pleasure or pain to all men. Second, it must be assumed that one man is equal to another for purposes of calculation. Equipped with these

---

[1] *Principles of Morals and Legislation*, p. 3.
[2] *Ibid.*, preface, p. xiii.
[3] *Traités de Législation civile et pénale*, vol. ii., p. 18.

ENGLISH POLITICAL THOUGHT

axioms, we can then go ahead and estimate the maxima for any given pleasure or pain. Finally, we can take all these maxima, and all our human units, and see how each unit can attain the fullest satisfaction of its wants. Our felicific calculus will have given us the formula and the fact of " the greatest good of the greatest number." Disorder will give place to order, and yet men remain miraculously the same.

Bentham, does, of course, admit a variation in individual sensibilities and in external circumstances,[1] but he maintains that for the purposes of the legislation some rough equality of pains and pleasures among men must be assumed, for there is otherwise mere chaos, the reign of accident. He did not indeed like the word equality. " La notion vague d'égalité, toute flatteuse qu'elle est, ne peut guère servir qu'à tromper, qu'à voiler le principe d'utilité, auquel il faut toujours en revenir."[2] But he thought the tendency of his time levelling. Though property is an essential of political life, each man should have property of about the same value, for do we not learn from the principle of utility that a man's pleasure from an increase of property varies inversely with the previous amount of property—that it steadily diminishes as he gets wealthier—that therefore the more equally property is distributed the more actual pleasure ?[3] Moreover, " in point of political discernment, the universal spread of learning has raised mankind in a manner to a level with each other."[4]

Now that he has his measure in the equality of men before Pleasure and Pain (a most revolutionary difference from Christian equality before God) Bentham has only to measure the value of different pleasures and pains. He was no man to content himself with the mere enunciation of a principle. No man loved more the infinite world of fact. Pleasure and pain are to be measured by their intensity, duration, certainty and uncertainty, propinquity or remoteness, and when

---

[1] *Traités de Législation civile et pénale*, vol ii., p. 19.
[2] *Tactiques des Assemblées législatives*, vol. ii., p. 293.
[3] Halévy, *op. cit.*, vol. i., pp. 77-79.
[4] *Fragment on Government* (ed. F. C. Montague), p. 155.

18

their long-run tendency is considered, by their fecundity and purity in addition to the foregoing.[1] Bentham lists fourteen simple pleasures, those of sense, wealth, skill, amity, good name, power, piety, benevolence, malevolence, memory, imagination, expectation, association, and relief; and twelve simple pains, those of privation, sense, awkwardness, enmity, ill name, piety, benevolence, malevolence, memory, imagination, expectation, and association. These in turn are subdivided. The pleasures of sense, for instance, include those of taste, intoxication, smell, touch, ear, eye, sex, health, and novelty.[2] All are elaborated, worked out and illustrated. There is something rather pathetic about Bentham's assurance that he has made the subjective objective, and therefore controllable. His " sample " of the " pleasures of a country prospect," listed under ii., 2, as " the idea of innocence and happiness of the birds, sheep, cattle, dogs, and other gentle or domestic animals "[3] is a great deal like Jeremy Bentham, and not at all like Lord Chesterfield.

The felicific calculus, once worked out, must be applied to this world. One thing at least was pretty clear. England did not operate on the principle of utility. The calculus showed that the pain inflicted on a man and on his dependants by depriving him of his life was far greater than the sum of the pleasure gained by the man from whom he stole a sheep and of the security gained by the state (i.e. pleasure divided among all the citizens). It would even show that the pleasure of a millionaire landlord in his wealth would not equal the sum of the pains of the agricultural labourers whom he kept in poverty. Bentham was not willing to go into the question as to why the principle of utility had been so long neglected, and he was somewhat surprised that it should be so much resisted. He was glad to steer clear of so metaphysical a question as that of the origin of evil, and rest on the simple fact that he at least knew what evil was.

In his earlier years, he hoped that by converting the rulers of England to the principle of utility he might make that

---

[1] *Principles of Morals and Legislation*, chap. iv.
[2] *Ibid.*, chap. v.   [3] *Ibid.*, p. 42 note.

principle prevail. He began with the benevolent despotism then in fashion. What was wrong in England was chiefly her laws, civil and criminal, an absurd mass of inconsistencies perpetuating old abuses, dealing out rewards and punishment with a shocking disregard for the greatest good of the greatest number. His first, and still his most readable work is the *Fragment on Government*, a devastating attack on the grandiloquent complacency of Blackstone. If the laws could only be codified according to the simple system he had worked out, men could be left to the natural pursuit of their own economic and cultural interests. Convert such able lawmakers as Lord Shelburne, and all will be well. Bentham, after bitter experience, found that the English ruling classes were not to be converted, and turned to the people. He ends, as we shall see, with a political programme as democratic as that of his old enemies, the Jacobins.

Yet too much can be made of Bentham's conversion to the Radical party. He never underwent that always rare conversion of the spirit whereby a man is led to repudiate his past desires. What time did to Bentham is really quite simple. He believed that certain legal reforms would make men behave in the way he wanted them to behave. Failing to get those reforms from the rulers of England, he sought to change those rulers, and thus necessarily added political reforms to his programme of legal reforms. He always had something of that philosopher's distrust of the crowd with which he began. " The bulk of mankind," he wrote in 1789, " ever ready to depreciate the character of their neighbours, in order, indirectly, to exalt their own, will take occasion to refer a motive to the class of bad ones."[1] He saw that quite ordinary men often failed to distinguish the useful from the harmful. Blackstone's style, he says, disguises his logical weakness, " so much is man governed by the ear."[2] He is tender towards the sophistry that the majority is necessarily right, but he admits that it is a sophistry.[3] He admits that " le tort du peuple n'est pas tant de murmurer contre

---

[1] *Principals of Morals and Legislation*, p. 136 note.
[2] *Fragment on Government*, p. 116.
[3] *Tactiques des Assemblées législatives*, vol. ii., p. 73.

des griefs imaginaires, que d'être insensible à de vrais griefs."[1] He can even be detected in a defence of prejudice not wholly reconcilable with his attack on Burke: "Beaucoup de préjugés sont des opinions saines . . . la somme d'idées que chacune peut acquérir par lui-même, ou verifier par son propre examen, est toujours très petite."[2] And elsewhere, in a chapter on "Égards dûs aux institutions existantes" he insists that the philosopher must not assume that men can be readily moulded, even in the direction indicated by the principle of utility.[3] He—or Dumont—even permits himself the epigrammatic remark: " la multitude ne sait pas douter."[4]

Nor is Bentham's attack on the Rights of Man inconsistent with his position as founder of the party of philosophical Radicalism. In the widest sense, as we shall see, the world he hoped to realize was not greatly different from the world Robespierre hoped to realize. You can, if you wish, so define " Nature " that it will describe the way of life signified to Bentham by the word " Utility." But what Bentham distrusted in the French revolutionary thinkers was their idea of liberty. He himself does not really believe in that anarchical aspect of liberty to be found in some of the work of Rousseau—in the *Discours sur l'inégalité* for example, though emphatically not in the *Contrat social*. Liberty in itself as a good, the romantic self-satisfaction of the ego in the contemplation of its own freedom, meant nothing for him. Adam Smith had taught him that men left to themselves would produce more wealth, and that freedom of exchange would most equally distribute that wealth. Therefore he believed in economic liberty. But morally men needed correction and guidance. Institutions must gently provide them with the proper rewards and punishments. Of the inmates of his Panopticon he wrote " Call them soldiers, call them monks, call them machines; if only they are happy, it signifies

---

[1] *Tactiques des Assemblées législatives,* vol. ii., p. 87.
[2] *Ibid.,* p. 233.
[3] *Traités de Législation civile et pénale,* vol. iii., p. 345.
[4] *Ibid.,* p. 349.

little."[1] It is misleading to talk, as the French do, of liberty as a " natural and imprescriptible right." A right must be based on a law enforceable by the courts. And " dire qu'une loi est contraire à la liberté naturelle, c'est simplement dire que c'est une loi. Car toute loi ne s'établit qu'au dépens de la liberté."[2] You must not ask whether a given law conforms to liberty or any other natural right, but whether it is useful. So little regard had Bentham even for that traditional and jealous English attachment to the liberty of the individual to be tried by his peers under common law that he wishes some kind of administrative law in England.[3]

A still greater objection to the French system than its confusion of rights and laws is to Bentham the metaphysical pretension to absoluteness that lies back of this confusion. To assert that anything is fundamental is to assert that it is eternal, unchanging. Bentham had as much dislike as Godwin for the notion that a law could be laid down in black and white, binding all men everywhere for all time.[4] Utility, he fondly hoped, was a principle that would enable men to make and unmake laws according to their inevitably varying needs and circumstances. Now, although one cannot, even by using a word like utility, escape the eternal problem of values, one can perhaps gain by its use a certain willingness to be guided by the present rather than by the past. Bentham's chief work, his elaborate study of jurisprudence in its widest sense, had precisely this effect. English law was still mediæval in its complexity, and especially mediæval in the moral absolutes on which its criminal code was based. Bentham was unquestionably the chief agent in initiating its adjustment to the England of the industrial revolution. In civil law, he insisted on efficiency, on the diminution by codification of the conflict of laws, on the lessening of delays, on the simplification of procedure, on the diminution of the expenses of litigation, on the especial need of clearing up the

---

[1] Quoted in Halévy, *op. cit.*, vol. i., p. 149.
[2] *Traités de Législation civile et pénale*, vol. i., p. 262.
[3] *Ibid.*, p. 325.
[4] *Ibid.*, *Sophismes anarchiques*, première partie, art. v.

complications of Eldon's Chancery, on the adjustment of English law to the new world of capitalist business. He never lost his distrust for lawyers and for what he deemed the abracadabra of the law. At bottom, his position here as elsewhere is that of eighteenth-century rationalism. If men will only think as clearly and as unemotionally about law as they do about physics, all will be well.

In the criminal law, he first brought home to his countrymen the standards of Beccaria and the Enlightenment. Crime is not an offence against an absolute God, but an obstruction to the happiness of the majority of the citizens of the State. A crime is really an act which causes so much more total pain than pleasure that the state must interfere to redress the balance, and punish crime. The aims of punishment are then first to create an actual pleasure, as when we feel that the criminal has got his deserts, and second, to prevent the recurrence of similar crimes. The ultimate aim of punishment therefore is the reform of the criminal. Bentham gives an elaborate list of the proper qualities of a satisfactory punishment, such as invariability, equality, commensurability with other punishments, exemplarity, frugality, subserviency to reformation, subserviency to compensation, popularity, and remissibility. On most of these scores, capital punishment comes off very ill, and Bentham would have none of it save in extreme cases.[1] Although these standards of punishment are worked out with an elaborate quaintness that makes them seem impractical, their general trend is that of modern criminal jurisprudence.

Bentham's more purely political programme conforms in the end pretty much to the programme of nineteenth-century Liberalism. He wants universal suffrage, a representative Parliament, a competent and responsible executive (he thinks little of the famous dogma of the separation of powers), and universal education, though not under State compulsion.[2] He wrote much on parliamentary procedure, and was the first to bring to this study a fruitful critical sense.

---

[1] *Principles of Morals and Legislation*, p. 197.
[2] *Traités de Législation civile et pénale*, vol. ii., p. 200.

The *Tactiques des assemblées législatives* can still be read with profit. He is at pains to justify himself against the reproach that a study of parliamentary procedure is merely an empty study of forms, and very properly points out that forms make all the difference between obstruction and efficiency, between palavering and debating. He comes more and more to distrust the exercise of political power by even the best of governments, though one suspects he never ceased to be a benevolent despot at heart. But unfortunately the benevolent of this world never seemed able to attain its government. In the present world, the government had best not interfere directly with individuals, except criminals, but it should in a fatherly way supplement the ignorance of its subjects by offering prizes for inventions, by acting as a clearing-house for scientific knowledge, by encouraging academies, agricultural societies and the like. He summed up his position when he commented on Bacon's *Leges non decet esse disputantes sed jubentes.* He should have added, says Bentham, *et docentes.*[1]

Within this gently paternal state the individual was to lead the good, the useful life. We must attempt some general appreciation of the ethical values Bentham thought were so clear and obvious in the pleasure-pain formula.[2] Now Bentham's ethics are really very temperate, almost Aristotelian in their acceptance of the natural man of judgment. He abhors any kind of asceticism, any attempt to deny value to sensual pleasure. He objects to the overtones of moral judgment which we find in words like " lust "; let us, he says, employ a phrase like " sexual desire," which simply describes a fact of Nature.[3] For that profoundly pessimistic current—perhaps the dominant current—in Christianity which utterly condemns the flesh he had a hearty dislike. For all such religions, religions which teach that " God has created a fund of suffering greater than that of enjoyment,"

---

[1] *Traités de Législation civile et pénale,* vol. i., p. 358.

[2] " . . . and *pain* and *pleasure* at least, are words which a man has no need, we may hope, to go to a Lawyer to know the meaning of." *Fragment on Government,* p. 121.

[3] *Principles of Morals and Legislation,* p. 106.

24

he invented the characteristic term of " caco-théisme."[1] His *Not Paul but Jesus* is a bitter attack on the man who thought it better to marry than to burn. He grew more bitter towards priests as he grew older, and thereby shocked many good Englishmen whose moral standards were on the whole like his own.

But the good life of the senses is by no means the life of unbridled indulgence in the crude pleasures of the senses. Like many rationalists of placid disposition, he makes his hierarchy of pleasures ultimately very Christian. He divides human motives into social (benevolence), demi-social (reputation, friendship, religion), anti-social (antipathy), and personal (sensual, power, money, self-preservation). The personal motives are indeed the " grandes roues " of human action, but the social and demi-social motives are absolutely necessary to control the personal ones. Bentham's most highly prized virtue is benevolence.[2] This eighteenth-century quality sometimes crops up in queer places, as when he condemns Roman lawyers for treating animals as things, and finds the story of Pasiphaë more moral than the practice of bullfighting.[3]

What Bentham thought useful was what are sometimes regarded as the typical middle-class virtues. Property is one of the necessities of the good life. One of the necessary springs of human action is the pleasure of security. Men must work, and they will not work for the simple pleasure of the work itself. But grant them through the law the assurance that work can be consolidated into property, and work will be done. Property then is not a natural right, but a consequence of morality. It follows then that Poor Relief is not a right, but an expedient to encourage labour and thrift. Bentham started the attack on the Speenhamland system which his party was to carry through. You must do something about the poor, of course, but you must always have in mind their moral reformation. In *Pauper Management Improved*, Bentham uses some typical and enlightening

---

[1] *Traités de Législation civile et pénale*, vol. i., p. 203.
[2] *Ibid.*, vol. ii., pp. 264-265.   [3] *Ibid.*, vol. i., p. 229.

C

phrases to describe how even in the workhouse the principle of the union of interest and duty may be furthered by the self-liberating principle, the earn-first principle, the piece-work or proportionate-pay principle, and the separate-work or performance-distinguishing principle.[1]

Bentham sketches what is really his Utopia in the third volume of the *Traités*, where he describes a state where the legal system will be at its maximum of efficiency. There will be no great crimes, no civil actions on points of rights, a simple legal procedure, no wars, very little government and hence very small taxes, free trade, a stable, non-partisan government (presumably of experts). It all reduces itself to " the absence of a certain quantity of evil." All this is perfectly possible, within the grasp of human intelligence and will. All else is a mere chimæra. Perfect happiness is a figment of philosophers; pleasure must always be bought by a certain amount of pain. There will always be accidents, and hence inequalities and jealousies among men. " Ne cherchons que le possible."[2] It is almost the Voltairean " il faut cultiver notre jardin." It would not have satisfied Carlyle.

It did, however, satisfy many Englishmen of the early nineteenth century. Bentham's influence was very great indeed. He wished to sweep away precisely those things that stood in the way of the English industrialist—feudal law, primogeniture, the tariff, apprenticeship, the old poor law, sinecures and extravagant government generally, nepotism in Church and State, the lack of enterprise characteristic of a landed aristocracy. He was already sure of the fact and possibility of progress, though biological discovery had not yet provided political thinkers with a satisfying theory of progress. He had parted definitely with the hindrances of Christian other-worldliness. Above all, by his insistence that the new order was in accordance with so English a thing as usefulness rather than with foreign and dangerous notions of right, he converted many a man frightened by the excesses of the French Revolution.

---

[1] *Works*, vol. viii.
[2] *Traités de Législation civile et pénale*, vol. iii., p. 394.

Of the two criticisms which we must pass on Bentham's system, only the first would have given him any concern. He would have objected strenuously to the reproach that he was a poor psychologist. The elaborate calculus of pains and pleasures he had worked out seemed to him a final analysis of what men really were. Yet to us it must seem strangely intellectualized. In the first place, we can no longer accept, even as a working hypothesis, the assumption that men are roughly alike in their desires. Even economics has abandoned its postulate of the *homo economicus*. The weaknesses of Bentham's psychology come out in a hundred places. He thinks theft originates in indolence and pecuniary interest, and that therefore the best punishment is hard labour, which hits at the weakness of indolence.[1] But a thief may be a kleptomaniac, or he may steal for the love of adventure, for the love of power, or for many other motives. Nor is unpleasant labour exactly a cure for indolence. He attributes a highly intellectual and unreal origin to his prejudice of authority. It is based on an " erreur de langage. Une idée fausse a produit une expression incorrecte, et l'expression devenue familière a perpetué l'erreur." The phrase " le vieux temps " refers really not to an *old* time, but to a *young* time, the time of the infancy and hence the incapacity of the race. The authority of tradition is therefore not the authority of age.[2] Duelling he attributes to the failure of the law to provide adequate substitutes—apologies, public atonement in suitably emblematic robes. For an insult to a woman, a man should be made to stand in public wearing female headdress.[3] He thinks that publishing the chemical composition of quack medicines is sufficient to prevent their sale.[4]

But the chief failure of Bentham's psychology comes out in his treatment of legal fictions, indeed of all words suggesting a meaning which logic strips them of. He rightly saw that one cannot think scientifically if one employs words

---

[1] *Principles of Morals and Legislation*, p. 196.

[2] *Tactiques des Assemblées législatives*, vol. ii., p. 28. Bentham may have taken this from Bacon—certainly a " highly intellectual " origin.

[3] *Traités de Législation civile et pénale*, vol. ii., p. 352.

[4] *Ibid.*, vol. iii., p. 150.

which carry eulogistic or dyslogistic overtones. What he objected to in terms like " power," " right," and " justice " was precisely the weight of human hopes and fears which distorts them, which moulds them so hopelessly to the private world of the individual who uses them. One cannot but respect his honest desire to use a terminology as much independent of human emotions as the symbols of mathematics. One may even grant that some such effort must be made by any critical thinker. But where Bentham errs is in his optimistic conviction that the majority of men need but to be told that they are using words as fictions instead of instruments of logic in order to cease such use of words. Granted that intellect and conscience in tireless union can do something to distinguish between fact and illusion in this world, it is too much to hope that many men can be capable of the effort. But to say that illusion is inevitable ought, in Bentham's terms, to mean that it is useful. That he would never admit.

Were we to phrase our second criticism so as to accuse Bentham himself of using a mere word, utility, for the sake of the pleasant overtones it conveys, we should be making too easy a point. The matter really goes deeper, beyond the point whither Bentham himself was desirous of trying to go. It is no doubt impossible for the human mind to face experience without sorting it into some kind of order. It is possible, though rare, for the individual mind to hold that its own order is purely provisional, and furthermore that it has no necessary validity for other minds. So completely sceptical a mind in politics, of course, would have to hold that no course of action could be prescribed for other people. It would have to hold to an anarchical individualism. Such minds are extremely rare. Most men construct, or acquire, an order—a set of values—which they wish to see realized in the world about them—in other words, which they wish to see other men live up to. For this order they commonly seek a sanction outside themselves. For a long time, God, the God of organized Christianity, had ordained this order. In Bentham's time, Nature was beginning to take God's place. Bentham himself preferred to find his master in

Utility. In any case, the root of the matter lies in the conviction that something greater than the individual, something to which he belongs, though only imperfectly, only with a part of his consciousness, is necessary to explain why other men, and even he himself, do not always so act that they have what they want. You cannot make anything of the difference between good and bad, natural and unnatural, or even between useful and harmful, unless you construct a pattern, or patterns, in the universe transcending immediate human sense-experience. Now Bentham wanted to keep his pattern, and at the same time retain his autonomous individuality. If he had remained consistently true to his denial of *community* among men, he must have ended a complete sceptic in politics. Either you must say that whatever a man wants at a given moment is what he thinks useful, in which case you are an anarchist; or you must say that he may want what is not useful, in which case you declare that there is something outside him superior to his will. Bentham, of course, held firmly to the latter position, at least in practical matters. Utility came in the end, as we have seen, to dictate pretty much what the Nature of the *philosophes* had dictated. Even natural rights, on which Bentham resolutely shut the door, he was forced to give entrance to in a less dignified way. For if you believe, as Bentham certainly believed, that men in power may try to force others to act in a way not in conformity with utility, then you must believe that utility insists on resistance. Unless whatever is, is right, then something else—something that actually is *not* in this immediate world of the senses Bentham thought he never left—must be right.

Bentham's refusal to admit that morality must necessarily transcend the flow of the individual's sense-experience is at the bottom of his difficulty with what M. Halévy calls " l'identification des intérêts." Bentham of course starts with the assumption that the individual who pursues intelligently—that is, in accordance with the dictates of utility— his own interests is perfectly moral. But if the interests of several men conflict? Bentham's only answer is that they do not know their true interests. Their governors, if only they are aware of the secrets of utility, can so arrange matters that such men will be guided insensibly into pursuing their true and unconflicting interests. But this solution is purely verbal, unless it is admitted that a man in society gives up a personal, private, immediate sense-interest for an impersonal general interest which is *his* only through the performance on his part of an act of faith or imagination, for a general interest which is not *his* in Bentham's nominalist philosophy. All social life therefore demands from the individual a sacrifice of his interests—his self-regarding interests in Bentham's phrase—which, contrary to Bentham's hope, he will not make on the bland assurance of his superiors that he is thereby following exactly the same interests he had given up. Some alchemy of the general will which Bentham denied is necessary to achieve this end. Bentham achieved some, indeed, of his ends, but only because his followers banded together in the kind of group he never understood, and followed with an irrational faith an abstraction he had also never understood, though he had made it—utilitarianism.

2. BROUGHAM[1]

" Great fluency of argument—such ingenuity as always convinces the reader that he could have said an equal number of equally plausible things on the opposite side of every question which he discusses—considerable rashness in stating decided opinions upon very difficult subjects—and, on all occasions, an exclusive attention to his own side of the argument—a certain facility in bringing together various details, which is apt sometimes to pass for the talent of forming large and comprehensive views, when in reality it

[1] Brougham published a formal treatise on *Political Philosophy* in three volumes in 1846. It is chiefly a manual of comparative government with some more general speculation. The student of Brougham's political ideas will need to supplement it from the four volumes of the *Speeches* (1838) and the three volumes of collected essays from the *Edinburgh Review* (1856). For critical comment see Aspinall, A., *Lord Brougham and the Whig Party* (1927); Bagehot, W., *Works*, vol. iii.

may only be an enumeration of particulars seen partially through the medium of some theory—a style, frequently declamatory, but always lively."[1] Thus artlessly did Brougham, in describing Dumouriez, describe himself. He had among contemporaries a reputation for unstable brilliance and unscrupulous self-seeking which, save for the brilliance, seems to-day pretty much deserved. In spite of his numerous writings on every possible subject, he has lived only as a skilful, if in the end unlucky, player in the game of parliamentary politics. It is a little difficult to-day to understand why he cut so great a figure among his contemporaries. Bagehot thought his success was due to the devil in him, to the uncommonly arresting and purely personal leer with which he looked upon a humdrum world. But there is little of the devil left in his written work. His essays and published speeches are about as dead as they can be.

This very evanescence of his work, however, makes it valuable to the historian of thought. Great works survive by cheating time—an achievement quite contrary to what the historian must set up as his goal. Therefore the survival in print of the writings of men like Brougham is singularly fortunate. Through him, we may come at the men on whom the impact of political theories—in this case largely those of Bentham—fell. Through him, we may escape in a measure from the worst predicament of the formal historian of thought, the difficulty of relating thought to action.

A hasty examination of the inconsistencies, the twistings and turnings of Brougham's career, his varied advocacies and loyalties, is at first sight disconcerting. To find a man seeking entrance to Parliament as a Tory, and when baulked turning Whig in a trice,[2] is troubling to one attempting to relate the terms Whig and Tory to specific views of life. For a man to attack the emancipation of the West Indian blacks as Jacobinism and some years later defend their emancipa-

---

[1] *Edinburgh Review* (1807), no. 20, p. 369.
[2] Aspinall, A., *Lord Brougham and the Whig Party*, pp. 14-16. The personal hostility of his Westmorland neighbours, the Lowthers, seems to be all that kept Brougham from Toryism.

tion,[1] at least suggests the possibility that interests colour his ideas. For one most immersed in the party battle to write as if party were an unnecessary evil[2] argues a willingness to allow fact and theory to rest in separate compartments. Brougham himself wrote that " opinions then are assumed, in order to marshal politicians in bands and separate them from others. Place is the real object; principle the assumed pretext."[3] This does not prevent him from devoting pages immediately following to defending the orthodox Whig view of the Whig party as the defender of the people, and of the Tory party as the agent of the Crown and the nobility.[4] There is no reason why we should disagree, as we must disagree in the case of Burke, with the contemporary opinion of Brougham as a person who fitted his ideas to his immediate convenience.

For if Brougham has no system, he certainly indulged in political generalizations. If those generalizations were of the kind he thought would directly advance his own standing in the political world, they are all the more valuable to us. He is a most useful barometer to measure the pressure of utilitarian ideas. He makes as clear as possible the process by which the ideas of Bentham came to be fitted to the hopes and aims of the English middle class. He once confessed that in his youth he had leaned towards the alarmist view of the French Revolution, and that only during the Regency had he become convinced of the necessity of reform in England.[5] That was the sort of thing that touched his hearers, for it was exactly what they had done.

Brougham is a good son of the Enlightenment. Politics, he insists without much attempt to prove his point (why prove the obvious ?), is capable of exact and scientific statement.[6] In the old days, men were content to accept it as a

---

[1] *An Enquiry into the Colonial Policy of European Powers* (1803), vol. ii. p. 259; *Speeches*, vol. ii., p. 138.
[2] *Political Philosophy*, vol. ii., p. 237.
[3] *Ibid.*, vol. i., p. 23.
[4] *Ibid.*, vol. i., pp. 55-62.
[5] *Speeches*, vol. ii., p. 614.
[6] *Political Philosophy*, vol. i., p. 4. *Edinburgh Review* (1803), no. 2, p. 361.

mystery. But now that physical science has emancipated human intelligence, men can examine into the grounds of their conduct, and order it in accordance with reason. " It may safely be affirmed, that hundreds nowadays discharge the sacred duty to themselves and their country, of forming their own opinions upon reflection, for one that had disenthralled himself thirty years ago."[1] Thanks to the labours of the thinkers of the last century, of Voltaire, " great and original in whatever pursuit," of Filangieri, " who of all writers before Bentham, comes nearest to the character of a Legal Philosopher,"[2] and of many others, we have clear standards of what is workable in politics. Brougham rejoices that " happily the time is past and gone when bigots could persuade mankind that the lights of philosophy were to be extinguished as dangerous to religion; and when tyrants could proscribe the instructors of the people as enemies to their power." " It is preposterous to imagine," he continues, " that the enlargement of our acquaintance with the laws which regulate the universe, can dispose to unbelief. . . . A pure and true religion has nothing to fear from the greatest expansion which the understanding can receive by the study either of matter or of mind."[3]

Indeed, it is to ignorance rather than to other human weaknesses that present political evils must be traced. Ignorance of the science of economics on the part of too many Englishmen of all classes explains our present unrest. If workmen would only read Malthus, they would limit their families; if they knew the " reasonable, indeed necessary rule which would confirm each man to living upon the produce of his own industry, or the income of his own property " they would welcome the new Poor Law.[4] " The rage against machinery; the objections to a free export of grain; nay, the exaggerated views of even just and true doctrines, as that which condemns the corn laws; afford

---

[1] *Speeches*, vol. i., p. x.

[2] *Ibid.*, vol. ii., p. 290. This is part of an introduction written as late as 1838.

[3] *Ibid.*, vol. iii., p. 150.

[4] *Political Philosophy*, vol. i., p. 18.

C*

additional illustrations of the mischiefs which ignorance of economical science is calculated to produce."[1] Brougham's economics, as the remark about the Corn Laws shows, was of the trimming variety. Finally, " an imperfect light is dangerous. In the twilight men's steps falter; and, as they dimly see, they doubtfully grope their way. Then let in more light! That is the cure for the evil."[2]

The light is the light of " General Expediency or Utility."[3] Brougham was not of the elect of Bentham's disciples, but he belongs to the school. He protests often enough against the abstract character of orthodox utilitarian philosophy. Bentham, he says, seemed " oftentimes to resemble the mechanician who should form his calculations and fashion his machinery upon the abstract consideration of the mechanical powers, and make no allowance for friction, or the resistance of the air, or the strength of the materials."[4] He forgets that he has to work with men, through men, upon men, and not with ideal beings fashioned to suit himself.[5] But these are just the commonplaces the man in the street was thinking about Bentham. They are not even wholly fair. What Bentham misses is precisely man's incapacity for devotion to an emotionally symbolized abstraction. In one sense, his man is not abstract enough. What Brougham did was to make the principle of utility coincide definitely with the unphilosophical aspirations of the English middle class.

Few statesmen, not even Macaulay, have said more flattering things about that class. " I speak now of the middle classes—of those hundreds of thousands of respectable persons—the most numerous, and by far the most wealthy, order in the community; for if all your Lordships' castles, manors, rights of warren and rights of chase, with all your broad acres, were brought to the hammer and sold at fifty years' purchase, the price would fly up and kick the beam when counterpoised by the vast and solid riches of those

[1] *Political Philosophy*, vol. i., p. 19.　[2] *Ibid.*, vol. i., p. 28.
[3] *Ibid.*, vol. i., p. 44.　[4] *Speeches*, vol. ii., p. 294.
[5] *Edinburgh Review* (1830), no. 103, p. 140.

middle classes, who are also the genuine depositaries of
sober, rational, intelligent, and honest English feeling. . . .
They are solid, right-judging men, and, above all, not given
to change. If they have a fault, it is that error on the right
side, a suspicion of state quacks—a dogged love of existing
institutions—a perfect contempt of all political nostrums.
They will neither be led astray by false reasoning, nor
deluded by impudent flattery."[1] Brougham rarely proposed
anything beyond the capacities or desires of these admirable
constituents. John Mill said of him, a trifle bitterly, " Lord
Brougham has fought, both frequently and effectively, on
the people's side; but few will assert that he often was much
in advance of them, or fought any up-hill battle in their
behalf."[2]

Brougham starts out with a very moderate programme of
parliamentary reform. In 1810, he finds even the younger
Pitt's a " wild scheme." He would not pull down, but build
up. The first object of reform is the limitation of the power
of the Crown, and only secondarily the improvement of
representation. The worst boroughs should be extinguished,
with compensation, the large towns, like Manchester,
Leeds, and Sheffield, gain representatives, and a copyhold
franchise be introduced in England.[3] By 1830 he has come
around to the Whig Bill. Rejected by his party, he maintains in 1838 that had always wanted household suffrage,
triennial parliaments, and, with qualifications, the ballot.[4]
He always trimmed on the ballot, and later abandoned it
entirely.[5] He was one of the first to suggest an educational
qualification for the suffrage.[6] A property qualification he
considers essential for a seat in Parliament, and is very
Whiggish in his contempt for the proposal of payment of
members. Politics as a paid profession he regards as an
inevitable restoration of eighteenth-century bribery and
corruption.[7]

[1] *Speeches*, vol. ii., p. 600.
[2] Mill, J. S., *Dissertations*, vol. iii., p. 8.
[3] *Edinburgh Review* (1810), no. 31, pp. 206-211. Aspinall, *op. cit.*, p. 27.
[4] *Speeches*, vol. ii., p. 554-555.   [5] *Political Philosophy*, vol. iii., p. 69.
[6] *Ibid.*, vol. iii., p. 82.   [7] *Ibid.*, vol. iii., p. 73.

On the subject of Poor Relief, Brougham is the perfect Benthamite. He must be one of the first to dwell sorrowfully on that blessed word, the " dole."[1] He even finds—the note is familiar—the position of the recipient of state aid enviable. The pauper " presumes to domineer over the honest and hard-working ratepayer, and the servant of the ratepayer, the overseer, whom he insults and tramples on."[2] The new Poor Law he asserts was " a proposition framed solely, and assented to solely, with this view, so help me, God! . . . with the view only, of benefiting the poor themselves."[3] Yet he had admitted in a commendatory review of Cobbett's *Cottage Economy* that " all substantial improvement in the character and conduct of the poor, must begin with an amendment of their condition; they must be enabled to live more comfortably, and they will soon have a greater respect for themselves.[4] As to how this improvement was to commence in an England where the free play of competition and the introduction of machinery were forcing wages below a standard of decency, Brougham was not clear.

Education seemed the simplest way out. To Brougham, as to so many of his contemporaries, education meant first of all indoctrination with the pleasing truths of economics. That popular education should lead to multanimity instead of unanimity was a proposition he never entertained. Yet his services to English education were considerable. He played a large part in the new movement for adult education, helped to found Mechanics' Institutes, and insisted that the technique of adult education must be considered a wholly new problem.[5] He was interested in all the educational theories of his day. He was particularly pleased with Owen's ideas, and wished to include infant education in his natural scheme. The years three to six he considered crucial, not so much for intellectual achievement, as for the establishing of sound health and morals. In the work of the Swiss experi-

---

[1] *Speeches*, vol. iii., p. 497.
[2] *Ibid.*, p. 490.   [3] *Ibid.*, p. 533.
[4] *Edinburgh Review* (1823), no. 75, p. 105.
[5] *Speeches*, vol. iii., p. 118.

menters he was struck with such happy details as the fact that at Hofwyl the boys learned arithmetic by counting the weeds they pulled.[1] He proposed in Parliament a national system of education. The compulsory principle was sternly rejected as contrary to individual liberty. There was to be a national Board of Education, but it was to have a purely advisory relation to the local schools. The Board would neither prescribe methods nor name teachers. It was to be a very unbureaucratic body indeed. Local authorities were to be encouraged to found new schools, and to improve old ones. Funds were to come from the reduction of charity of all kinds to an absolute minimum.[2] He called to the public attention by Parliamentary investigation and by pamphleteering the abuses into which the endowed schools and colleges had fallen. The publication of details such as that at Winchester boys swore, according to a mediæval statute, that they could not command five marks (about £3 6s.) income, and yet averaged a yearly expenditure of sixty guineas, was the first step in a reform of such foundations.[3]

He proposed many other reforms of obviously Benthamite inspiration. Although a lawyer, he disliked the complexity of the English legal system. He objected to the differences between the English and Scotch codes on marriage, divorce, and illegitimacy, and sought to have the law of family unified in both countries.[4] He sought the disestablishment of the Irish Church, a body which he declared to rest on " the foulest practical abuse that ever existed in any civilized country."[5] He was less outright towards the English Church, but his attitude towards that body was always thoroughly Erastian. The Church was morally useful, but it certainly needed reforming. There was no reason why Parliament should not abolish plurality, adjust stipends, and otherwise do for the Church what the Reform Bill would do for the State.[6]

---

[1] *Edinburgh Review* (1818), no. 61, p. 159.
[2] *Speeches*, vol. iii., pp. 276 ff.
[3] *Letter to Sir Samuel Romilly on the Abuse of Charities* (1818).
[4] *Speeches*, vol. iii., p. 433.   [5] *Ibid.*, vol. iv., p. 64.
[6] *Edinburgh Review* (1832), no. 111, pp. 203 ff.

Of Brougham's economic theories we have already had several examples. He came into real public importance by carrying through what Castlereagh at once saw was the first great victory of the commercial and industrial interest over the landed aristocracy—the repeal of the Orders in Council in 1812.[1] He ridicules the Tory ministry as ignorant and " romantic " supporters of an outworn mercantilism. These economic illiterates still hold to the grand motto—" All trade, and no barter, all selling and no buying; all for money, and nothing for goods."[2] Yet he defended the Corn Laws as an exception to the rule, as providing an " advantage of a higher nature " in ensuring the national food supply in war time.[3] He was a devout Malthusian. He held as a truism that men " should be employed and paid according to the demand for their labour, and its value to the employer."[4] Men have no rights against the iron law of wages. No doctrine more " monstrous " than " that all accumulation of capital is a grievance to them, robbing them of their just rights; that every man has a title to that which he renders valuable by his labour; that the amount of his remuneration for his work must be ascertained, not by the competition in the market of labourers and employers, but by the personal wants and wishes of the former."[5]

The rôle of the State should thus be limited to the prevention of actual violence and to the encouragement of education. The final test of a good government is its " cheapness."[6] Naturally enough the Colonies must go by the board. Brougham is a determined Little Englander. Colonies are a useless expense. It is absurd to encourage artificially the timber trade with Canada, when a better market lies at hand in the Baltic. Canada should be left to go its own way, and, once raised to an equality with England by Free Trade, it will enter into the natural community of nations.[7] Brougham sketches with all the confidence of a

---

[1] Aspinall, *op. cit.*, p. 25. [2] *Speeches*, vol. i., p. 567.
[3] *Speeches*, vol. i., p. 568. [4] *Ibid.*, vol. iii., p. 484.
[5] *Edinburgh Review* (1832), no. 111, p. 259.
[6] *Political Philosophy*, vol. i., p. 64.
[7] *Speeches*, vol. iv., p. 304.

Cobden—with more confidence, since he did not attempt to make the experiment—a world where national rivalry, limited now to trade and culture, has resulted in universal peace.

Brougham is at his weakest when he leaves specific proposals and attempts to analyse the ultimate basis of state action. The *Political Philosophy* is a woeful piece of work. He seems to start with the assumption that man is gifted with the power of ruling his own conduct so that the pursuit of his own interests coincides with the interests of all. To the State as a corporate body he assigns no real existence. He violently dislikes the City-State, for the " evils of petty, contracted ideas which such a narrow community engenders, and especially for the restlessness which arises among all the people, when each takes as much interest in the State's concerns as if they were his own."[1] He takes individual liberty to be the ultimate good in society. And liberty is good because it is *natural*—that is, in conformity with the universal law of progress through competition. Freedom of competition, or the career open to talents, is thus the first thing we must seek in a society. This competition is not limited, but rather ensured, by the institution of private property. Property is the essential reward and incentive for struggle. Liberty thus implies not equality, but inequality. Free competition will ensure that the gifted few put forth their best efforts, and society will acquire its natural aristocracy. To protect the property of the gifted few against the envy of the many, the State with its machinery of rights and power is necessary. The efficient State is one where the holders of sovereign power and the natural aristocrats are one and the same.[2]

Brougham repeats at great length somewhat stale reflections from Locke and Montesquieu as to the nature of the

---

[1] *Political Philosophy*, vol. iii., p. 53.

[2] Brougham's doctrine of sovereignty is Austinian. *Political Philosophy*, vol. i., p. 66. It is interesting to note that Bentham himself had doubts about sovereignty. Some person or persons must indeed give commands, but for himself, he would not undertake to find a sovereign in the United Provinces, in the Helvetic or even in the Germanic body. *Principles of Morals and Legislation*, p. 218 note.

ENGLISH POLITICAL THOUGHT

best government. He has no doubts about the separation of powers, and concludes that all in all a mixed government of the English type is the best. The world is no doubt gradually approaching democracy, and in England great concessions must be made to democratic demands, such as that for universal suffrage. But the old English love for compromise has been the secret of English success. No great reform of the House of Lords is needed, for that body is essential to a mixed government. As long as you have a landed interest, you must allow it to be represented. The Whig party has always maintained that Lockian theory of checks and balances under which England has prospered. Throw into the balance a little more weight to allow for the new middle classes, and you will have done all that is possible to improve the condition of England.

Brougham's shallowness comes out strikingly in some of his general observations in the *Political Philosophy*. " The same persons," he says, " who being unfit to be themselves trusted with power would ill use it, are very capable of making a good choice enough of a representative."[1] A democracy, he thinks, is " more certainly pure than in any other form of government "; and it has the additional virtue of great cheapness.[2] Legislative bodies should rightly have the power of approving or rejecting appointees of the executive. In a conflict between them, " neither party obtains the result most desired, but a person is chosen against whom neither has any very insuperable objection; and the probability is that a better choice is made than if either singly had selected."[3] Comment on this in the light of American history is hardly necessary. He abounds in commonplaces like " It often, indeed, happens, that the same refinements which enlarge the intellect and polish the manners of a community, relax its love of independence, and prepare the way for encroachments upon its rights."[4]

Yet Brougham is the new Whig almost as definitely as

---

[1] *Political Philosophy*, vol. iii., p. 56.
[2] *Ibid.*, vol. iii., pp. 111-115.   [3] *Ibid.*, vol. ii., p. 10.
[4] *Edinburgh Review* (1830), no. 103, p. 157.

40

Disraeli is the new Tory. He preserved with great care all the fine platitudes, all the compromises of true Whiggism, and yet gave room for the newer energies of the makers of the industrial revolution. He insisted that the old Whig coterie could no longer hope for successful grasp of power in a Parliament which the revolutionary and Napoleonic wars had hardened into a Tory preserve. The Whigs must go to the country. They must consult people " out of doors." Brougham himself, in spite of ridicule, set the example of frequent tours of speechmaking. Party organization must take full advantage of the Press. The Whigs must go half-way towards the Benthamites, must adopt the principle of utility as the proper measure of what is safe. Revolutions occur only when the political aristocracy is not the natural aristocracy. The successful manufacturer is now part of the natural aristocracy of England. Make room for him, then, and he will prove to be a good Whig after all.

It is hardly necessary to point out how politic this advice was, and how closely it corresponds to the development of England. But Brougham was in no sense of the word a feeling man. There is no trace in him of sympathy for the plight of the English working man, quite swept away from his moorings by the achievements of Brougham's natural aristocracy of manufacturers. He would indeed educate the working man. But education is a singularly vague word—vaguer even than most of the phrases of the great revolutionary movement of the time. Brougham's education seems to have meant, beyond the three r's, only the moral platitudes of the Enlightenment, a suitable dash of science, and a great deal of current economics. This was not a very useful programme for the hand weaver or the agricultural labourer. Nor was it wholly acceptable to many more articulate Englishmen. We shall hear enough of that opposition between *laissez-faire* and intervention which runs throughout the century. But even in the early nineteenth century, there was something in the dogmatic individualism of new Whigs like Brougham and Macaulay that left many of their educated countrymen profoundly dissatisfied. Many and very different motives went into this opposition; indeed one

41

of its weaknesses, in contrast with the school of *laissez-faire*, was its varied composition. But Brougham illustrates perfectly one of the elements from which it was a revulsion. His is the hard complacency of the *arriviste*. What he sought above all things was a technique for getting ahead. Even the disappointments of his prolonged old age failed to leave him any serious doubts as to the career open to talents.

Now, though economics and biology conspired throughout the century to justify the notion that human existence is above all a struggle, there was, as there always has been, an ultimate of human consciousness, a conviction that life is a sharing in an order. Only in such an order is struggle dignified by discipline into conformity with what is really human. Brougham, indeed, like all the other defenders of the ethics of scramble, would have asserted that he, too, was defending an order, a better order than that of the present, a highly practical order because it accepted men as they were, and did not attempt to repress their desires. Now it is clear that some men's desires, if realized, will baulk the desires of other men. Possibly the old Christian hierarchical order, which implied the forceful suppression of certain human desires by the organized group, was wrong. But Brougham and his fellows were equally wrong in supposing that no desires needed suppression. They did not indeed act on that supposition as regards the desire of working men to combine to raise wages. They did not really live up to Macaulay's dictum that the cure for the evils of freedom lies in more freedom. At bottom, they would use the power of the group to encourage what they liked and to discourage what they disliked. But their likes and dislikes, their whole system of values, left out too much. It included too many of the values of unrest, and not enough of the values of rest; it provided for achievement, but not for renunciation, for getting and not for spending. By what seems an inescapable tendency of human thought, they were driven to an optimistic, scientific monism resting inconsistently enough on an atomistic individualism. But the individual can never adjust himself to a monistic universe. He must be ever aware of the possibilities of optimism and pessimism, of liberty and authority, of competition and co-operation. Our final criticism of Brougham must be commonplace enough; he thought he had obtained in the career open to natural talents a universal measuring-rod, a measuring-rod which could somehow become a moral law. He would people the world with ultimate Broughams.

3. OWEN[1]

Not the least of the puzzles which this world presents to the purely speculative mind is the occasional combination in one person of the successful man of affairs and the crank. It seems almost axiomatic that to make money requires a certain hard-headed acceptance of the world as it is, a distrust for anything unusual, anything not entertained by the men with whom one has business relations. That, for instance, a self-made, successful banker should be a British Israelite, and hold earnestly that the Anglo-Saxons stem from the lost tribes of Israel, deepens his success into a greater mystery than ever. Perhaps after all the academic critic is too little a mystic; what makes him a critic is an absence of certain appetites, and a consequent inability to appreciate certain values as ends of action. Even the most modest critical effort simplifies the world out of all proportion. Unpleasant though the reflection may be, there is some truth in the romantic dichotomy between thought and action. Consistency is a criterion of thought, but not of business success. Certainly no thinker would have entertained the incredible scheme of Cecil Rhodes for a *pax Anglo-Saxonica*, nor would he have dispatched Mr. Ford's peace ship. It is possible to maintain that such men make their millions with the sensible part of their minds, and their schemes with the visionary part. On the other hand, it is

---

[1] Though he started late in life, Owen wrote a vast amount. He repeated himself, however, even more than most active reformers, and almost all his ideas can be found in *The Book of the New Moral World*, 7 parts (London, 1836-1849). This may be supplemented by the *New View of Society* (1813-1814), obtainable in the Everyman's edition (1927). See Podmore, F., *Robert Owen*, 2 vols. (1906) ; Cole, G. D. H., *Robert Owen* (1925) ; Beer, M., *History of British Socialism*, 2 vols. (1923), vol. i.

possible that the modern world of business is not a sensible world, and that common sense really is not a gift necessary for great success in it.

At any rate, Robert Owen was the kind of man we have described. He made a great deal of money as a cotton manufacturer, and he spent it all in what he regarded as a quite similar, if more neglected, kind of manufacturing—the manufacturing of men of virtue. England's most famous Utopian Socialist was one of Brougham's natural aristocrats of commerce. A poor draper's apprentice, he saved a little capital, borrowed more, and set himself up in Manchester as a maker of textile machinery. He was successful enough to gain the confidence of his associates, and was soon able to take over with some partners the cotton mills at New Lanark in Scotland. His methods with his workmen were indeed rather more paternalistic than current economic theory thought desirable; but they brought profit to the establishment, and encouraged Owen to believe he had found a cure for the evils of society. He neglected his own business more and more in favour of his new apostleship. From an attempt to convert the rulers of England to his new system he passed on to an attempt to realize it in practice in Indiana. The failure of New Harmony deprived him of most of his capital. The last thirty years of his life were devoted to a rather pathetic, but not wholly fruitless series of Radicalisms, in which the grand Utopia, though postponed, was never out of sight. Trade unionist, co-operationist, Socialist, freethinker and finally spiritualist, he was still the Owen of the *New View of Society*.

That new view was as old as Locke and the French encyclopædia, in some ways as old as the Stoa. But Owen's downrightness of statement and his absolute self-assurance almost persuade his reader that he has made a discovery. This is the grand principle, as self-evident as the proposition that a straight line is the shortest distance between two points, that " any general character, from the best to the worst, from the most ignorant to the most enlightened, may be given . . . to the world at large, by the application of proper means; which means are to a great extent at the command and under the control of those who have influence in the affairs of men."[1] Or, as he again stated it, that " the character of a man is, without a single exception, always formed for him; that it may be, and is, chiefly created by his predecessors; that they give him, or may give him, his ideas and habits, which are the powers that govern and direct his conduct."[2] This is in a very naked form the environmentalist belief (one hesitates to presume to label it a fallacy) which in one shape or another lies beneath all programmes of reform. In this outright form it is hardly fashionable to-day, though few men have held to it more tenaciously than the very modern behaviourist school of psychologists.

The child, then, is capable of becoming whatever his environment makes him. This is not to say that he may become anything at all. Owen insists that the possibilities of human life are limited in one direction by the inexorable (but beneficent) laws of Nature.[3] In another direction, they are at present limited by the accumulated weight of past environment, by the errors and vices which go by the name of tradition and convention.[4]   Since from birth onward a person's acts are determined by his environment, good or bad, it follows that the common opinion, enforced by organized religion, that men are morally responsible for what they do is erroneous. In this error, indeed, lies the origin of evil. For primitive men were endowed with imaginations stronger than their reason. Unable to understand the laws of Nature, they invented theologies which placed them, as children of God, outside the law of Nature, and therefore able to choose between one act and another. Thus there was introduced the whole apparatus of secular and religious government with which man cheats himself. " *All* institutions and external circumstances of man's formation have been direct emanations from these early, crude, and most grievous errors of our ancestors."[5]

---

[1] *New View of Society*, first essay.
[2] *Ibid.*, third essay.
[3] *Lectures on an Entire New State of Society* (1828), p. 200.
[4] *New View of Society*, third essay.
[5] *Manifesto of Robert Owen*, p. 8.

Owen admitted, with a rather touching regard for consistency, that he himself was " a man whose organization *at birth*, and character *from birth*, has been formed *for* him."[1] But apparently in him Nature contrived, especially at New Lanark, to form a man determined wholly according to her own laws. Obviously it was his mission to open the eyes of his fellows to the badness of their environment, and to persuade them that their children, at least, must be subjected only to the kind of environmental influences which Owen's lucky acquaintance with the law of Nature revealed to him. Owen was wholly justified, given his premises, in assuming the *rôle* of a Messiah, and he bore the *rôle* with an ingratiating mixture of assurance and humility.

Now it follows indisputably that if men as they now are act under all sorts of evil influences, to allow them to do what they want to do is no way out at all. *Laissez-faire* means necessarily *laissez faire au mal*. The one way out is for the emancipated few—at the start, perhaps, the emancipated one—to draw from a knowledge of Nature a scheme of social environment which will impel men to good acts rather than bad, and to subject them to this environment. The new society will be not individualist, but collectivist. " If there be one closet doctrine," writes Owen, " more contrary to truth than another, it is the notion that individual interest, as that term is now understood, is a more advantageous principle on which to found the social system, for the benefit of all, or of any, than the principle of union and mutual co-operation."[2] Far from distrusting legislation, we must admit that only through good legislation can we overcome human weaknesses inherited from a vicious past. " The extent of the benefits which may be produced by proper legislative measures, few are yet prepared to form any adequate idea of. . . . [Such are] laws to prevent a large part of our fellow-subjects, under the manufacturing system, from being oppressed by a much smaller part . . . laws to prevent the same valuable part of our population from being perpetually

---

[1] *Signs of the Times*, p. 9.
[2] *Report to the County of Lanark*, p. 31.

surrounded by temptations, which they have not been trained to resist, and which compel them to commit actions most hurtful to themselves and to society."[1]

Before we attempt to understand the details of this legislative programme, the spirit behind it, and the way Owen hoped to realize it, we shall do well to consider what he found chiefly wrong in the England of his day. His own writing is almost equally balanced between criticism of existing society and description of a good society. First, this laborious England, of which the Manchester people are so proud, is a poor and inefficient England. Its lauded economics of competition is an economics of waste. Thanks to the use of machinery, invented by men in communion, through science, with the secrets of Nature, it produces more goods than the old England. But thanks to the stupidity of its Government, its morals, and its religion, it produces far less than it might produce, and it shares that production unjustly and wastefully. In the first place, thousands of able-bodied men are non-producers, living on the industry of others. There are far too many retail merchants. " Of these [retail] shops there are probably much more than fifty for one that would be required, under an arrangement formed on a knowledge of the Science of Society."[2] Moreover, selling under the present competitive system demoralizes the seller. It makes him servile, and later, if he amasses money, overbearing.[3] Then there are the professions, most of which, save those of engineering, medicine, and teaching, are useless or harmful. Lawyers, soldiers, officers and men of the navy, and priests are a total waste. Even those properly useful professions which minister to science are corrupted by the economic system. Fifty to sixty per cent. of what the professions cost society at present could well be saved.[4] Finally, the landlord and the *rentier* are most obvious parasites.

In this competitive society there arise inevitably certain desires which, translated into values, lead to still more waste.

[1] *Address on the Opening of the Institute at New Lanark*, p. 16, 17.
[2] *Lectures on an Entire New State of Society*, p. 22.
[3] *Book of the New Moral World*, part ii., p. 23.
[4] *Ibid.*, part ii., p. 19.

Men wish to gain purely external and meretricious marks of distinction. Snob-value arises, and the stupid race of fashion. Under a proper system, only essentials would be produced. By standardizing production for a fixed market, Owen estimates the total cost of production could be cut to one-quarter of what it now is. Even in agriculture, the principle of all wheat and no truffles would tremendously increase production.[1] The stock objection of those who hold that poverty is inevitable is thus seen to have no force. Under properly guided production and distribution, there would be abundance for all. Malthus is right about present society; increased production will but multiply the poor. But he and all such " learned, inexperienced men " are wrong when they apply their ideas to the New Society.[2] Finally, under the present system, a premium is put on buying cheap and selling dear, unaccompanied by moral considerations. Moreover, the poor naturally emulate the rich in their desire for ostentation. The result is a wasteful flood of flimsy goods, even adulteration and poisoning.[3]

This society has created the factory system, and the factory system has created the new poor. Owen felt deeply what so many quite different men felt, that the life of the English working man was an intolerably inhuman life. If this is what machines must bring with them, it were better they had never been invented. " Except for the future advantages to be obtained from it [the factory system] . . . it would have been well for the world if it had never been known."[4] Moreover, the ruling, that is, the capitalist classes, are really injuring their own immediate interests by exploiting the labouring classes. In permitting themselves to make use of the competition of labourers to keep wages down to a minimum, they are stupidly limiting the market for the goods they trade in. Owen is of especial interest in the history of economic thought for his emphatic defence of a theory of wages which has since found defenders even among

[1] *Book of the New Moral World*, part ii., p. 20.
[2] Cole, G. D. H., *Robert Owen*, p. 144.
[3] *Book of the New Moral World*, part ii., pp. 22-24.
[4] *Manifesto of Robert Owen*, p. 12.

orthodox economists. " The markets of the world are created solely by the remuneration allowed for the industry of the working classes, and those markets are more or less extended and profitable, in proportion as these classes are well or ill remunerated for their labour."[1] High wages therefore increase consumption and demand, and maintain high prices. They also permit the labourer to maintain himself in better health and spirits, and therefore to produce more. The notion that the labourer's gain is the capitalist's loss is as old-fashioned and wrong as the mercantilist theory that trade involves loss to one party to compensate for gain to another. Orthodox economists never wholly adopted Owen's optimistic theory of wages, but they are to-day much nearer to his position than to that of the old " iron law " of wages.

The economic basis of English society then is clearly bad; but economics rests ultimately on moral values. Men create and share the kind of wealth they think worth having. The moral basis of English society must therefore be wrong. To cap matters, these morals are incorporated in, and enforced by, a religion which represents the culmination of evil. In his earlier days, Owen kept fairly quiet about religion, in deference to the prejudices of the influential men from whom he hoped to gain support. But in his later years he attacked organized Christianity with a fervour that made him one of the important figures in the history of English rationalism.[2] Owen agreed with Bossuet that the multiplication of sects was in itself a proof of error; but he refused, unlike Bossuet, to accept one form of Christian belief as nearer truth than another. Christianity makes the fundamentally erroneous assumption that men are morally responsible for their acts. It therefore puts them under the power of a priesthood which can dictate what is moral and what is immoral. Had priests understood true morality, they might have brought about the new social order. But they were tied down to the second great error of Christianity, its distrust of the flesh. They

[1] *Report to the County of Lanark*, p. 12.
[2] See the *Investigator* (a rationalist periodical), 1st December 1858.

decreed that certain natural human desires were immoral,
and that the man who followed these desires was guilty of
sin. Especially in the matter of sex relations have priests
imposed false standards on man. They have " arranged a
legal and *unnatural* intercourse of the sexes, under the
supposition, that human nature was formed with the power
to love or hate, or to be indifferent, in its sexual feelings, at
the will or pleasure of the individual. . . . They thus
greatly diminished the enjoyment of the social intercourse
between the sexes, and estranged their minds from each
other, making them to feel and act sexually more foolishly and
irrationally than all other animals."[1]

Christian morals, then, are necessarily morals of fear and
repression. They mete out rewards and punishments (in
themselves always bad) according to standards no human
being can attain. The inevitable result is the shocking gap
between the ethics of Christ and the practices of Christians.
Hypocrisy becomes part of the necessary adjustment between morals and reality. Meanwhile the essential energies
of man, all his healthy desires and ambitions, drive him to
the creation of modern industrial society in which men
compete where they should unite, and unite (as in maintaining sex prudery, for instance) where they should compete.

Owen then, opposes natural man to the unnatural man
created by society. If one must deal with schools and labels,
one may say that he belongs to the school of Rousseau, and
that he accepts the doctrine of the natural goodness of man.
But Rousseauism is not quite the simple thing such critics
as Mr. Irving Babbitt conceive it to be. Above all, and
especially in Owen's hands, Nature does not insist that a
man should have whatever he wants at a given moment.
Owen does not deny reality to the moral struggle. He
merely employs for a set of values a word with eulogistic
connotations, enjoying especially fortunate, if somewhat
vague, relations with that natural order for which science is a
search. The struggle between natural and unnatural is as

---

[1] *Lectures on an Entire New State of Society*, p. 77.

real as the Christian struggle between good and bad. What is really important is not the labelling of a man as a "naturalist," but the understanding of what he means by Nature. Nor need we be disturbed by Owen's attribution of a rigid determinism to the operations of Nature. Calvin attributed quite as rigid a determinism to the operations of God. But the choice between good and evil was as real to one thinker as to the other. Neither ever confounds for a moment the desirable with the inevitable.

Before we attempt to do Owen the justice of examining into the specific content he gave the word "nature"— before we study the details of his new moral world—we must look briefly at his celebrated experiment at New Lanark. Here is to be found the modest but quite definitely realized model of his Utopia. When Owen took over the works at New Lanark from the Quaker Dale, he found what was considered a superior factory village. Housing conditions were extremely bad, and many families had but one room. Sanitation was neglected. Refuse of all sorts accumulated in heaps before the doors of the cottages. Dram-shops abounded, and the Scottish Saturday night debauch was an established institution. Pilfering of the company's goods by employees caused serious loss. Factory life did not suit the Lowlanders, and labourers had to be imported from the destitute highlands. Even so, much reliance had to be placed on the labour of parish apprentices, chiefly recruited from Edinburgh and Leith, who were taken at the ages of five to eight, articled for a period of from seven to eight years, and subjected to a working day of eleven and a half hours. Dale was a humane man, however, and had insisted that the children be given a little schooling at the close of their day's work. It seems almost unbelievable that, out of some three thousand children who passed through this frightful process in twelve years, only fourteen died.[1]

Within a few years, Owen had turned this dirty little

---

[1] Brief accounts of conditions at New Lanark before Owen's arrival, and of his own work there, will be found in the biographies of Owen by G. D. H. Cole and by F. Podmore.

village into one of the wonders of Europe, a place of pilgrimage for English earls and Russian grand dukes. And the company paid better dividends than ever. Owen began by sanitary reform. He provided for the orderly disposal of waste, and forbade household refuse-pits in front of the cottages. He built new houses, and eventually gave each family several rooms. He lectured to his employees on " Order and Cleanliness," but at first to no avail. The good Scotch housewives insisted on their right to do as they would with their own. But gradually he overcame the hostility of his people in this respect as in others. He instituted committees of villagers with powers of inspection, drew up a code of sanitary rules, required houses to be cleaned once a week and whitewashed once a year, and finally got his people to feel proud of the neatness of the community. He sold good whisky at reasonable prices, and drove the small dram-shops out of business, partly by forbidding them on company territory, partly by underselling them. Drunkenness—active and obvious drunkenness—he punished by successively increasing fines culminating in dismissal. (It is probable that one reason for his success was that he soon pruned out the more recalcitrant and independent spirits.) Pilfering he stopped by a careful checking system at the factory. He increased production by methods which the present independence of the workers would make impossibly childish to-day, but which worked at New Lanark. He established, for instance, what he called " silent monitors " —blocks of wood painted white, yellow, blue, or black, according to the achievements of the operative, and hung before his place in the factory.

A good environment was obviously doing wonders at New Lanark. But after all Owen's adult human material had been, and was still in a measure, subject to other and less happy influences. Children were better subjects for his experiments. Surely if he could have charge of their education from the beginning, they could be brought almost wholly under a good environment. Owen early began to take charge of the education of the children of his operatives. It was as an educational experiment that New Lanark gained its European reputation, and it was through education that Owen worked up to his wider programme. A brief glance at his ideas on education will provide a natural introduction for his complete social system, for the socialist society which he held up in contrast to the competitive society he lived in.

" Children are," writes Owen, almost as if he had never had any, "without exception, *passive* and wonderfully contrived compounds."[1] So varied is the external world with which they come into contact, so many different experiences impress themselves upon each child, that no two of them ever grow up alike. The last thing we need worry about, even though we assume identical capacity at birth, is that children will attain a monotonous and unprogressive uniformity. Our task is merely to see that the inevitable multiplicity of experiences which will mould men shall be a good multiplicity of experiences. Now children are influenced from birth. The first three years are in many ways the most important. And it is precisely in these years that the ignorance of parents and nurses does the greatest damage. You must either convert the parents, or remove the children as much as possible from parental influence.[2] Owen came to believe the latter alternative the only possible way of effecting the transition from the old to the new society,[3] and even at New Lanark he established forerunners of the modern nursery school. Infants must be treated as the little animals they are. They must have plenty of outdoor exercise, good food, light clothing, and at first very little purely intellectual training. He doubts whether, in the final state of society, " books will ever be used before children attain their tenth year.[4] Boys and girls will be brought up together to have no sense of shame at their external sexual differences.[5] There will be no rewards and no punishments, since these suggest a moral autonomy no human being possesses. The consequences of a bad act will be made so clear that no child will

---

[1] *New View of Society*, second essay. The italics are mine.
[2] *Ibid.*, third essay.
[3] *Lectures on an Entire New State of Society*, p. 82.
[4] Owen, Robert Dale, *Threading my Way* (1874), vol. i., p. 140.
[5] *Lectures on an Entire New State of Society*, pp. 105-107.

wish to repeat the act. Moral indoctrination will be limited
to the clear exposition of the Golden Rule.[1] The teacher, of
course, must guard his own conduct carefully. He must ex-
hibit none of the vices present society forces on man. "He who
has seen no anger, will he be liable to feel resentment? He
who has been witness to no deceit, will he be untruthful?"[2]
The child must be taught the useful and the decorative arts,
as well as the mere abstract learning of the past. Indeed, the
curriculum at New Lanark included, in addition to reading,
writing, and arithmetic, geography (taught as far as possible
from models and illustrations), ancient and modern history,
natural history (with the use of specimens), religion, sewing,
singing, dancing, and military drill. Above all, the first
principle to be maintained is: " Never to demand attention
from a child to any subject unsuited to his years or capacity,
or to require it from him, on any occasion when it is not
spontaneous."[3] Owen would still be ranked among " progressive " educators.

Owen's success at New Lanark was so great that he felt he
could not limit himself to so small a field. But if society was
to be regenerated a series of such small experiments must be
initiated. You could not really reform a Leviathan like
modern England *en bloc*. This is the starting-point for
Owen's famous scheme for a model community. Once
started, such a community would breed others, and in the
end the world would be covered with a network of such
communities. The important thing was to work out a complete scheme for the initial community. Owen altered a
detail here and there in the course of his long career, but in
the main his constructive scheme follows the lines laid down
in his *Report* of 1816 to the county of Lanark.

On a territory agriculturally rich enough to support about
1,000 or 1,500 people, a new village will be built. The
buildings will be constructed around a central parallelogram
devoted to lawns and gardens. They will include living-
quarters with common kitchens, dining-rooms, and recre-
ation-rooms, but providing separate apartments for each

[1] *New View of Society*, first essay.
[2] *Lectures on an Entire New State of Society*, p. 116.   [3] *Ibid.*, p. 118.

family. A school, a community hall, and other necessary public buildings will complete the parallelogram. Barns and workshops will be built a little apart. The community will be self-supporting as far as possible in regard to food. Owen even defends spade culture as the most productive form of agricultural labour. The machine age is not wholly repudiated, however. Each community will manufacture in model factories what its resources best provide it with. Free trade between communities will then ensure an ample supply of such goods for all.

Children are to be separated from their parents at the age of three, though of course they will see a great deal of them in the normal community life. For the next five years, these children will be taught according to the scheme of education we have just outlined. From their eighth to their twenty-sixth years they will make their major contributions to the productive activity of the community. That is to say, they will take part in the agreeable tasks of educating their juniors, of cultivating the fields, and of manning the workshops. From their twenty-sixth to their thirty-first years they will take charge of the distributive system of the community. This work is really very simple, requires less of the physical energy of youth, and will ripen them in knowledge of their fellows and prepare them for the next stage. In this next stage, from their thirty-first to their forty-first years, they will take charge of local government, and make use of their greater leisure to cultivate the arts and sciences for their own sake, and not for teaching. From their forty-first to their sixty-first years, they pass on to the control of what may be called the foreign relations of the group, and, of course, continue to cultivate their abundant leisure. After they attain the age of sixty, they retire from active participation in affairs.[1]

Owen goes into infinite detail in his pamphlets on this model society. We cannot here follow him into these complexities. We must content ourselves with touching upon certain aspects of his schemes which throw light on his

---

[1] *Book of the New Moral World*, part v., chap. vii.

general principles. In the first place we must note that he does very little to controvert stock objections to the economics of Communism. Work he of course admits is essential to production. But invention, which is a free flowering of human curiosity, has made actual labour much less arduous than it once was, and will continue increasingly to do so. Moreover, much work, if not most work, is pleasant when it is the free choice of the workman. Owen would recognise with Fourier and with Morris that the agreeableness of work is an important factor in assuring production. But he assumes that his educational system will be adequate to train willing workmen. Greed, or even lust for power, he will not admit as a necessary economic incentive. Such motives are a product of the old bad system, and will not even be in the vocabulary of his perfectly taught children. Indolence, when it crops up, will be regarded as a minor disposition to crime, and so treated. All that we now consider as criminal will be held in the new state as pathological. His council of elders will remove to the hospital all whom it considers " physically, intellectually, or morally diseased."[1] Nor will there be any difficulties with the economics of distribution. Owen once worked out a system of pricing based on the quantity of labour involved in production, and even established a short-lived labour exchange on this principle.[2] In his ideal community, however, he is apparently willing to allow the individual to draw upon the public stores as he likes.

For politics as such, Owen had the confident indifference evident also in Fourier. The complexities of modern legislative systems are made necessary by the whole fabric of error we are trying to maintain. The legislative aid of Parliament may be necessary in certain stages of transition to the new society. But once the model communities are operating, politics will be simple. The one principle Owen accepts for his political arrangements is that of age. Political authority in the community will rest in a council composed of all members, men and women, between the ages of thirty and

---

[1] *Book of the New Moral World*, part vi., p. 77.
[2] See Cole, *op. cit.*, pp. 143 ff.

forty. Presidency of this council, which carries with it what may be called the formal sovereignty over the group, lies with the oldest member. This council, after free debate, will make the simple decisions necessary to regulate the community. Owen was no democrat, and did not even bother with the problem of majority decisions. At New Harmony, the democratic constitution of the town gave him much annoyance. If he is pressed, he will admit a patriarchal theory of the State. The governing council is to regard the community as a family, and to rest its decisions ultimately on the wisdom of its oldest member. Relations between nuclei —the word is Owen's—are to be managed in a similar way by a council composed of members of the local councils who have passed the age limit of forty. He is not very clear as to the composition of these councils, nor as to their territorial extent. They will be chosen by common accord, and will take age into very serious consideration. Their ultimate scope will include the whole world.

For the family as he knew it Owen had little regard. That his own family life was apparently happy will perhaps disturb the psychologist, but we may presume here to remain undisturbed. Indissoluble marriage in our present society, writes Owen, is clearly bad. Men and women now enter into marriage for reasons too unrelated to their sex-life to make it a successful institution. Even in the ideal community, external circumstances may alienate a couple. Divorce at the will of either party is thus essential.[1] The children are to be brought up under the control of the community, so that they form no hindrance to free divorce. Moreover, Owen shares the belief of all defenders of complete sexual freedom that, under such conditions, and with a proper sexual education, actual maladjustments between men and women will virtually cease. For the sacred associations of the English home Owen has no regard at all. Family life is stuffy and inefficient. Most women are bad cooks, and poor housewives. His communal apartments will be better managed, better heated, more economical in every way, than the small

---

[1] *Lectures on an Entire New State of Society*, p. 76.

D

houses of the present. Privacy in sleeping-quarters is all that human beings require. Community meals and community recreation will afford a far more interesting social life than the present system can afford.

Finally, we come to the individual himself as a moral being. We have said that Owen regards human beings as identical at birth. That is perhaps not wholly true. " Perfect equality," he writes, " is incompatible with the condition of human life, but there will be the nearest approach to it in practice, that the difference of age and *original organization* will admit."[1] But this admission is hardly more than a concession to common sense. After all, children are sometimes born crippled, or feeble-minded. Owen makes some rather unscientific suggestions in the direction of eugenics. He shares the hopeful, if mystic, belief that a proper sex ecstasy will produce superior children. He goes so far as to contrast our success in animal breeding with our failure in human breeding.[2] But apparently he is unwilling to draw up a precise scheme for mating given human beings. That, too, will be left in the ideal state to the workings of a beneficent Nature. Inequalities at birth are not very great, anyway. Certainly no men are so superior to their fellows as to merit exceptional monetary reward. Owen is a pretty complete egalitarian.[3]

Liberty, too, he regards as essential to human life. " Freedom of action is essential to health and to the full enjoyment of animal and mental existence. It is the natural right of all animals, limited only by their action not being injurious to others."[4] This is the familiar and inconclusive formula we shall have to analyse in the work of its most famous exponent, J. S. Mill. Freedom of speech is to Owen even more indispensable than freedom of action. All varieties of opinion must be encouraged. Argue with error, but do not seek to silence it. No man can help holding an opinion. " To say to a man, ' You should not believe as you

---

[1] *Lectures on an Entire New State of Society*, p. 148. The italics are mine.
[2] *Book of the New Moral World*, part iii., p. 7.
[3] He believes, of course, in sex equality *Ibid.*, part iv., p. 47.
[4] *Ibid.*, part iii., p. 70.

do,' is as silly as to say, ' You are too short, you ought to be tall.' "[1] Yet he refuses to accept the shibboleths of the French Revolution. " Liberty cannot be given to the robber or murderer. Equality cannot take place between St. James's and St. Giles's. Fraternity can never arise between filth, grossly bad habits, self-degradation,—and cleanliness, superior habits and manners, and rational self-respect."[2] That is, liberty, equality, and fraternity are commonplaces of the New Society. But as applied to the present society they are misleading phrases in which men take a vain delight. We can only achieve the New Society by training the young in accordance with specific values suggested by these phrases. The authority of the wise will impose true freedom on the unwise.

Owen loathed all kinds of violence, and even as an agitator did little directly to sharpen class antagonisms. Yet in spite of the Utopian character of his teachings, he is an important figure in the history of the English Labour movement. The innocent unreality of his philosophy as a whole need not conceal the fact that he had a hand in beginning a number of experiments more fruitful than New Harmony. His curiosity and his enthusiasm led him into many paths, not all of which have proved by-paths. Mr. Cole has pointed out his services to education, to workers' co-operation, to trades unionism (his was the first attempt at " one big union "), and, through his son, Robert Dale Owen, to the movement for birth control.[3] Owen, with the Chartists and the early trade union leaders, helped to create that quite un-Victorian *milieu* of independent working-class thought in which, rather than in the work of men like Carlyle, Ruskin, and Disraeli, lies the true origin of the modern English Labour movement. Nor is much of his economic thought as unorthodox to-day as it was in 1830. Only our Eldons will take great exception to his indictment of the competitive system.

What seems now most old-fashioned in his thought is his

---

[1] *Book of the New Moral World*, part vi., p. 16. [2] *May Meetings*, p. 25.
[3] Cole, *op. cit.*, p. 242.

confidence in Nature as the eighteenth century understood the word, and his firm assurance that there is " one right way " in politics.[1] Yet, even though we hardly dare accept Nature's simple scheme as Owen did, even though we cannot assume environment to be as omnipotent as he thought it, we have to-day swung back a little towards him from the extreme biological determinism of the later nineteenth century. Even the phrase " social science," which he did much to popularize, has acquired a new prestige, and a not wholly new content, as the " social sciences."

Owen merits a certain immortality quite apart from the swing of the pendulum which has brought Manchester economics into disrepute. For he had one of the attributes of the true thinker. His curiosity exceeded his moral fervour. He had indeed enough of the latter quality to deserve the title of crank, but never that of dogmatist. He was very sure that he had discovered the one right way, but fortunately he was never very sure as to just what way he had discovered. He knew at least that it was not the common way. Owen kept to the last, as his excursion into spiritualism shows, that curious freshness which belongs to the inventor. He stuck to the framework of his generalizations, but he was always altering the details. The true dogmatist—and most men are, perhaps fortunately for the stability of human society, true dogmatists—sums up his habits in universals to which he gives emotional allegiance. Owen's habits were always changing, even though his habit of mind remained unchanged. He was thus saved from a devotion to routine erected into a universal. A universal must, from its very definition, be shared. Owen, though he had disciples, never really had a school, as Bentham did. He was always footloose and free, not a member of society. His self-confidence was never re-enforced by adhesion to a genuine group, and therefore never wholly satisfied. Nonconformity drove him perpetually into a revision of his schemes and a reassertion of his originality.

[1] " There is but one rational mode by which the business of the human race can be performed. *There is only one right way* " (*Book of the New Moral World*, part vi., p. 5).

4. COBBETT[1]

To write about Cobbett as a political thinker implies, in a sense, a false start. For, properly speaking, Cobbett never thought at all. Let us hasten to add that this remark is not a snobbishly intellectualist condemnation of Cobbett, but an attempt to give to the word thought a decently precise meaning. To think implies an effort on the part of the thinker to construct a coherent scheme out of the material of his experience, yet independent of his desires. The possibility of complete detachment on the part of the thinker may well be an illusion, but it is an indispensable illusion. Without it, thought is as immediate, as private, and as unreal as the rest of our sense-experience. Now Cobbett never made any attempt to get outside himself. His responses to experience are as self-centred as a child's. He was naturally enough never really troubled by the reproaches of moral inconsistency to which his career gave rise, and which were on the whole unjust; but, had he been able even to suspect the meaning of the phrase, he would have been equally untroubled by the reproach of logical inconsistency. Put him over against Bentham, Brougham, and Owen, and the contrast is remarkable. Each of these former drew certain assumptions from his temperament and experience; but they erected on these assumptions systems which have a certain amount of what the world has agreed to call logical consistency. Cobbett, too, harboured innumerable generalizations; and he could draw logical inferences in specific cases. But he has nothing like a system. His judgments of value have a peculiar directness and privacy. He actually *felt* about ideas the way most men—and none more strongly

---

[1] Cobbett's sons reprinted in six volumes (*Selections from Cobbett's Political Works*, edited by J. M. and J. P. Cobbett, London, 1835-1842) the most important of his journalistic writings, both of the Peter Porcupine period and of the *Political Register* period. The *Advice to Young Men* (1829; reprinted by the Oxford University Press, 1906), the *Rural Rides* (1830; in Everyman's Library, 1912), and the *Cottage Economy* (1822) are necessary to a fuller understanding of Cobbett as a person and as a moralist. See Melville, L., *Life and Letters of William Cobbett in England and America* (2 vols., 1913); Carlyle, E. I., *William Cobbett* (1904); Chesterton, G. K., *Cobbett* (1925).

than Cobbett—feel about food and drink. He disliked paper money exactly as he disliked tea. There is no separating the operations of his consciousness. To say that he was prejudiced is quite inadequate. He was not even capable of framing a notion as to the difference between a prejudiced judgment and an unprejudiced one. He was always " morally certain "—that dreadful, and in this world perhaps the sole, form of certitude.

This childish directness which could never distinguish between an appetite and a principle has given Cobbett's work the charm it holds for such men as Mr. Chesterton. Cobbett affords a standing invitation to paradox. Any critic can find him as full of surprises as a human being can be. He had no interest in the imaginative literature of his time; yet in one of the most obvious senses of the word, he was more romantic than Keats or Shelley. For romanticism was in part an attempt to recapture the childhood of the race. Cobbett was—though Wordsworth would have been horrified at the thought—the " mighty prophet, seer blest " of the famous ode. Now this kind of romanticism seeks the richness of sense-life not staled by unduly analytical reflection. It would revive, if we may use the word without Christian overtones of condemnation, the sentient animal in man. Animals are notoriously conservative. They like to be comfortable and undisturbed. Cobbett was a true conservative. What he valued was the good, simple, hearty life of the Englishman of fable—good food, good drink, good labour of the soil that pricks the appetites, the comfortable family life of the den. It is the intellect that finds satisfaction in novelty. Bodily necessity may be the mother of protest, but not of invention. The scheming intellect, then, is the real radical. Now Cobbett lived in a very radical and very uncomfortable age. All the old ways were disappearing. Englishmen were drinking tea and other slops; even their beer was brewed for them, and was acquiring a synthetic, manufactured flavour. Cobbett hated machinery as an animal must hate a treadmill. Moreover, the good life of the human animal, at least, must be a tribal life. Part of its satisfactions must lie in loyalty to a fixed and recognizable group. But the industrial revolution was successful only because it broke up the fixed loyalties of old England. The model for the factory was not, and could not be, the mediæval parish. Therefore the conservative Cobbett—and this is a paradox Mr. Chesterton makes the most of—became the leading English Radical. But he was a Radical only in the shallow and obvious sense of the word which involves resistance to the existing order. He was a peer of Bentham's only in that he wanted very much less of that of which the utilitarians wanted a great deal more. That both Cobbett and the utilitarians hoped a reform of Parliament would give them what they wanted afforded an accidental common rallying-point.

Cobbett notoriously began his career as a Tory of Tories. Few writers were more vituperative towards the French Revolution, that compound of " Atheism, Robbery, Unitarianism, Swindling, Jacobinism, Massacres, Civic Feasts, and Insurrections."[1] Later he could write of that movement: " In judging the French Revolution, we are not to inquire what fooleries or violences were committed during its progress; but, we are to ask, what has it produced in the end ? " In the end, he continues, it has destroyed Bourbon tyranny and given the land to the peasant. The Revolution is justified in its results.[2] Yet few men, not excepting Burke, deserve less to be called turncoats. Cobbett's conversion does not even, as does the conversion in the other direction of the Lake poets, present a subtle problem in psychology. He is an articulate Tory first in America, where the enemies of the England he could not help loving were democrats, Jacobins. On his return to England, he naturally continued to support the Tory party. But as early as 1804[3] he began to distrust Pitt for his financial measures and his obvious leanings towards the commercial classes. Cobbett was a Tory because he supposed the Tories, like himself, wanted

---

[1] *A Bone to gnaw for the Democrats* (1797), p. 12.
[2] *Selections from Cobbett's Political Works* (ed. J. M. and J. P. Cobbett), vol. vi., p. 219. Written in 1821.
[3] See *Political Works*, vol. i., and especially the third and fifth of the *Letters to William Pitt.*

to retain the old England of the soil, the England of manly rural simplicity, the England of hearty squires and heartier yeomen. Melville's impeachment opened his eyes to the existence of financial corruption which he simply had been too faithful to see.[1] The Tory party was sold to the " fundlords " as completely as the Whigs. Seats in Parliament were actually advertised *for sale* in the London dailies.[2]

How could one who loathed the cash nexus defend such a state of affairs ? Cobbett clung hopefully a while longer to his benefactor Windham. But by 1807 he has given up hope in the Tories. The *Political Register* has turned to the people of England, still uncorrupted at heart. Their governors have betrayed them. Reform is the only way out. We may take Cobbett at his own word, when, in reply to the *Elements of Reform*, a pamphlet in which his enemies reprinted some of the bitterest tirades of Porcupine against reformers, he asserted that he had mistaken his men, but not his goal. " The doctrine of *consistency*, as now in vogue, is the most absurd that ever was broached. It teaches, that, if you once think well of any person or thing, you must always think well of that person or thing."[3] You change your mind, not Yourself.

Cobbett had those gifts of the artist which are indispensable to the journalist and agitator, and which were so sadly lacking in the utilitarians. He could be interesting because he could use hard, tangible phrases that got to work at once on the senses of his readers. He could move men because he felt as they did. He could create in thousands and thousands of men that almost magical cohesion which it is out of the power of the thinker to create. The *Political Register*, become proudly *Twopenny Trash*, was the first really popular English journal. After all, the men of England were animals like himself. They, too, found the industrial revolution uncomfortable. It is one of the ironies of history that he pushed them on towards the political capping of the new movement, towards that Reform of 1832, which is the

---

[1] *Political Register*, 27th July, 1805.   [2] *Ibid.*, 9th May, 1807.
[3] *Political Works*, vol. iii., p. 237.

English Revolution of 1789. The survival of mediæval land tenure in France, and the complete failure of its aristocracy to adjust itself to the new commerce, gave the French Revolution an emotional hold over ordinary Frenchmen which enabled its leaders to overcome the inertia of the many, and achieve the rare miracle of a violent social and political change. In England, conditions for such a miracle were lacking. Thanks to Cobbett, however, Englishmen became excited over the Reform Bill. He made reform seem the common thing, the *res publica* which it was not.

Any study of Cobbett's political ideas must be an analysis of his likes and dislikes. It must try to illustrate concretely the daily life of his old England, which was simply an extension to others of his own daily life. The basis of that life was domestic. Cobbett valued highly all that Owen so disliked in the family. " Give me, for a beautiful sight, a neat and smart woman, heating her oven and setting in her bread! And, if the bustle do make the sign of labour glisten on her brow, where is the man that would not kiss that off, rather than lick the plaster from the cheek of a duchess."[1] He loved young children, and writes reverently of their " almost boneless limbs " and touching helplessness.[2] This he characteristically erects into a moral absolute. " I never knew a man that was good for *much* who had a dislike for little children; and I never knew a woman of that taste who was good for anything at all."[3]

Women he worshipped after a satisfying image of his own. " It is, I should imagine, pretty difficult to keep love alive towards a woman who *never sees the dew*, never beholds the *rising sun*, and who constantly comes directly from a reeking bed to the breakfast table, and there chews about, without appetite, the choicest morsels of human food."[4] Women must be pure. " It is not enough that a young woman abstain from everything approaching towards indecorum in her behaviour towards men; it is, with me, not enough that she cast down her eyes, or turn aside her head with a smile, when she hears an indelicate allusion: she ought to appear *not to under-*

---

[1] *Cottage Economy*, p. 77. [2] *Advice to Young Men*, section 247.
[3] *Ibid.*, section 179. [4] *Ibid.*, section 106.

D*

stand it, and to receive from it no more impression than if she were a post."[1] She must love her children, and suckle them herself. Cobbett devoted a sermon to " The Unnatural Mother," which shows him at his most domestic. " The motives [for employing a wet-nurse] are two in number, the one, that her *beauty* may not suffer from the performance of her most sacred duty; the *other*, too gross, too beastly, to be named, except within the walls of a brothel. Let it be observed, however, that, as to the first motive, it is pretty sure to *fail*, if beauty be valued on account of its power over *the husband*. For, the flame of love being past, the fire is kept alive by nothing so effectually as by the fruit of it; and, what becomes of this, if the child be banished to a hireling breast ? "[2]

For Cobbett's was a highly decent, almost Victorian, nature. There are no pathological depths in him. He never behaves the way pessimistic Christian ethics assume it is natural for the human animal to behave. His appetites are all healthy. Gluttony he abhors as " the indulgence beyond the absolute demands of nature."[3] He asserts proudly that he never " spent more than *thirty-five minutes a day at table*, including all the meals of the day."[4] He never played cards, nor wasted time in public houses.[5] He estimates that the fifteen pounds a year the average man throws away in public houses would amount, in the course of a tradesman's life, to a decent fortune for a child.[6] Men spend too much time outside the family circle. He himself had never been an absentee husband. Much of his work was written while the babies were crying—that never disturbed him.[7] He thought the text beginning " Go to the ant, thou sluggard " one of the most beautiful ever penned.[8]

Domestic happiness and natural sobriety formed the foundations of his good life. Work, for its own sake, was an essential. " To wish to live on the labour of others is, besides the folly of it, to contemplate a *fraud* at the least, and, under

---

[1] *Advice to Young Men*, section 90.   [2] *Sermons*, p. 227.
[3] *Advice to Young Men*, section 24.   [4] *Ibid.*, section 30.
[5] *Ibid.*, section 34.   [6] *Ibid.*, section 171.   [7] *Ibid.*, section 258.
[8] *Sermons*, p. 121.

certain circumstances, to meditate oppression and robbery."[1]
And this must be independent work, work like that of the
farmer who reaps where he has sown. It must rest on the
institution of private property. These independent workers
are united in a society by common tastes, by common for-
bearances, and by a common love of country. Cobbett never
worried over the intellectual opposition between the individual and the group. " A man is so identified with his country,
that he cannot, do what he will, wholly alienate himself from
it: it can know no triumph, nor any disgrace, which does
not, in part, belong to him: parents, brethren, relations,
friends, neighbours, make, all taken together, a good half
of one's self."[2]

Cobbett, as we have said, never thought of criticizing, or
rounding out this moral world of his into a system. He loved
the look of the English countryside. He also wanted
Englishmen to produce their own food. When, therefore,
he ardently defends live and wasteful hedges in contrast to
dead and efficient fences, he simply sinks the weaker desire
in the stronger.[3] He ought to have felt some sympathy—if
sympathies only went by ought to's—for Samuel Johnson,
whom he nevertheless calls " old dread-death and dread-
devil Johnson, that teacher of moping and melancholy."[4] He
disliked the false modesty of " genteelisms " and attacked
expressions like " small-clothes "[5]; yet in the very same
passage he denies that any modest woman could allow a man
to attend her at childbirth. He would have none of Jenner's
vaccination—naturally enough he distrusted physicians—
but he defends inoculation with smallpox itself.[6] Perhaps
the most striking example of his inability to allow facts to
influence his judgment is his determined insistence that,
census figures to the contrary notwithstanding, the population of England had not greatly increased between 1801 and
1821.[7] Since England took a century, he says, to grow from
five millions to eight, it could not possibly have grown from

---

[1] *Advice to Young Men*, section 13.   [2] *Emigrant's Guide*, p. 5.
[3] *Rural Rides* (edited by Pitt Cobbett), vol. i., p. 50.   [4] *Ibid.*, vol. i, p. 48.
[5] *Advice to Young Men*, section 239.   [6] *Ibid.*, sections 261-265.
[7] *Political Works*, vol. vi., p. 346.

eight millions to eleven in twenty years. This is not *a priori* reasoning; it is pure romance.

When Cobbett ventures, as he has to venture, into political generalizations, this picturesque immediacy of judgment betrays him. These generalizations carry with them concrete consequences. They influence, according to a law of their own, the very world of likes and dislikes which for Cobbett never changed. The social contract theory and the patriarchal theory do not affect political practice in the same way. Cobbett, as a matter of fact, held them both in a fraternal and unnatural embrace. His political theories are, to use the cant word, rationalizations. But rationalizations do a work of their own in this world, a work Cobbett simply could not understand. Property he thought with Locke was crystallized labour. To live without labour he thought immoral, " unless you have ample fortune whereon to live clear of debt."[1] That rigid adherence to his definition of property would destroy most property in his England apparently did not enter his mind. He did not like property in stocks and bonds, because he did not like the new rich. He thought men of property should care for the poor. He wanted the poor to be self-respecting, and to own a little property of their own. It is all very confusing, and very well meant.

Cobbett accepts an extraordinary amount of the fashionable political theory of the Enlightenment. " These truths are written on the heart of man : that all men are, by nature, *equal*; that civil society can never have arisen from any motive other than that of the *benefit of the whole*; that, whenever civil society makes the greater part of the people *worse off* than they were under the Law of Nature, the civil compact is, in conscience, dissolved, and all the rights of nature return; that, in civil society, the *rights and the duties go hand in hand*, and that, when the former are taken away, the latter cease to exist . . . rights going before duties, as value received goes before payment."[2] Freedom he defined as Macaulay might have defined it: " Freedom is not an empty sound; it is not an abstract idea; it is not a thing

---

[1] *Advice to Young Men*, section 13.   [2] *Ibid.*, sections 334, 335.

that nobody can feel. It means, and it means *nothing else*, *the full and quiet enjoyment of your own property.*"[1]

Now these free and equal men, banded together under the social contract, each with his own property, will govern themselves by a representative Parliament. "The great right, therefore, of *every man*, the right of rights, is the right of having a share in the making of the laws, to which the good of the whole makes it his duty to submit."[2] This right is no mere abstract principle. It is a practical matter, for a man who pays taxes should help decide how much he pays and for what purpose the money is spent.[3] Once the whole people share in determining taxation, a lessening of governmental expenditure is inevitable. Cobbett actually uses the Broughamese phrase to describe the ultimate end of government—"cheapness."[4] His government will not even interfere to provide compulsory education. "The general taste of parents and their naturally high opinion of their children's capacities, are quite sufficient to furnish the schools, without the aid of another Act of Parliament and *another cursed tax.*"[5] Finally, he is an exponent of Free Trade.[6]

This is certainly a pretty complete outline of a *laissez-faire* political philosophy, most of it, let it be noted, in Cobbett's own words. Nothing could be more contrary to what Cobbett really wanted. He had, it is true, that English devotion to the yeomanry ideal, that notion of the individual independent in the castle of his home, which gives a more than abstract force to his distrust of the State. He had an unquestioning devotion to the historical paraphernalia of English rights. But above all he hated the England of fund-lords and manufacturers, and he loved the England of the common people. To protect the common people, to restore them to what he imagined had been their old status, he is willing to use any possible method. " I wish to see the poor

---

[1] *A History of the Protestant Reformation in England and Ireland*, vol. i, section 456.
[2] *Advice to Young Men*, section 336.   [3] *Ibid.*, sections 348, 349.
[4] *Legacy to Parsons*, p. 182.   [5] *Political Works*, vol. ii., p. 289.
[6] *Letters on the Late War between Great Britain and the United States*, p. 141.

men of England what the poor men of England were when
I was born," he said in a famous phrase.[1] He is an interventionist in spirit. The tragedy of his life lies in his conviction that the Reformed Parliament would intervene as he
desired. He lived to see that Parliament, of which he was a
member, pass the new Poor Law.

This desire to intervene in the free play of economic life
to protect the poor comes out in all his work. He admired
the Church of the Middle Ages because it was the "guardian
of the common people," and he is as bitter as Disraeli on the
spoliation by which the English Reformation robbed a
common thing for the good of a few.[2] Absolute ownership
of the land is un-English. "Men lawfully possess only the
USE of land and of things attached to the land; and they must
take care that in USING them, they do not do injury to any
other part of the community, or to the whole of the community
taken together." Cobbett brings forward a long list of
things a man may *not* do with his own—such as producing
unnecessary noises, smoke, other nuisances, allowing stal-
lions to roam on commons, and so on; he concludes that
landlords may not drive tenants and cottagers off their land,
that on the contrary they must provide for them.[3] "That
there ought to *be no legal provision for the poor and destitute*;
that all such provision is *essentially bad*; that such provision,
even for the aged and infirm, ought not to be made; and that
even the *giving of alms to the wretched is an evil*: these asser-
tions of MALTHUS and BROUGHAM . . . demand a serious,
and, at the same time, an indignant and scornful, refuta-
tion."[4] Cobbett was even willing to achieve his desires by
so revolutionary a step as expropriation. He suggests that,
if conditions get worse, it may be necessary to make every
tenant of house or land worth less than ten pounds a year an
owner in fee-simple, indemnifying the present owners with
money saved by Governmental economies.[5] His natural

[1] *Political Works*, vol. ii., p. 285.
[2] *A History of the Protestant Reformation in England and Ireland*, vol. i.,
section 456.
[3] *Legacy to Labourers*, p. 73.   [4] *Ibid.*, p. 100.
[5] *Political Works*, vol. v., p. 392.

conservatism comes out in his respect for a real landed
aristocracy, for an aristocracy built on the true patriarchal
principle. He contrasts the old " resident *native* gentry,
attached to the soil, known to every farmer and labourer
from their childhood, frequently mixing with them in those
pursuits where all artificial distinctions are lost," and the
modern non-resident gentleman, who merely recuperates on
his acres from city dissipations.[1]

Nor are Cobbett's economic notions orthodox. Something
—he is never quite sure what—must call a halt to the immoral expansion of wealth. He looks back fondly on the
mediæval prohibition of interest, and regrets that men have
abandoned the teaching of the Fathers in this as in so many
other respects.[2] Paper money and the whole machinery of
credit he loathed. It made possible the sponging existence
of the speculator. It upset everyone with the false hope of
unearned riches. Accidental success in the hurly-burly
turned " those whom nature and good laws [note the
phrase " nature and good laws "] made to black shoes,
sweep chimnies or the streets," into men " rolling in car-
riages, or sitting in saloons surrounded by gaudy footmen
with napkins twisted round their thumbs."[3] Paper money
brought inevitable inflation, and inflation benefited the
adventurer, the man whose assets were as mobile as his
principles, and injured the sober, steady man whose assets
were fixed. It injured the workman, for wages never rise as
rapidly as prices. Yet deflation would bring an unearned
gain to all those who had lent money to the nation at the high
price level. Cobbett's remedy was characteristically simple
and unburdened with theoretical scruples: reduce the
interest rate on the national debt.[4] He thought no other
solution possible, and offered to allow himself to be broiled
alive if the return to a gold basis as provided for in Peel's
Bill proved possible.[5] Cobbett never understood the incredible powers of the new industry. In the end, England actually produced enough new goods to balance the increase in

---

[1] *Rural Rides*, vol. i., p. 46.
[2] *Advice to Young Men*, section 63.   [3] *Ibid*, section 69.
[4] *Political Works*, vol. vi., p. 179.   [5] *Ibid*, vol. vi., p. 42.

the quantity of money brought on by the expenses of the Government in the Napoleonic wars. The new wealth undoubtedly created the world of speculation Cobbett disliked; it undoubtedly corrupted, and then destroyed, his beloved rural England; but it certainly was no fiction.

Cobbett's great failure, after all, was a failure of the understanding. So many of his outraged feelings are the feelings of all honest men that we are inclined to over-much sympathy with him. We, too, dislike the England of his wrath, " the capacious jails and penitentiaries; the stock exchange; the hot and ancle and knee-swelling, and lung-destroying cotton-factories; the whiskered standing army and its splendid barracks; the parson-captains, parson-lieutenants, parson-ensigns and parson-justices; the poor rates and pauper houses; and by no means forgetting, that blessing which is peculiarly and doubly and ' gloriously ' protestant, the NATIONAL DEBT."[1] But our sympathies, and the attraction which so able a master of the concrete in words must have for us, ought not to conceal from us Cobbett's weakness as a prophet. With his diagnosis of the political and social evils of his time we may easily agree. In the name of economic freedom, men were exploiting other men. Somehow, the assurance of regularity had gone out of life. For that part of their nature that demands something fixed and eternal, men could find no satisfaction. Cobbett, though he never used the phrase, was as aware as St. Simon or Comte that what his century lacked was a unified scheme of social reconstruction, a universal faith.

But any such faith is a constructive effort of the whole of man's faculties. Men build abiding faiths out of the world of sense-experience in which they live. But what gives to faith an apparent independence of the chaos of experience is the intellectual effort which has gone into the absorption of this experience. In spite of what is still current opinion to the contrary, effective human belief has always an element of reason. For human reason alone can make the adjustment between novelties forced on human experience—the

[1] *A History of the Protestant Reformation in England and Ireland*, vol. i., section 93.

72

machine, for instance—and habit. Now Cobbett, as we have tried to show, never made this effort of adjustment. In purely personal terms, he merely growled at being disturbed in his habits. In a wider sense applying to the system of ideas he had after all to work with, he sought to maintain the old frame of society, the old specific adjustments to a given situation, and to destroy, or neglect, he was never quite sure which, the new situation. He says definitely that he never sought to *change* or *destroy* the institutions of England, but to do away with innovations upon them, the encroachments of aristocracy, and especially of the usurers' aristocracy, new treason laws, combination laws, Bourbon-police laws, taxation, standing armies, *agents provocateurs*, and so on.[1] Most deeply rooted in Cobbett was that kind of moral solipsism which is the source of much of what goes by the name of Conservatism. He could never even admit the existence of moral values outside himself. Therefore the question of adjusting his scheme of values to altered conditions never troubled him. For as Cobbett lacked the intellectual detachment which would have allowed him to criticize his own habits, so he lacked the imaginative capacity which would have enabled him to salvage those habits, in part at least, in a new faith.

He was, however, too uncomfortable to keep quiet. The very intensity with which he felt a conservative's unhappiness in a changing world prevented his making the compromises with novelty by which most conservatives cheat themselves. He was no Eldon. Something had to be done. We have already explained the pathetic fervour with which he took up the Radical cause. His blundering enthusiasm led him to do the thing most contrary to his ultimate hopes. Were he alive to-day, he would surely be even more unhappy than he was in the England of the Regency. Yet most of what he fought for politically has been achieved. The men of England were no Cobbetts. They were either far more flexible, or far more cowardly, than he. The England of universal suffrage has not proved to be the England of *Cottage Economy*. Just why Cobbett was so wrong cannot be

---

[1] *Legacy to Labourers*, pp. 5-17.

73

answered in a formula. Yet it seems most likely that he carried the natural conservatism of the average man to heroism. We may worship heroes, but we do not imitate them. Not even the Englishman will really die for his beer. Indeed, the only kind of heroism that comes near being practical is heroism in defence of the abstract. Cobbett was too attached to common things to be a successful defender of them. We return to his fundamental failure—his failure to use his intellect to correct, build up, and render systematic, and thus shareable with other men, his prejudices.

5. COLERIDGE[1]

Not the least of the difficulties confronting the study of political ideas is the virtual impossibility of exact definition of some of its most indispensable terms. One cannot get far in the subject without having recourse to the word conservative. Now the man in the street, and the dictionary too, are agreed in defining a conservative as a man who supports the existing political system and resists any change in that system. But, as we have seen, only third-rate minds like Eldon's and Croker's come somewhere near satisfying this definition in the first third of the nineteenth century in England. In the modern world, at least, very few articulate persons have been willing to defend the existing order *in toto*. We shall have to extend our definition of conservative from the mere question of change to that of the quality of change. We shall have to admit the existence of several kinds of conservatives, insufficiently described without the addition of a qualifying epithet.

First, there is the ordinary conservative, the conservative of the dictionary. He is the man who, from satisfaction with

---

[1] Coleridge's mature political philosophy is best studied in *On the Constitution of the Church and State* (1830). Some of his milder Jacobinical thought may be found in his daughter Sara's collection of his *Essays on his own Times* (1850). Much of *The Friend* (1837), and *The Statesman's Manual : A Lay Sermon* (1816), is of political import. See Mill, J. S., " Coleridge " in *Dissertations*, vol. ii. ; Cobban, A., *Edmund Burke and the Revolt against the Eighteenth Century* (1929), chap. vi., Brinton, C., *Political Ideas of the English Romanticists* (1926), chap. ii.

existing conditions, or from mere inertia of mind and will, accepts things as they are. He rarely takes the trouble to commit himself to paper, but he exists in great numbers. Such men may be Bolshevists in modern Russia, Fascists in modern Italy, and Republicans—or Democrats—in modern America. Their constancy, and therefore their susceptibility to definition, lies in their temperament, not in their tenets. Second, there is the conservative of the flesh. He is the man who, living in a time of transition, carries over from his youth certain desires and satisfactions, hardened into habits, which can only with difficulty be realized under the new order. The more sheltered his youth, the more exceptional his environment, the more definitely he comes into conflict with the world of his maturity. It is impossible, also, to avoid the conclusion that some men are born with a temperamental opposition to things as they are. Such men may sometimes adopt a purely abstract scheme of better things, and become true radicals. Or they may root their ideas in an imaginary, or only partly real, past, and become conservatives of this second kind. Cobbett, with his whole background of Farnham life, was a pure conservative of the flesh, not untouched by a temperamental opposition to things as they are. Third, there is the philosophical conservative. He is the man who works out a consistent and timeless generalization applying to the behaviour of men in politics. The details of his scheme must vary with the political conditions to which he applies it. But the central point is the same. The philosophical conservative distrusts his fellow men. He is therefore on the side of authority as opposed to liberty. Since any given authority usually has its foundations in the past, he is commonly a defender of the past. But it is not resistance to change so much as the conviction that any change will destroy authority and free the way to untrustworthy individual desires that marks him out as a conservative. Now most modern anti-authoritarian movements stem from the optimistic eighteenth-century trust in the goodness —or the usefulness—of the desires of the common man; and most modern authoritarian—that is, philosophical conservative—movements stem from the two great pessimistic opponents of this eighteenth-century doctrine of the natural goodness of man, Burke and Maistre. In the England with which we are concerned in this chapter, Coleridge is the greatest disciple of Burke. Coleridge was so far from being contented with the England of 1830 that he fails entirely to conform to the dictionary definition of the conservative as the man who accepts the established order. But he is certainly a philosophical conservative. His figure rounds out pretty completely a study of English political thought from Bentham to the passing of the Reform Bill of 1832.

In spite of John Mill's essay, Coleridge is not always given the place he merits in the history of English political thought. His fame as a poet has delivered him over to purely literary critics. His failure as a metaphysician has unduly discredited all his prose writings. Yet his influence as a political moralist was very great indeed. He, one suspects, rather than Mrs. Taylor, was responsible for the conversion of John Mill from Bentham's doctrinaire atomism to a more critical conception of the relation between society and the individual. Through his influence on Maurice and hence on Kingsley, he is one of the founders of Christian Socialism in England. The debt of the Oxford movement to him is not inconsiderable. Even Carlyle, in spite of the ungraciousness of his famous description of the sage of Highgate, owed more than he admitted to Coleridge. The settled form which philosophical conservatism took in nineteenth-century England, that Tory democracy which is still far from dead, finds its pattern in the work of Coleridge.

Like his fellow poets, Wordsworth and Southey, Coleridge was a Jacobin in his youth. The promise of the French Revolution was too great to be resisted by a well-wisher of his kind. Coleridge never had that touching humanitarian affection for his fellow men that inspired Bentham, but he did want men to be happy and well behaved. With him Jacobinism was what Taine claimed it commonly is, a disease of youth. He was simply overcome by a contagion of hope. What he sought for in the French Revolution, and in its democratic frame of government, was a stable society in which the conflicting passions of men would be stilled in obedience. He himself could never trust his own instincts, let alone those of other men. Opium-taking hardly leads to the good life according to the utilitarians. Coleridge sought a discipline in the French Revolution. He found Napoleon, and a kind of discipline he did not like. He therefore abandoned his youthful faith, and sought another.[1]

This faith is fairly completely expounded in his *Constitution of the Church and State* of 1830. Coleridge was seeking for an answer to the question: How can selfish, unruly, natural men live together in such a way as to prevent their mutual extermination ? Man, left to himself, is *homini lupus*. What was the Committee of Public Safety but a pack of wolves ? Yet such committees are fortunately rare phenomena. On the whole, men manage to get on in civil society much better than a study of the psychology of individuals would lead us to fear. The commonwealth is a better thing than its separate members. Men are more than men because they must live up to a certain standard set for them by the State. It is this standard that we commonly call the constitution.

Now what, in 1830, is the constitution of England ? It is obviously not the existing government. There is inherent in the notion of a constitution an element of moral ordering. Now the acts of a given set of men—and especially the acts of such men as have governed England from the younger Pitt through Liverpool to Wellington—do not in themselves provide a moral code. At worst—and in 1830 we are almost driven to use this phrase in describing the work of the long Tory rule—they may be based on a hand-to-mouth expediency which is content to stumble along without actually falling. No, the constitution of England is an idea in the full philosophic acceptance of the term. It is a regulative principle from which men may stray, as they stray from the Ten Commandments, but to which human reason must always, in the long run, bring them back. Coleridge was much attached to a distinction between *reason* and *understanding* based on the German distinction between *Vernunft* and

---

[1] His Jacobinism, which is pretty ordinary as to content, may be studied in his Bristol publications, the *Conciones ad Populum*, and the *Watchman*, in *Essays on his Own Times*, vol. i.

Verstand.[1] We cannot afford to go too deeply into the metaphysical distinctions here involved. Briefly, Coleridge asserts that understanding, the reason of the *philosophes* and the Benthamites, deals with means and not with ends, that it tells us how to get what we want, but that it does not tell us what we ought to want. True reason, however, deals with ends, and somehow guides men's wants. It explains our judgments of *value*, not indeed according to crude logic— this is the weapon of the mere understanding—but according to something more deeply human than logic. It is Pascal's *esprit de finesse*, and not his *esprit de géometrie*.

This true reason is in a sense a racial inheritance. Its judgments have gathered strength and body for us from the Greeks onward. Through reason we may learn what the constitution of England really is; but we must not take the present as our guide. That is to make the error of the utilitarians. We must seek the constitution of England in the whole past of the race, just as we must seek its literature in its whole past. The constitution thus arrived at will be an idea, a creature of the mind, if you like, but therefore far more real than an object of present sense-experience.[2] Equipped with this idea, we may then judge contemporary politics in accordance with it. We may decide what are legitimate institutions, and what are mere excrescences. We may retain and develop the former, and prune away the latter.[3]

There are, says Coleridge, and always have been, three estates in England, " the first being the estate of the land-owners or possessors of fixed property, consisting of the two classes of the Barons and the Franklins; the second comprising the merchants, the manufacturers, free artisans, and the distributive class "; and the third being the National Church.[4] The first two he groups together as the Proprietage, the third forms the Nationality. He distinguishes carefully, if not very satisfactorily, between the Church of Christ, which is not of this world at all, and the National

---

[1] *The Statesman's Manual : A Lay Sermon*, Appendix C.
[2] *Constitution of the Church and State* (edited by H. N. Coleridge, 1839), p. 19.
[3] *Ibid.*, p. 20.   [4] *Ibid.*, pp. 45-47.

Church, which is concerned with the better ordering of this world. Historically, ministers of the Christian word have in England, by a fortunate accident, been members of the Nationality, or National Church,[1] and at present this Nationality, where it has not been completely perverted to other ends, is limited to these ministers. But this total coincidence of membership is not necessary, nor indeed desirable. The Nationality is in idea a group of men exempted by a secured income from the play of economic competition, and devoting their lives to maintaining and increasing the spiritual possessions of the race. These men are, in the widest sense, men of learning. They are members of what Coleridge calls the Clerisy, clerks in the mediæval sense in which any educated man was a clerk. Especially since the Reformation, such men have in increasing numbers entered the economic struggle, and doctors, lawyers, teachers, scientists, and engineers—members of what we now call the liberal professions—are considered on the same independent footing as merchants and artisans. The fund of the Nationality, however, has been in great part perverted to the selfish uses of the Tudor aristocracy. Only clergymen are now supported by this fund. And even in this use there is much abuse—absenteeship, plurality of benefices, misappropriation of the funds of the great schools and colleges. To return to the Constitution of England, we must at once restore this fund, and see that it is used, first, to support revived and truly liberal institutions of higher learning; second, to maintain a pastor, presbyter, or parson in every parish; third, to maintain a schoolmaster in every parish.[2] We may then hope to restore learning gradually to its old freedom from the pressure of economic life. We may make the liberal professions into careers of disinterested investigation.

The other two orders make up what Coleridge calls the Proprietage. The first order is divided into that of the Barons, and that of the Franklins. The Barons, with their great and assured incomes from the land, are the chief

---

[1] *Constitution of the Church and State*, p. 59. [2] *Ibid.*, p. 56.

element in the stability of England. They stand wholly for permanence. Lifted above the rest of their countrymen, they are peculiarly the trustees of its institutions, and sit by themselves in Parliament in a separate house. Only slightly below them in rank, wealth, and prestige are the Franklins (the country gentlemen of other writers). These Franklins, too, make a group interested above all in permanence. But they are nearer the third estate than the Barons. Their children, indeed, will often pass over into the ranks of the third estate. Since the Franklins are too numerous to form a house of their own, they send to Parliament the knights of the shire. By an often-noticed good fortune of the English political constitution, these knights of the shire sit with the representatives of the personal, or mercantile, interests in the same House. This personal, or mercantile, interest is the last element in English society. Its property is not in immovable land, but in goods. Its interests are all in progress, in change. Any business is in a sense a speculation, and therefore you will not find in business men that sober, conservative adherence to established ways you will find in the landed division of the Proprietage.

Within the Proprietage, then, the two forces essential to a stable, but not decaying, society, the forces of permanence and of progression, are suitably balanced. The Proprietage itself, whose interests are, in the neutral sense of the word, selfish and worldly, is balanced by the Nationality, or the Clerisy, whose members are free to devote themselves to things of the spirit. As regards individuals, of course, these groups or interests are not hard and fixed castes. Any advanced state must provide something like the career open to talents. Yet however much they may " modify and leaven each other," they will never do so completely, " but that the distinct character will remain legible."[1]

This outline of the English Constitution is not in all respects as new as its terminology. It owes much to the familiar theory of checks and balances. But Coleridge is far from repeating the formula of Locke and Montesquieu. In the first place, his concept of the *rôle* of the Clerisy was new.

---

[1] *Constitution of the Church and State*, p. 28.

Again, his theory of the regulative action of the idea of the constitution involves a notion of the State quite different from that commonly held in the previous century. Though he rejects the Rousseauistic social contract as falsely pretending to an historical origin, and as starting from a false individualism, he insists that the State is based on " the idea of an ever-originating contract " which elevates the individual from a thing to a person. Without this idea, you have no commonwealth, but only a slave-plantation.[1] The State thus exists because a man is a moral entity. The test of an act of the Government then, is not whether it interferes with the crude freedom of the individual to follow what his understanding tells him is his interest, but whether it conforms with the morality dictated by his reason. Coleridge dodges the difficulty which Rousseau faced. He does not insist in so many words that State action may conform to a reason, to a morality, that the individual is too limited to appreciate. But there can be no doubt that he accepts the implications of his idealistic conception of the State. When the natural leaders of the State are convinced that a course of action conforms to true morality, they are justified in imposing this course on their fellows.

As a matter of fact, Coleridge, true to his idealistic position, will not admit that, however much individual interests may actually clash with a given state action, there is in a properly constituted society any antithesis between the individual and the group. If you act on utilitarian assumptions, you do of course get such a clash. But the utilitarians assume individuals to be sovereign and equal, and therefore their group is a fiction. Actually, the individual is, as a moral person, linked to a group which has a life of its own. The society which Coleridge describes in terms of Nationality and Proprietage he conceives to be endowed with the reality human imagination gives to such abstractions as Justice, Right, and Beauty. The individual is fitted into such a society by the absolute fact of *value*. Such a society—and we must not be afraid of the word—is properly hierarchical. The best must indeed come to the top. But it

---

[1] *Constitution of the Church and State*, p. 15.

will not come to the top in the senseless competition of flesh with flesh. In a struggle determined by the uncensored desires of the majority, Shakespeare would be worsted by the merest penny-a-liner. True superiority must rest on the respectful subordination of the inferior.

We have thus arrived at the central point of Coleridge's political philosophy. The State is " a moral unit, an organic whole."[1] The individual's place in the State is ultimately determined by his value to the State. This value is an absolute of experience, like any other moral judgment. What we call the rights and duties of the individual—the two are inseparable[2]—are the external, tangible marks by which we may know whether that individual has his proper place in the State. It is misleading to say that men have *equal* rights and duties, but we must say that all have *equally* rights and duties. The landed gentry have rights to their property. The agricultural labourers have no such rights. But the landed gentry have also the duty of using their property as a trust so that the agricultural labourers may not fall into the condition of mere beasts. So, too, with education. No man has an unconditional right to an education. He has only a certain given capacity for education. The gifted few will devote themselves to philosophy and science, and attain to a position in the Clerisy. This position will carry with it the right to support from the fund of the Nationality, and the duty to use learning in accordance with true reason for the good of all. The many will not receive the ridiculous education proposed by Brougham and his like—the popularizing even of so limited a study as science is inevitably its plebification—but will be taught the sober and obvious facts of Christian subordination.[3]

Coleridge's position is that of the Tory democrat. The few must govern, but in the interests of all. Nay, only the few know fully the interests of all. But it is essential that the few realize that their position is a fiduciary one. Once you accept the fact of human inequality, and at the same time

[1] *Constitution of the Church and State*, p. 117.
[2] *Essays on his Own Times*, vol. i., pp. 6-29.
[3] *Constitution of the Church and State*, p. 71.

throw all human activity open to unlimited competition, you get the shocking rule of might evident in modern England. The great tragedy of the success of the " mechanico-corpuscular theory " of the eighteenth century is the hold it has gained on the English upper classes.[1] They have come to believe that they are responsible to themselves alone for their possessions. But they must be made to realize that if they have more than is necessary for their own wants, more than their own wants must be felt by them as their interests.[2] They must learn that " the possession of a property, not connected with especial duties, a property not fiduciary or official, but arbitrary and unconditional, was in the sight of our forefathers the brand of a Jew and an alien; not the distinction, nor the right, nor the honour, of an English baron or gentleman."[3]

The results of this betrayal of their trust by the natural guardians of the people is visible everywhere in the England of 1830. Not even Cobbett exceeded Coleridge in the vehemence of his condemnation of the new industrial society. " Then we have game laws, corn laws, cotton factories, Spitalfields, the tillers of the land paid by poor rates, and the remainder of the population mechanized into engines for the manufactory of new rich men;—yea, the machinery of the wealth of the nation made up of the wretchedness, disease, and depravity of those who should constitute the strength of the nation! Disease, I say, and vice, while the wheels are in full motion; but at the first stop the magic wealth-machine is converted into an intolerable weight of pauperism."[4] Or again: " Gin consumed by paupers to the value of about eighteen millions yearly: government by clubs of journeymen; by saint and sinner societies, committees, institutions; by reviews, magazines and above all by newspapers: lastly, crimes quadrupled for the whole country, and in some counties decupled."[5]

---

[1] *Constitution of the Church and State*, p. 68.
[2] *A Lay Sermon addressed to the Higher and Middle Classes on the Existing Distresses and Discontents* (1817), Introduction.
[3] *Constitution of the Church and State*, pp. 44-45.
[4] *Ibid.*, p. 66.   [5] *Ibid.*, p. 70.

Now such conditions are the inevitable result of the philosophy of *laissez-faire*. But this philosophy has won its way by no mere force of abstract ideas. It has prevailed in England because it corresponds to, and expresses, the interests of a class. Ever since the miscalled Glorious Revolution of 1688, the trading classes, the third estate of the nation, have been gaining a disastrous predominance. Englishmen are devoured by a desire for gain. What should be but a part of the State has taken command of the whole. Land and learning alike are sacrificed to trade.[1] This is a corruption of the true constitution of England. The true constitution can only be restored if the landed interest and the Clerisy co-operate. But landed gentry and men of learning must first purge themselves of the commercial taint. They must abandon the struggle for wealth, and be content with what they have. Specifically, they must curb economic competition by legal regulation of hours and conditions of labour, by inspection of factories and output, by setting standards in the good old mediæval way. Above all, they must recognize that the constitution of England is a regulative norm superior to any momentary combination of interests. Thus they will check the present omnipotence of a Parliament devoted to the interests of trade. Coleridge has no use for what he regards as the utilitarian theory of sovereignty. The true sovereign in England is not the Parliament, but the whole body of the English people rightly functioning in accordance with the idea of its constitution.[2]

Coleridge, then, maintains the idealistic position that the State is a moral entity transcending the sense-experience of its members, that the good of the State is also the good of its members, but that this good is not ascertainable by the individual who follows the mere dictates of his own senses, and that, since most men are constantly tempted so to follow the dictates of their senses, the virtuous and enlightened few must use the machinery of the State to enforce right conduct on the many. But, as he also maintains, this enforced right

---

[1] See especially the *Lay Sermon . . . on the Existing Distresses and Discontents*.

[2] *Constitution of the Church and State*, chap. xi. " The Omnipotence of Parliament."

conduct is what the many, too, in so far as they are men and
not animals, really know instinctively (not with their lying
understandings) to be what they want. This State will be
hierarchically organized; the privileged few will govern in
accordance with the best inheritance of their predecessors,
in accordance with that right frame of political society of
which the past gives the surest, though not the whole, sign. It
is tempting to conclude this summary of Coleridge's thought
with the neat generalization that with him, as with other
thinkers, idealistic metaphysics and Conservative politics
are necessarily united. The conservative is an idealist, the
liberal an empiricist. But as we shall see, T. H. Green had
an even more soundly idealistic metaphysics than Coleridge,
yet he always considered himself a Liberal in politics. The
truth is that a man's metaphysics seem sometimes to be not
the most fundamental thing about him; or better, perhaps,
that the opposition of idealist and empiricist is only one
aspect of the complexities of the human temperament.

The generalizations of ethics, and therefore of politics, are
capable of infinitely varied adaptations to the temperament
of the individual. It is fairly safe to conclude, however, that
the opposition between pessimist and optimist in ethics
translates itself in politics into the opposition between Conservative and Liberal. Any ethics involves a distinction between good and bad, between what might be and what is. That
whatever is, is right, is a formula to which a man's metaphysics
may logically lead him, but which no man really attempts to live
by. Now there is curiously little actual difference in the
modern Western world, at least, as to the specific content
of the better order. Bentham ultimately measured pain and
pleasure much as the Christian estimates vice and virtue.

Where men do chiefly differ is over the way in which this
better order can be realized. Some men believe that the
individual has the capacity to attain to this order by following
something within himself—instinct, common sense, reason.
That which history has accumulated outside the individual,
and which society as now organized would have him conform
to, is somehow inferior to himself. Convention is evil, revolt
against convention good. In degrees varying from pure

anarchism to mild liberalism, such men hold that the best course of action is to trust the individual to work out his own destiny. Other men believe that the individual is somehow inferior to his social inheritance. The man who acts according to something within himself—instinct, common sense, reason—is likely to do evil. Convention is the product of a wisdom not visible in any one man at any one time, let alone in masses of men. What saves man in this world is his willingness to obey a will which, in his inmost consciousness, he realizes is superior to himself, though at the same time mysteriously a part of himself. In degrees varying from benevolent despotism of the one to a mild conservative respect for what is established, such men hold that the best course of action is to maintain obedience to a specific code. This code is assumed by most conservatives to be more or less the prevailing code. But as we have seen, many conservatives would seek that code in the recent, or even in the far, past. Even when a thinker pretends to formulate his own code, as did Plato, it is not an abuse of the term to call him a conservative. It is possible metaphysically to reconcile liberty and authority, as Rousseau did in his famous phrase about forcing a man to be free. But in this world, the specific test is reasonably clear: shall the individual do what he wants to do, or shall he do what another, or others, want him to do? Now Coleridge, in the last resort, wants men to obey others. Those others are the gentlemen and the scholars of England. If the common men of England are in revolt against their superiors, it is because their superiors have been false to their past. Reform is necessary, but it is an aristocratic and not a democratic reform. To restore obedience you must restore what is worth obeying.

Disraeli, and indeed Carlyle, said little more than this. It seems probable that some men will always say it. Whether they will be listened to or not probably depends on circumstances the social scientist can only incompletely analyse. At any rate, as time went on the nineteenth century paid increasing attention to the philosophy of authority. Coleridge to-day is far less old-fashioned than Bentham. Nationality and Proprietage seem less remote than *laissez-faire*.

86

CHAPTER III

CHARTISM

THE inevitable subjectivity of historical judgments can hardly appear more clearly than when an attempt is made to change the quantitative measurement of time in a qualitative one. Centuries prove recalcitrant enough to qualitative estimate. Certainly the nineteenth century, if it has a life of its own, does not begin with 1800 nor end with 1899. One could defend an eighteenth century lasting from 1715 to 1789, and a nineteenth century lasting from 1789 to 1914. The subdivision of a century is even more difficult. Dicey's familiar symmetrical division of the nineteenth century in England into three more or less equal parts is in many ways a happy one. Certainly 1832 is an inescapable boundary-mark. Yet the second Reform Bill is by no means as significant as the first, and one may find Dicey's choice of the middle 'sixties as a dividing-mark a bit too symmetrical.

For the study of English political thought, at least, the period between the passage of the first Reform Bill in 1832 and the dying-out of Chartist agitation in the Christian Socialism of the early 'fifties, has certain marked characteristics. In these twenty years, there was always present in men's minds the possibility that the English working classes would assume political power, perhaps even by some kind of violence. The condition-of-England question was still open in all its details. Could the ruling classes, even with the aid of the newly enfranchised middle class, maintain their old position ? The failure of the monster petition gave a pretty satisfactory assurance that they could. After the turn of the half-century—the Exposition of 1851 is an excellent landmark here—men settled down to work out the Victorian compromise. Victorian civilization is something more than a mere struggle. It is a brief, but real, moment of social equilibrium, comparable in a way to the Augustan age of Pope and Walpole. It is a definite order, a hierarchy of a kind, a society in which an old aristocracy maintained itself by the politic adoption of the ethical and æsthetic standards

87

of a middle class whose interests it contrived to make its own.

This Victorian compromise grew out of the conflicts of the 'thirties and 'forties, but it was very far from getting itself established in that period. There was still the possibility in men's minds, as long as Chartism was alive, as long as the Oxford movement was still young, as long as Free Trade was an aggressive crusade with ambitions no more limited to England than the ambitions of the great Revolution had been limited to France, as long as Christian Socialism was both Christian and Socialist, that England would undergo a complete social transformation. Many of the political thinkers of the Chartist era continued to live and write long after 1850. Many of them came to alter their ideas under new influences. But all of them were formed in the stress of the 'thirties and 'forties, and all of them wrote with the apostolic fervour born of conflict. Later Victorian writing has not quite this consciousness of new worlds to create. It is combative and critical enough, but it is far less hopeful of immediate change.

We shall, then, in this chapter, concern ourselves with the thinkers whose world was formed for them by the passage of the Reform Bill of 1832, and who in turn formed the world we call Victorian. They show the multanimity characteristic of modern thought. They are, like all thinkers, in part the product of social forces which the most optimistic rationalist would not dare maintain they wholly controlled. They are very far from forming anything like a school. But they do have in common a preoccupation with a condition-of-England question which the Reform Bill of 1832 had made only the more acute. They are all confronted with the industrial revolution as a *fait accompli*. England can no longer grow food enough to support her population. She cannot immediately, at least, become again the green and pleasant land of Cobbett's hopes. But she cannot remain the England of slums, of strikes, of periodic unemployment. She cannot remain in unnatural conflict with herself. Mill, Cobden, Kingsley, Disraeli, Newman, and Carlyle have this in common—they are all conscious architects of a new England.

I. MILL[1]

John Stuart Mill's career is not infrequently explained as the gradual, but never complete, emancipation of an emotional nature from a precocious and narrow rationalism. Indoctrinated rather than educated by his father, he underwent in his youth a nervous crisis which nearly destroyed him, and which we can quite easily describe as emotional starvation. Released from this crisis by the work of Wordsworth and Coleridge, he was partially converted to the transcendentalism of Carlyle. Then followed a gradual return to the intellectual position of his youth, as he found Carlyle's ethics and politics more and more authoritarian and pessimistic, more and more turned towards the doctrine of renunciation of this world. In this middle period, the period of his great writings, his rationalism was tempered with a sympathy for the oppressed, a devotion to the life of the spirit, which he attributed to the influence of his wife. After her death, he again took refuge in emotion, and ended, in the posthumous *Three Essays on Religion*, with a timid mysticism where faith is rather pathetically disguised as hope.

Now there can be no doubt that an unresolved dichotomy underlay Mill's curiously irresolute and troubled philosophy. Nor can there be any doubt that much of the explanation of this dichotomy is to be found in an education certainly not suited to a subtle-minded and by no means emotionally barren nature. But the conflict so evident in Mill's work goes deeper than dissatisfaction with the education imposed

---

[1] The essentials of Mill's political thought are in the *Utilitarianism* (1863), *Liberty* (1859), and *Representative Government* (1861), conveniently issued together in one volume in Everyman's Library. The *Autobiography* (1873) and certain of the essays, notably those on Bentham and on Coleridge reprinted in the *Dissertations and Discussions* (4 vols., 1859-1875), are indispensable to an understanding of how Mill's ideas were formed in the Chartist period. Critical comment on Mill is abundant. See Stephen, L., *The English Utilitarians* (1900) vol. iii.; MacCunn, J., *Six Radical Thinkers* (1907); Whittaker, T., *Comte and Mill* (1908); Neff, E., *Carlyle and Mill* (1927); Stephen, J. F., *Liberty, Equality, Fraternity* (1874); Harrison, F., *Tennyson, Ruskin, Mill* (1899).

E

on him by his father. His greatest gift, after all, was a lively intellectual curiosity. He had one of the attributes of the sceptic, a sense of the incompleteness of any formulated truth, of the possibility that the opposite of what he was affirming was true also. Here he found himself in conflict, not only with the finalities of philosophic Radicalism, but with the appetite of his time for finalities of any sort. Mill was not so much a baulked mystic as a baulked sceptic; and he was baulked as much by the spirit of the age as by the spirit of his party, as much by Carlyle and Kingsley as by Bentham. He had to believe in something. He satisfied himself by holding inconsistent, and even quite contrary, beliefs. Hence the ease with which a lawyer-like mind such as Fitzjames Stephen's could demolish the essay *On Liberty*.

Mill never ceased to believe in individual liberty. This belief he anchored partly in a determined empiricism. The difference between the two schools of philosophy, that of Intuition and that of Experience and Association, he says, " is not a mere matter of abstract speculation; it is full of practical consequences, and lies at the foundation of all the greatest differences of practical opinion in an age of progress."[1] And again, " the notion that truths external to the mind may be known by intuition or consciousness, independently of observation and experience, is, I am persuaded, in these times, the great intellectual support of false doctrines and bad institutions."[2] Now the existence of the individual is a *datum* of sense-experience. If you start with a belief that this individual is formed by circumstances over which, as the ultimate reality, he has control, then you may hope by altering circumstances to alter the individual. If, however, with the intuitionists, you assume the individual to be the creature of circumstances erected into absolutes, like Church, State, Tradition, and the like, you bar the way to any improvement in his status. Mill was wrong, as T. H. Green was to show, in assuming that philosophic idealism is necessarily hostile to individual liberty, and to self-improvement on the part of the individual. But he held to this belief with determination.

---

[1] *Autobiography* (ed. by H. J. Laski, 1924), p. 232.   [2] *Ibid.*, p. 191.

His individualism, has, however, another root. He believed as intensely as did Acton that power corrupts, and that absolute power corrupts absolutely. He writes of " the greater mental honesty, and amenability to reason, of the better part of the working class." But, he continues, " may not this reasonably be ascribed to the fact that they have not yet, like the others, been corrupted by power ? "[1] Again, he writes: " It is a universally observed fact that . . . the disposition to prefer a man's selfish interests to those which he shares with other people, and his immediate and direct interest to those which are indirect and remote, are characteristics most especially called forth and fostered by the possession of power."[2] This distrust of power is not merely the other side of a trust in ordinary men. We shall see that Mill was very far from an optimistic view of human nature. It is rather the assertion of an intellectualist fear of this rough world of the appetites. Mill's devotion to individual liberty was not without its roots in nihilism. Human selfishness was somehow a less dreadful thing if left unorganized, uncombined with other human selfishnesses.

Mill then was an individualist because he held the individual to be an ultimate reality, and because he feared the power of organized individuals. But there is still another source of his individualism. He was too good a child of his age to doubt the fact of progress. Progress is innovation, and innovation is always the work of the individual, never that of the tribe. The only test of the value of an innovation is its value in use. Therefore there must be complete liberty for experimentation. Only in full conflict with the old can the value of the new be determined. Society must tolerate, nay encourage, the solitary individual in his conflict with society. For the only alternative to innovation is not stability, but decay. This argument is not new with Mill, but it finds in the *Liberty* its classical exposition.

Even on its positive side, then, Mill's love of liberty is in a sense impure. It is compounded of shrinking from conflict

[1] *Letters* (ed. by H. S. R. Elliott, 2 vols., 1910), vol. ii., p. 45.
[2] *Representative Government*, chap. vi., p. 252.

and difficulty, a temperamental sympathy for the oppressed and suffering, an intellectual devotion to the metaphysics in which he was brought up, a conviction of the value of novelty. But it lacks much of the emotional intensity of devotion to an abstract yet satisfying ideal evident in the eleutheromania of Shelley and even of Byron; it has none of the brash assurance of the born fighter, of the man who has pushed his way to material success, like the confidence of Brougham in *laissez-faire*; it has not even the calm assurance of a single-minded rationalism like that of Bentham. On what we may call its negative side, Mill's doctrine of liberty is still further qualified and obscured.

In the first place, he profoundly distrusted human beings as he knew them. Liberalism is a comfortable doctrine only for the optimist, and Mill was no consistent optimist either of the head or of the heart. " But ordinary human nature is so poor a thing,"[1] he writes almost in passing, as of something to be accepted without discussion. And in a letter to Florence Nightingale he writes, " for no earthly power can ever prevent the constant, unceasing, unsleeping, elastic pressure of human egotism from weighing down and thrusting aside those who have not the power to resist it. Where there is life there is egotism, and if men were to abolish every unjust law to-day, there is nothing to prevent them from making new ones to-morrow."[2] Men are stupid and selfish as individuals, mediocre and stodgy as a mass.[3]

Mill's contempt for the many takes on not infrequently a priggish quality a trifle annoying in one professedly not allied with the Deity. " J'ai refusé de rien faire," he writes to Littré concerning his Westminster candidature, " de ce que font ordinairement chez nous les candidats. Je n'ai fait que ce qu'ils ne font guère, c'est à dire, une profession de foi parfaitement sincère."[4]

This sense of his fellow creatures' weaknesses seems an insecure foundation for a belief in their liberty. But Mill's inconsistency lies deeper. He professes, as we have seen,

[1] " The Claims of Labour," *Dissertations and Discussions* (1874-1875), vol. ii., p. 288.
[2] *Letters*, vol. ii., p. 102. [3] *Liberty*, chap. iii., *passim*. [4] *Letters*, vol. ii., p. 30.

to base his ethics on the empirical position. Good and evil
are but the successful or the unsuccessful manipulation of
their environment by human beings guided to a greater or
less extent by their reason. What we denominate better is
no absolute divulged to us by a power above reason, but
simply the result of past and present experimentation. Mill
is an instrumentalist. We learn what is good for us ethically
as we learn to use light and heat. Good and bad are subjective only in the sense that all quality is subjective. Thanks
to the principle of association and the fact of racial experience, something like a code of morals—though never a
fixed and unchanging code—can be worked out. The contents of this code are determined by the experience of the
best and wisest. " Those who are equally acquainted with,
and equally capable of appreciating and enjoying, both, do
give a most marked preference to the manner of existence
which employs their higher faculties."[1] Stoic and Epicurean
experience have combined with Christian experience, so that
" in the golden rule of Jesus of Nazareth we read the complete spirit of the ethics of utility."[2]

Instrumentalism then leads to the same goal as intuition-
ism. But Mill continued to abhor the notion of an absolute
not attained to by the ordinary operations of logic. " I
found by actual experience of Hegel that conversancy with
him tends to deprave one's intellect. . . . For some time
after I had finished the book all such words as *reflection*,
development, *evolution*, etc., gave me a sort of sickening
feeling."[3] Yet Mill himself develops in the essay on Coleridge, and in the essay *On Liberty*, a theory of the derivation
of truth from the conflict of opposites which might almost be
called a common-sense Hegelianism, an Hegelianism without the trappings of idealistic phraseology. Freedom of
discussion is essential because any one set of beliefs is one-
sided, contains but part of the truth. " Where there is
identity of position and pursuits, there also will be identity
of partialities, passions, and prejudices; and to give to any

---

[1] *Utilitarianism*, chap. ii., p. 8.   [2] *Ibid.*, p. 16.
[3] *Letters*, vol. ii., p. 93.

one set of partialities, passions, and prejudices, absolute power, without counter-balance from partialities, passions, and prejudices of a different sort, is the way to render the correction of any of those imperfections hopeless."[1] It is true that Mill values this conflict for its moral use in keeping the individual intellectually alive. It is true that he recoils in horror from the possibility that it is " necessary that some part of mankind should persist in error to enable any to realize the truth."[2] But he retains the necessity of conflict between half-truths in order to produce something nearer to whole truths.

Mill strays even farther than this, however, from a consistent empiricism. He was never wholly happy in a belief that evil is a mere maladjustment of the human animal to its environment, and that the cure for evil lies in the environment. He always distrusted nature. He writes of " the course of nature, of which so great a part is tyranny, iniquity, and all the things which are punished as the most atrocious crimes when done by human creatures, being the daily doings of nature through the whole range of organic life."[3] Man is potentially at least so much better than his environment, so much better than himself. It is tempting for a restless, curious, dissatisfied intellect to take refuge in the belief that man is not wholly the creature of this world of the senses. Mill yielded to the temptation. He became, indeed, a Manichæan. God is good, but not all-powerful. The evidence of design in the universe points to a God, but to a God who had to confine himself to contrivance, in itself an indication of limitation of power. " A creed like this," he wrote, " allows it to be believed that all the mass of evil which exists was undesigned by, and exists not by the appointment of, but in spite of, the Being whom we are called upon to worship."[4]

Manichæanism is not a very subtle nor a very imaginative faith; but it is definitely a theology, an assertion that sense experience and association are not the whole range of human

[1] Essay on Bentham, *Dissertations and Discussions*, vol. i., p. 404.
[2] *Liberty*, chap. ii., p. 103. [3] *Letters*, vol. i., p. 156.
[4] *Three Essays on Religion* (1874), p. 116.

consciousness. It implies a definite sanction for moral judgments, and, one would think, a very definite limitation on the liberty of the individual. God surely cannot wish us to leave men free to do wrong. As a matter of fact, Mill's theology ripened too late to affect his politics seriously. But the temperamental inclinations that drove him to admit the possibility of a living God are evident throughout his life. His doctrine of liberty is tempered constantly by the excellence of his intentions and his hopes. Moreover, he lived in a time when liberty, having been more nearly realized in economic life, at least, than ever before, seemed not to be working out entirely as a sensitive man might wish. Mill early concerned himself with the condition of the English working classes, and never allowed his economic theories to interfere with his desire to improve this condition. It is a commonplace that successive editions of the *Principles of Economics* admit more and more collectivistic elements. In the end, Mill even went back on his old wages fund theory, and admitted that trade unions may raise wages.[1]

We have found that what may be called the psychological background of Mill's idea of liberty is singularly complex. His utilitarian heritage, his empiricist metaphysics, his conception of progress through solitary genius, his very refinement of thought and feeling, put him on the side of individual freedom. But these same elements, given a very slight twist by an inquiring intelligence, could very well argue against individual freedom. Utilitarianism might find individual freedom producing something less than the greatest good of the greatest number. The empiricist might find the slums of Manchester forced on his attention even more successfully than the achievements of Free Trade. Progress through individual initiative might run up against the dead weight of a free majority. Refinement was certain to be shocked into pessimism by the spectacle of men freely competing with one another in the England of 1830. Mill's whole political thought—that of the essay *On Liberty* as well as that of the *Representative Government*—exhibits in fact

---

[1] See the essay on "Thornton on Labour," *Dissertations and Discussions*, vol. v.

and in detail the confusion we have already found in his personality.

The famous formula of the *Liberty* is after all but a formula to which almost any actual course of action can be made to conform. " The sole end for which mankind are warranted, individually or collectively, in interfering with the liberty of action of any of their number, is self-protection. . . . The only purpose for which power can be rightfully exercised over any member of a civilized community, against his will, is to prevent harm to others. His own good, either physical or moral, is not a sufficient warrant."[1] Now this can be, as Mill surely intended it to be, an assertion of the moral autonomy of the individual, the corner-stone of a faith in the common-sense notion of liberty of thought and action. And in the chapter on " Applications "[2] Mill does make an honest effort to apply it in this sense. Drunkenness in the individual is clearly not a concern of the State's. Yet " the making himself drunk, in a person whom drunkenness excites to do harm to others, is a crime against others." Therefore the law is justified in putting such persons under special legal restriction.[3] All we need do is stretch the point a bit further, assert that all drunkenness implies danger to the sober, and we can justify even that " Maine law " of prohibition Mill so disliked. So, too, with education. The State must interfere to prevent the selfish man from harming his children by neglecting to send them to school. Compulsory education, carefully devised to avoid bureaucracy, must be provided. Nay, more, " to bring a child into existence without a fair prospect of being able, not only to provide food for its body, but instruction and training for its mind, is a moral crime, both against the unfortunate offspring and against society; . . . if the parent does not fulfil this obligation, the State ought to see it fulfilled, at the charge, as far as possible, of the parent."[4]

In spite of the final qualification, this is a very great step towards collectivism. Mill could not quite accept the consequences of the assertion that men can be free to do evil. Nor

---

[1] *Liberty*, Introduction, p. 72.   [2] *Ibid.*, chap. v.   [3] *Ibid.*, p. 153.   [4] *Ibid.*

could he, even though he distrusted the State, quite bring himself to refuse its aid in destroying evil. With all his ingenuity, he could not wriggle himself out of the predicament in which all speculation on the question of liberty and authority must find itself: either liberty is desirable regardless of its consequences, or it is desirable only when its consequences are good. If you accept the second alternative, you have merely pushed the question back to your distinction between good and evil. Your adjustment between liberty and authority is none other than your moral code.

Again, Mill concludes in the *Representative Government* that only through the active participation of the citizens of a State in its government can human beings be made properly " self-protecting " and " self-dependent."[1] But instead of what we might expect from this premise, a straightforward defence of universal suffrage, equal electoral districts, the ballot, and the rest of the paraphernalia of philosophic Radicalism, we have a scheme of government brought forward, the main purpose of which is to prevent the tyranny of the majority. Plural voting, the number of votes depending on education and character, and proportional representation (Hare's plan) are proposed. The ballot is attacked as a dangerous concession to human selfishness even more than to human cowardice.[2] Indeed, Mill's typical hesitancy comes out very well in his treatment of the ballot. Men—even men of the lower classes—are no longer to be intimidated by fear of their superiors. But they are selfish at heart. Publicity, however, is a possible check on selfishness. Men are ashamed to be as bad in public as they might be in private. Therefore, no secret ballot. But Mill stops comfortably short of where this reasoning might lead him. If men so acting in common are somehow better than each would be individually, is not society better than the individuals that make it up? Is it not absurd to base one's philosophy on the autonomy of the individual if you think him at his best only when he ceases to be autonomous, and acts with other men?

---

[1] *Representative Government*, chap. iii, p. 208.   [2] *Ibid.*, chapters vii, viii, *passim.*

E*

The very puzzlement so obvious in Mill's work makes him a thoroughly representative Englishman of his time. Intellectual honesty so sheared his generalizations that they came perilously close to those attained by mere intellectual inertia. Mill, who prided himself on independence of judgment, on being himself one of the solitary thinkers with whom men must eventually catch up, was really a very good Victorian. He was not, indeed, without certain seminal ideas, ideas which have had a very real influence. But taken as a whole, his political and moral standards are those professed by large numbers of his fellows. The *Representative Government*, doubts as to the rule of the majority and all, is pretty much a platform for nineteenth-century Liberalism both in England and on the Continent. But it is not a prescient book, in the sense that Burke's *Reflections* is a prescient book. Neither Mill's hopes nor his forebodings are quite pertinent to-day.

We have said that Mill brought forward certain seminal ideas. Now these ideas were assimilated rather to his temperament than to any systematic philosophy. They are not often clear-cut, nor always consistent. But Mill's mind was fertile enough, if not always penetrating. He achieved something like the common touch, and his writings were widely read. Therefore his espousal of certain causes is perhaps the most important thing for us in his political thought.

The first of these causes, in his own eyes, was that of woman's rights. Mill's relations with Mrs. Taylor, who ultimately became his wife, afford a very curious psychological problem. But for us, it is enough to note that he early gained from her the conviction that women are in many respects morally superior to men, and that therefore they should have full legal and political equality with men. He is definitely one of the pioneers in the movement for woman's suffrage.[1] Yet even here he lacks prescience. Mill's estimate of women, where it is not purely the reflection of his relations with the high-minded and consecrated Mrs. Taylor, is that of any right-thinking Englishman of

---

[1] See *The Subjection of Women* (1869).

the day. " The common voice of mankind," he thinks, proclaims women " superior in moral goodness."[1] Especially are women superior to men in their emancipation from the lower pleasures of sex. Women have made love the high spiritual thing it can be. Men are still too commonly mere beasts. Those who cry out that Malthus would suppress natural human delights have an unworthy standard. " The conduct, which it is reckoned so cruel to disapprove, is a degrading slavery to a brute instinct in one of the persons concerned, and most commonly, in the other, helpless submission to a revolting abuse of power."[2] The emancipation of women, therefore, will mean the emancipation of so many more good desires, good instincts. Sex tyranny like that of the present is bad, just because it is a tyranny. But it is worse than other tyrannies, because we know for sure that the good is kept down by the bad. There is no difficulty in applying the principles of the essay *On Liberty* to women.

Another cause to which Mill devoted himself from his youngest days is compounded of his sympathy for women and his desire to lift the standard of life of the labouring classes. Mill is one of the leaders of the movement for birth control. He is not, strictly speaking, a neo-Malthusian. As can be seen from the above-quoted passage, he had none of Mr. D. H. Lawrence's exalted appreciation of the value of sex intercourse. He always retained a distrust of what seemed to him a low instinct, and his ideal was what Malthus regarded as the best of the preventive checks, moral restraint. But he was no censorious Puritan. The iron law of wages which he held in his earlier days left no possible source of improvement for the labouring classes except the limitation of their numbers. Even after he modified somewhat that iron law, he still felt that permanent improvement in the condition of the poor must be accompanied by a reduced birthrate. He did, indeed, see that even slight improvements in the standard of living of the poor tended to make them more provident, more anxious to guard their gains.[3] Moral

---

[1] *Letters*, vol. i., p. 161.
[2] *Principles of Economics*, book ii., chap. xi., 6.
[3] " The Claims of Labour " (1805), *Dissertations and Discussions*, vol. ii.

restraint is most desirable, but, as a necessary step to this, artificial limitation of births must be welcomed.

Mill's interest in the labouring classes was lifelong. From a pretty doctrinaire adhesion to *laissez-faire* he passed through encouragement to unionism (accompanied by a distrust of the oligarchical tendencies of skilled labour), to an active sympathy with Socialism as a form of co-operation. The State he never ceased to distrust, and the Socialism with which he sympathized was undoubtedly something like guild Socialism in an unformulated stage. As early as 1848 he wrote of a reviewer of his *Principles of Economics*. " He gives a totally false idea of the book and of its author when he makes me a participant in the derision with which he speaks of Socialists of all kinds and degrees. . . . They [Socialists] are the greatest element of improvement in the present state of mankind."[1] And in his autobiography he wrote of himself and his wife that " our ideal of ultimate improvement went far beyond Democracy, and would class us decidedly under the general designation of Socialists."[2] But there is hesitation here, too. Mill could not quite bring himself to trust in the organization of a Socialist state from existing human material. Anything like the Marxian class war shocked him profoundly. Class interests were inevitable at present, but they were the " sinister interests " of Bentham, only to be lessened by the free play of competition. His Socialism was Utopian in the sense that it demanded for its realization human beings of superior moral qualities. In practice, it led him to sympathize, somewhat inconsistently, with the essay *On Liberty*, with Factory Acts, proposals for insurance against sickness, accident, and old age, Sanitation Acts and the like. It led him into active participation in the movement for land reform, a movement which aimed at the breaking up of large estates and the restoration of the peasant farmer. He helped draw up the programme of the Land Tenure Reform Association, which included the abolition of primogeniture, the State administration of waste lands and commons, the encouragement of small holdings, and a mild

---

[1] *Letters*, vol. i., p. 138.   [2] *Autobiography*, p. 196.

form of the single tax, involving State expropriation of the unearned *future* increment on land, in so far as that proves ascertainable.[1]

Finally, Mill's insistence on the place of minorities in the State gives him a right to figure among the founders of modern pluralism in politics. Here, too, we must not expect any clear-cut doctrine. Mill did not concern himself with the problem of sovereignty as such. But one of the most consistent elements in his thought is the distrust of the tyranny of the majority, a phrase which he did much to popularize in England. His review of de Tocqueville's *Democracy in America* in 1840 dwelt upon the phrase at length.[2] The *Representative Government* is largely a search for expedients to prevent democratic levelling—Hare's plan, educational qualifications for voting, property qualifications, plural voting, protection of minorities. Mill held on purely moral grounds as firmly as any Darwinian could hold on biological grounds, that variation is indispensable to existence. For want of " a social support, a *point d'appui*, for individual resistance to the tendencies of the ruling power," he wrote, " the older societies, and all but a few modern ones, either fell into dissolution or became stationary (which means slow deterioration) through the exclusive predominance of a part only of the conditions of social and mental well-being."[3] The only true safeguard for variation is a moral one; a people must be educated to be tolerant of all kinds of social experimentation. " No society," he wrote in a famous phrase, " in which eccentricity is a matter of reproach can be in a wholesome state."[4]

A word must be said as to Mill's position on one of the unavoidable questions of political theory—the *rôle* of ideas in actual politics. He had no blind faith in the power of reason. " Ideas, unless outward circumstances conspire with them, have in general no very rapid or immediate

---

[1] See the papers on Land Reform, *Dissertations and Discussions*, vol. v.

[2] *Dissertations and Discussions*, vol. ii.

[3] *Representative Government*, chap. vii, p. 268.

[4] *Principles of Economics*, book ii., chap. i., paragraph 4 (p. 130 of " People's edition " of 1867).

efficacy in human affairs."[1] What matters is power, and power is a material, an economic thing. He says in the *Autobiography* that he early became convinced "that government is always either in the hands, or passing into the hands, of whatever is the strongest power in society, and that what this power is, does not depend on institutions, but institutions on it."[2] That power in his day he recognized was the middle class. "To most purposes, in the constitution of modern society, the government of a numerous middle class is Democracy. Nay, it not merely *is* Democracy, but the only Democracy of which there is yet any example: what is called universal suffrage in America arising from the fact, that America is *all* middle class."[3] Yet he was very far from depreciating the value of the instrument of thought. Thought ultimately formulates our beliefs, and, as he says in a striking phrase, "one person with a belief is a social power equal to ninety-nine who have only interests."[4] Thought is essentially an aristocratic thing, in the good sense of the word. It is therefore important to encourage thinkers. The old rationalist comes out occasionally in the chastened Victorian. "If it were possible," Mill writes in his diary in February 1854, "to blot entirely out the whole of German metaphysics, the whole of Christian theology, and the whole of the Roman and English systems of technical jurisprudence, and to direct all the minds that expand their faculties in these three pursuits to useful speculation or practice, there would be talent enough set at liberty to change the face of the world."[5]

The abiding impression left by Mill's work is that of a mind of transparent honesty in a state of extreme tension. That tension is the result of a conflict between the dogmatism imposed on him by his environment and the scepticism natural to his temperament. Mill was no more comfortable

---

[1] "The Claims of Labour," *Dissertations and Discussions,* vol. ii., p. 269.
[2] *Autobiography,* p. 137.
[3] Review of de Tocqueville's *Democracy in America* in *Dissertations and Discussions,* vol. ii., p. 99.
[4] *Representative Government,* chap. i., p. 183.
[5] *Letters,* vol. ii., p. 369.

in his surroundings than was Carlyle. He had a firm sense of " the extraordinary difference in value between one person and another."[1] But surely this value was not market value ? It could not be measured in the rough conflict of worldly interests. Was it not ultimately unmeasurable in terms of positive scientific knowledge, and thus a matter of faith ? But faith in such values is really only a form of scepticism as regards the possibility of erecting a fact into a value. Such faith is perfectly consistent with what is commonly called an open mind. Mill's mind was usually very open, but rather in spite of himself. He once wrote: " I not only have never seen any evidence that I think of the slightest weight in favour of Spiritualism, but I should also find it very difficult to believe any of it on any evidence whatever."[2] And so the wan theism of his last years is the final refuge of a mind that never had quite the courage of its own doubts.

2. COBDEN[3]

To come to Cobden after Mill is to realize fully the variety of human personality we are forced to catalogue under common political labels. For Cobden, as well as Mill, was one of the men who helped transform Whiggism into nineteenth-century Liberalism. Both men agreed as to the fundamentals of free trade and foreign policy. Both, though they were under Tory suspicion as dangerous Radicals, now seem sober and English enough. Yet Cobden is, compared with Mill, a simple and untortured soul. His political generalizations were few and clear-cut, always in the service of a definite end. He seems to have none of Mill's doubts and fears. To study Cobden's ideas is to study the

---

[1] *Representative Government*, chap. xii., p. 320.   [2] *Letters*, vol. ii., p. 109.
[3] Cobden's *Political Writings* were collected in two volumes (London, 1868). The tract on *Russia* in the first volume is perhaps most representative. His *Speeches* (ed. by Thorold Rogers and John Bright, 2 vols., 1870) are also essential. See Morley, J., *Life of Cobden* (2 vols., 1881-1882); MacCunn, J., *Six Radical Thinkers* (1910); Rogers, Thorold, *Cobden* and *Modern Political Opinion* (1873); Hobson, J. N., *Richard Cobden : The International Man* (1918).

intellectual equipment of the political agitator, of the man of action. Mill never really left his desk, even to sit in Parliament. Cobden, self-made success in the business of cotton manufacturing, was always in the thick of the political struggle. He is a far better index of the mind of the ordinary Liberal than is Mill.

Cobden's life was ruled by two master ideas, Free Trade and non-intervention. Free trade seemed to him to stand out in the pages of Adam Smith and his successors as one of the triumphant achievements of the human mind, comparable to the work of Galileo and Newton. But he admits that its full force came home to him from his experience as a manufacturer, from his awareness of the needs of his fellow workers. " I am afraid," he said of the anti-Corn Law agitation—and the use of the word afraid is illuminating, " that most of us entered upon this struggle with the belief that we had some distinct class-interest in the question, and that we should carry it by a manifestation of our will in this district, against the will and consent of other portions of the community."[1] Cobden, as we shall see, had no difficulty in finding an ethical justification to calm his fears of acting selfishly. Meanwhile, we must note that he and his Leaguers carried the abolition of the Corn Laws by a striking manifestation of the workings of the group will in politics. The Anti-Corn Law League remains one of the most illuminating subjects to which the student of politics can turn. Its methods compare favourably—in many senses—with those of the Anti-Saloon League in America. It started with a clear theoretical basis, which men like Cobden adopted admirably to the comprehension of the common man. It never lost sight of the material interests on which it was founded. Its propaganda was persistent and abundant. Its organization was compact and centralized without being tyrannical, and it cut clean across party lines which stood in its way. We cannot here go into the details of this agitation. Typical of its methods, however, was Cobden's device of using the actual constitutional framework to secure his

---

[1] Quoted in Morley, J., *Life of Cobden* (1-vol. edition, 1906), p. 141.

end without appearing to subvert or even to modify the constitution. The Reform of 1832 had stopped so far short of household suffrage that much of the strength of the League in the mill towns could not go to the polls. This was especially true of the counties. Cobden hit upon the expedient of creating forty-shilling freeholds for the express purpose of securing a qualification to vote. Funds were secured, lands bought and parcelled out. Cobden even urged his followers to buy freeholds for their adult sons, and give them these instead of nest-eggs in stocks and bonds. In this way hundreds of votes were created in critical constituencies.[1]

Cobden found for Free Trade a justification in the law of Nature which lifted the whole struggle out of the narrow bounds of selfish interests. The struggle is not, as the Tories make it out to be, between the landed interest and the commercial interest. " In every instance where the farmers have been plunged in the greatest distress and suffering, it has been in the midst of the most bountiful harvest, and in the most genial seasons. Any man who takes these facts alone must have a very undue and irreverent notion of the great Creator of the world, if he supposes that this is a natural or a designed state of things. No; there is an unnatural cause for this unnatural state of things. . . . The law which interferes with the wisdom of the Divine Providence, and substitutes the law of wicked men for the law of nature."[2] This law of Nature, then, is the law of God. " To buy in the cheapest market, and sell in the dearest. What is the meaning of this maxim ? It means that you take the article which you have in the greatest abundance, and with it obtain from others that of which they have the most to spare; so giving to mankind the means of enjoying the fullest abundance of earth's goods, and in doing so, carrying out to the fullest extent the Christian doctrine of ' Doing to all men as ye would they should do unto you.' "[3]

---

[1] See Morley, *op. cit.*, chap. vi., and Jordan, H. D., " Political Methods of the Anti-Corn Law League," *Political Science Quarterly*, vol. xlii., pp. 58-76.
[2] *Speeches*, vol. i., p. 68.   [3] *Ibid.*, vol. i., p. 385.

The Corn Laws are thus bread taxes laid on the food of all Englishmen for the immediate benefit, not of the farmers, but of the few great landlords. Agriculture itself will benefit ultimately from the abolition of protection. Free farming from its feudal limitations, open it to competition, and you will get able and enterprising farmers and a free flow of capital to what is after all " the most inviting business of all."[1] Cobden, as well as Cobbett, was of South of England farming stock, and he always retained a love of the English countryside and of the English peasantry. He never considered himself an enemy of old England.

Nor will repeal of the Corn Laws redound simply to the benefit of capitalists. It means " increased trade, and the claim of a right, besides, to exchange our manufactures for the corn of all other countries, by which we should very much increase the extent of our trade. How can this be done, unless by an increased amount of labour ? How can we call into requisition an increased demand for labourers without also increasing the rate of wages ? "[2] Low wages have never made the profits of English manufacturers. Any increase in production is bound to be shared by capitalist and labourer alike. Free trade, then, is to the interest of all Englishmen. It is " something more than a remedy for present evils." Cobden was perfectly sincere in believing that " a moral and even a religious spirit may be infused into that topic."[3]

For free trade is no merely English question. England, thanks to the glorious work of men like Watt and Arkwright, has achieved a position of world leadership in industry which is really a mission. " In the present day, commerce is the grand panacea, which, like a beneficent medical discovery, will serve to inoculate with the healthy and saving taste for civilization all the nations of the world."[4] And again, " Free trade! What is it ? Why, breaking down the barriers that separate nations; those barriers, behind which

[1] *Speeches*, vol. i., p. 404.   [2] *Ibid.*, vol. i., p. 6
[3] Quoted in Morley, *op. cit.*, p. 126.
[4] *Political Writings*, vol. i., p. 45.

nestle the feelings of pride, revenge, hatred, and jealousy, which every now and then burst their bounds, and deluge whole countries with blood."[1]   Well might he write that it was his favourite sentiment that " Free trade was the international law of the Almighty."[2]

Cobden's second great cause, that of international peace through non-intervention, is thus the logical consequence of his devotion to free trade. War is the product of the unnatural rivalries of the old ruling classes of Europe. Nurtured in feudal pride, trained to regard the career of arms as honourable, ignorant and contemptuous of trade, those in power in Europe, and even in England, accept war as a matter of course. They proceed on the false assumption that the interests of their countries are best served by the harm of other countries. Even in economics, this notion is incorporated in the mercantilist system, which still rules the mind of the upper classes. But the truth is that the interests of nations, like the interests of individuals, are not naturally antagonistic. " I likewise assert that the honest and just interests of this country, and of her inhabitants, are the just and honest interests of the whole world."[3]

Now this truth, incompletely received everywhere, has, thanks to the industrial revolution, obtained a slight hold in England. International peace through international free trade is not at once attainable. But England can and must set the necessary example of abandoning the old system of national aggression. Her present *rôle* must be that of an educator of the world, and to fulfil this *rôle* she must adopt a resolute policy of non-intervention in European affairs. That English intervention has been in the past, and is still, justified by her statesmen on moral grounds only makes matters worse. English sympathy with Poland, for instance, is often inspired by the most laudable motives, and is felt by excellent men. But at best, such men are presumptuous. They are assuming an omniscience into the ways of Providence not granted to men, save to those who buy in the

---

[1] *Speeches*, vol. i., p. 79.   [2] *Political Writings*, vol. ii., p. 110.
[3] *Speeches*, vol. ii., p. 27.

cheapest, and sell in the dearest, markets. At the worst, such men are inspired by a blind hatred of Russia and a sentimental attachment to the oppressed.[1]

At the core of English foreign policy is to be found a doctrine in which a false morality appears as a disguise for a mistaken pride and an equally mistaken sense of interest—the doctrine of the balance of power. The first step in a reform of English foreign policy must be the destruction of this doctrine. In the first place, this balance of power is a chimæra. It never had that kind of political reality which incorporates itself in laws and institutions. It was never maintained for any length of time. The whole history of the eighteenth and early nineteenth centuries is a series of wars in violation of the principle of the balance of power.[2] The real reason why England supported the principle was first, a selfish desire to keep down the more enterprising nations of the Continent, and second, a vainglorious desire to play the part of policeman and peacemaker. The " balance of Europe " meant a desire to see England hold the balance, to dispense justice in a way consoling to her pride.[3] But, says Cobden in one of those neat phrases which explain his hold as an agitator, even for such misguided men to-day, " I presume it is not intended that England should be the Anacharsis Clootz of Europe."[4]

It follows that England's colonial policy has been as mistaken as her foreign policy. In defiance of economic laws, she has annexed lands in every quarter of the globe, regardless of their suitability to white settlement. She has attempted to bind her colonists to her by all sorts of artificial ties. She has indulged in a foolish pride at the mere extent of her possessions. Her ambition for territorial conquests has made her one of the chief violators of that balance of power she pretends to maintain. The seizure of Gibraltar is on a par with the seizure of Silesia.[5] History shows that colonial ambition is the grave of national prosperity. " Spain lies, at

---

[1] *Political Writings*, vol. i., pp. 7 ff.
[2] *Ibid.*, especially the pamphlet *England, Ireland, and America*, vol. i.
[3] *Ibid.*, vol. i., p. 257.   [4] *Speeches*, vol. ii., p. 7.
[5] *Political Writings*, vol. i., p. 261.

CHARTISM

this moment, a miserable spectacle of a nation whose own
national greatness has been immolated on the shrine of
transatlantic ambition. May not some future historian
possibly be found recording a similar epitaph on the tomb
of Britain ? "[1] Cobden was always a Little Englander. The
colonies, left to shift for themselves, would by the workings
of economic law remain good customers of England, and yet
cease to involve her in international difficulties.

England, then, must abandon the game of international
politics. She must confine herself to a small and efficient
armament to be used purely to defend herself from actual
aggression. Incidentally, this would mean a vast economy,
a liberation of resources, human or material, which would
enormously increase her wealth. She would then be able to
promote the cause of world peace in two ways. In the first
place, by adopting complete free trade she would set an
example to the whole world. Her traders would carry everywhere goods which no ambassador ever carried. " Not a
bale of merchandise leaves our shores, but it bears the seeds
of intelligence and fruitful thought to the members of some
less enlightened community."[2] By this example, by encouraging propaganda for free trade throughout the world,
and by concluding, wherever possible, treaties of commercial
reciprocity, she would gradually convert the world. Secondly,
freed from the incubus of militarism, her diplomatists would
support any move that promised to promote peace. Instead
of into secret alliances, she would enter into treaties
limiting armament by agreement. The excellent example
of the agreement between England and the United States,
whereby the Great Lakes have been freed from armed force,
could be followed even with the hereditary enemy, France.[3]
At home, the successful methods of the Anti-Corn Law
League could be used for a Peace League. Men could be
brought to see that wars and tariffs are equally unreasonable
and equally unnecessary.

The Crimean War hurt Cobden deeply, but it did not
cause him to revise his ideas. He was more certain than ever

[1] *Political Writings*, vol. i., p. 25. [2] *Ibid.*, vol. i., p. 45.
[3] *Speeches*, vol. i., p. 468.

that the true interests of the English people lay in free trade and non-intervention. The war itself was the best proof of that. But the middle class in England was still capable of being taken in by aristocrats like Palmerston. The remedy was for the middle class to take stock of itself, to be true to itself. Cobden's two great ideas have a common origin——his devotion to a way of life he believed to be that of his class. He is as class-conscious as any Marxian. His favourite phrase, indeed, is " the middle and industrious classes." Between the employer and the labourer there is no real opposition of interests, and Tory politicians who try to stir up such opposition and align the labouring class with the aristocracy are simply playing their old selfish game.[1] The middle and industrious classes are united in true solidarity against the frivolous ruling class. " In ordinary times we are governed by classes and interests, which are insignificant, in real importance, and as regards the welfare of the country; and if we did not occasionally check them——if we did not, from time to time, by the upheaving of the mass of the people, turn them from their folly and their selfishness,——they would long ago have plunged this country in as great a state of confusion as has been witnessed in any country on the Continent."[2] And again, " You have had your government of aristocracy and tradition; and the worst thing that ever befell this country has been its government for the last century-and-a-half."[3]

Cobden, however, is no political revolutionist. At bottom, he thought Government of little importance in an industrious country. Once reduced to its necessary minor functions—— a process going on rapidly nowadays——and it might be left to frivolous people. Extension of suffrage is indeed necessary as a final check on the aristocracy; but its results will be a further diminution of the importance of Government, and of course further economies in administration.[4] No, the important thing for England is a continuation of the silent rule of Nature as embodied in her middle and industrious

[1] *Speeches*, vol. ii., p. 469.
[2] *Ibid.*, vol. ii., p. 492.   [3] *Ibid.*, vol. ii., p. 484.   [4] *Ibid.*, vol. ii., p. 472.

classes. Here is to be found the " wealth, intelligence, and productive industry " which has made modern England the envy of the world.[1]

Cobden was the perfect Philistine of Matthew Arnold's indignation. When he used the phrase " middle class " he meant a whole scheme of values, an appreciation of this world, which goes far beyond economics. Arnold and other critics have perhaps not been wholly fair to this scheme of values; yet, especially on the æsthetic side, it is curiously narrow. Cobden much preferred the Hudson to the Bosphorus.[2] Picturesque dirt simply annoyed him; industrial dirt, the dirt of the English slums, also annoyed him. It is quite unjust to Cobden to imply that he was satisfied with the physical side of the industrial revolution in England. But he wanted chiefly sanitary reform, neatness, efficiency. With the æsthetic revolt against the factory, as with the æsthetic appreciation of the Middle Ages, he had no sympathy whatever. Classical antiquity moved him only to reflect on the perversion it had worked in English education. " What famous puffers those old Greeks were! " he wrote from the Levant. " Half the educated world in Europe is now devoting more thought to the ancient affairs of these Lilliputian states, the squabbles of their tribes, the wars of their villages, the geography of their rivulets and hillocks, than they bestow upon the modern history of the South and North Americas, the politics of the United States, and the charts of the mighty rivers and mountains of the new world."[3]

Cobden was a utilitarian in that narrow sense of the word Mill so regretted. From Rome he wrote, " These stately and graceful aqueducts are nearly the only ruins which excite feelings of regret, being perhaps the sole buildings which did not merit destruction by the crimes, the folly, and the injustice which attended their construction, or the purposes to which they were devoted."[4] Similarly, he has nothing but praise for the United States. Extensive travel

---

[1] *Speeches*, vol. i., p. 413.
[2] Morley, *op. cit.*, p. 72.   [3] *Ibid.*, p. 80.   [4] *Ibid.*, p. 435.

in America only confirmed his opinion that the Americans were " the best people, individually and nationally."[1] Some of his judgments on America, indeed, make rather strange reading. What he admired most in American Government was its " strict economy."[2] He liked American men, but he could not discover anywhere a " wholesome, blooming, pretty woman."[3]

Yet on the whole Cobden's judgments are consistent. Roman Catholic countries he dislikes because they are unprogressive, because they have no factories, no steadily expanding trade.[4] The chief trouble with Ireland is that she has never had a middle class.[5] So in the Levant an erroneous religion has been an instrument of oppression. Substitute the Bible for the Koran, and you have taken the first step towards awakening these people.[6] Material prosperity in a State is an essential index of progress. And progress is an attribute of life. " We must not stand still, or imagine we can remain stereotyped, like the Chinese; for, if we ever cease to progress, be assured we shall commence to decline."[7]

This progress is also of course moral progress. The industrial revolution will re-enforce and not destroy Christian ethics. Cobden was always a sincere believer. But his Christianity failed to make him a pessimist. " Very few men," he said, " are, from connection or prejudice, monopolists, unless their capacity for inquiry or their sympathies have been blunted by already possessing an undue share of wealth."[8] In general, " it is certain that in this world the virtues and the forces go together, and the vices and the weaknesses are inseparable."[9] Cobden held that vague faith in progress and that very definite moral code with which Victorian society tempered *laissez-faire*. He distrusted government, as did Mill, because he felt that competition in business encouraged the free acceptance of Christian

---

[1] *Political Writings*, vol. i., p. 130.
[2] *Ibid.*, vol. i., p. 132.   [3] Morley, *op. cit.*, p. 38.
[4] *Political Writings*, vol. i., p. 55.   [5] *Ibid.*, vol. i., p. 52.
[6] *Ibid.*, vol. i., p. 33.   [7] *Speeches*, vol. ii., p. 303.
[8] *Ibid.*, vol. i., p. 212.   [9] *Ibid.*, vol. ii., p. 106.

morality, while the privileges of political place encouraged the monopolistic vices. It is a position extremely difficult to hold to-day, for experience has taught us that men are not to be separated as political and economic animals. But it was a position held by many Englishmen of the last century. And to a surprising extent they lived up to it.

For nothing is more misleading than to regard men like Cobden as simple exploiters of the poor, salving their consciences by conformity to middle-class decency. Cobden's thought is full of concern with the condition-of-England question. "I have travelled much," he wrote, "and always with an eye to the state of the great majority, who everywhere constitute the toiling base of the social pyramid; and I confess I have arrived at the conclusion that there is no country where so much is required to be done before the mass of the people become what it is pretended they are, what they ought to be, and what I trust they will yet be, as in England."[1] He continues by insisting as emphatically as Disraeli or Carlyle ever did that England should cease trying to improve the negroes and reform the Poles, and devote herself to her own poor. He admits that labour is not pleasant under the new conditions, contrasting the " natural labour of agriculture " with the " more confined and irksome pursuits of the factory or workshop."[2] He notes how the " old shopkeepers " visited and helped their poorer neighbours, and how the " new shopkeepers " scarcely know the names of their nearest neighbours.[3] He writes from Germany of the English " shopocracy " who, " if they were possessed of a little of the *mind* of the merchants and manufacturers of Frankfort, Chemnitz, Elberfeld, etc., would become the De Medicis, and Fuggers, and De Witts of England, instead of glorying in being the toadies of a clodpole aristocracy, only less enlightened than themselves."[4]

Child labour he regards as an unquestioned evil. It is not an economic, but a medical problem. No child should work at all in cotton mills until the age of fourteen, and thereafter

[1] *Political Writings*, vol. i., p. 490.
[2] *Ibid.*, vol. i., p. 112.   [3] *Ibid.*, vol. i., p. 126.
[4] Quoted in Morley, *op. cit.*, p. 134.

its work should be lighter than that of adults. Yet he would not prevent child labour by legislation stopping the machines after certain hours. He opposed the ten-hour law for adult labour as a relic of the feudal ages. He wanted to cultivate in the English labourer " the love of independence, the privilege of self-respect, the disdain of being patronized or petted, the desire to accumulate, and the ambition to rise." He will not think so ill of the labourer as to imagine that, once he is aware of the evils of child labour, he will not keep his children from the factory.[1] Education, too, is a prime necessity. Cobden prefers voluntary education at the cost of parents, and thinks that if you have good schools they will be filled. But as a *pis aller*, if workmen won't send their children to school, he is willing to compel them to by law, and admits that he will not be squeamish about oppressed liberty.[2]

Nor was Cobden unaware of the possible dangers of Free Trade. He knew that he was helping to build up an England entirely dependent on outside sources for food. If nationalist wars were to continue, and with them commercial blockades, he admits: " I should shrink from promoting the indefinite growth of a population whose means of subsistence would be liable to be cut off at any moment by a belligerent power, against whom we should have no right of resistance."[3] He was alive also to the other danger that menaced an English industrial state—the cutting-off of her markets by the growth of industry elsewhere. The American tariff, he insists, was forced on the United States by the unwise policy of England in the Napoleonic wars. America is already on the way to manufacturing her own goods, to the detriment of English industry.[4] Yet here, too, his optimism overcame his fears. International agreement will end commercial blockades; economic common sense will keep the naturally agricultural states from attempting industrial expansion, and thus preserve English markets. Already it is clear that Russian attempts to develop manufacturing are doomed to failure.[5]

---

[1] Morley, *op. cit.*, Appendix A.   [2] *Speeches*, vol. ii., p. 580.
[3] *Political Writings*, vol. ii., p. 17.   [4] *Ibid.*, vol. i., p. 307.
[5] *Ibid.*, vol. ii., p. 121.

CHARTISM

One reads Cobden to-day with a strange sense of following an idyll. There was little enough idyllic about Cobden's career as an agitator and a debater. He was as far as possible from quiet content with the England he lived in. He was a reformer, a fighter, scornful of Utopias. Yet what he fought for seems now as impossibly simple as any Utopia. The English middle class seems no longer the elect of a God happily conversant with the works of Adam Smith. The problems of government seem no longer reducible to the problem of eliminating government. International relations seem now to require something more than the substitution of the commercial traveller for the ambassador. Still, there is no more reason why the modern critic should patronize Cobden for his politics than for his clothes. Both may seem odd and remote now. But that remoteness is almost a precise measure of their fitness. To him and to his contemporaries Cobden's idyll was as real as the Albert Memorial. It was a faith that sent them busily to work, sure that their work was somehow more than work, that it had a value and a permanence. Surely we ourselves are not so exempt from the need for such a faith as to scorn it in others ?

3. KINGSLEY[1]

Kingsley seems to-day even stranger and more remote than Cobden. His opinions were driven by his enthusiasm to that pitch of exaggeration in which the type becomes the caricature, and thereby ceases to be typical. It is tempting to select some of these opinions, and hold them up gleefully as Victorian. Here really is proof of the fact which a decent critical scepticism is constantly tempted to deny, that the Victorians were quite as bad as all

---

[1] For Kingsley's political thought two novels, *Yeast* (1848), and *Alton Locke* (1850), and the letters in *Charles Kingsley, his Letters and Memories of his Life* (ed. by Mrs. F. E. Kingsley, 2 vols., 1871), are essential. His contributions to the Christian Socialist journal, *Politics for the People* (1848-1849), are not easily accessible. See Cazamian, L., *Le roman social en Angleterre* (1904) ; Harrison, F., *Studies in Early Victorian Literature* (1895) ; Stubbs, C. S., *Charles Kingsley and the Christian Social Movement* (1897).

that. " There were two Dover coachmen—twins. One drove the up-coach, the other the down, for thirty years, so that they never saw each other night or day, but when they whirled past once a day, each on his box, on their restless homeless errand. They never noticed each other in passing but by the jerk of the wrist, which is the cant sign of recognition among horse-driving men. Brutes! the sentimentalist will say—for they were both fat, jolly men! And when one of them died, the other took to his bed in a few days, in perfect health, and pined away and died also! His words were ' Now Tom is gone, I can't stay.' Was not that spirit love ? That story always makes me ready to cry. And cases as strong are common."[1] Or again: " I say that the Church of England is wonderfully and mysteriously fitted for the souls of a free Norse-Saxon race; for men, whose ancestors fought by the side of Odin, over whom a descendant of Odin now rules."[2] Finally—though the list might be prolonged indefinitely—mind makes the body, not body the mind; therefore beautiful souls like Burns, Raphael, Goethe and Shakespeare—especially Shakespeare, who combines all perfection of mind and body in himself— have beautiful faces. Raphael's is " a face to be kissed, not worshipped."[3]

The temptation to hold Kingsley up as a Victorian must be overcome. He was a man, not a period. He had, it is true, a horror of social nonconformity. His friend, Thomas Hughes, writes that " to less sensitive men the effect of eccentricity upon him was almost comic, as when on one occasion he was quite upset and silenced by the appearance of a bearded member of Council [on Working Men's Associations] at an important deputation, in a straw hat and blue plush gloves. He did not recover from the depression produced by those gloves for days."[4] Especially in his later years, this love of conformity makes him a useful index for

[1] Charles Kingsley, *Letters and Memories* (ed. by Mrs. F. E. Kingsley), vol. i., p. 83.
[2] *Ibid.*, vol. i., p. 253.
[3] Kingsley, C., *Literary and General Lectures and Essays* (1898), p. 128.
[4] *Letters and Memories*, vol. i., p. 269.

the social historian. But the emotions that went into his political philosophy are strongly personal, and we shall do well not to sink him in historical generalizations. The habits into which he moulded his desires are indeed social and representative; the desires themselves are far too intense to be given a common label.

Kingsley appears in the history of thought as a Christian Socialist. He did indeed abandon the cause pretty completely after the early 'fifties. And he is by no means as profound a thinker as his master, Maurice. Yet he had a far larger audience than Maurice or any other of the group. He is a more useful figure for the student, not of the currents of professional philosophy and theology, but of ideas as they descend to the crowd. Kingsley is for our purposes an essential figure. He will stand for one kind of reaction to the problems of the industrial revolution in the mid-nineteenth century. His partial abandonment of the Socialist solution is in itself a valuable fact. It is one more contribution to an understanding of the Victorian compromise. With the caution that a large part of Kingsley belongs to the psychologist or even to the psychopathologist, and that therefore we must not take him *en bloc* as typical of an age which he often caricatures rather than represents, we may proceed to the study of what Christian Socialism meant to him.

Perhaps the best introduction to such a study will be an analysis of *Alton Locke*, a programme novel that made a great stir in its day, though it is now relegated to histories of English literature. Alton Locke is a poor tailor, orphaned of his father, a small and quite unnecessary retailer, and brought up by his mother, a hopeless, narrow Calvinist. The boy is early obliged to earn his living as a tailor. He learns from personal experience the horrors of a sweated trade, where even the best masters are forced by competition to treat their workmen not as men, but as animals. Thanks to a chance meeting with a Scotch bookseller, Sandy Mackaye, a Carlyle turned Chartist, he is able, though with great difficulties, to follow his natural bent for learning. He meets Chartist fellow workmen, is fired with the cause of the oppressed, and writes poetry under this inspiration. On a visit to the Dulwich gallery he meets the lovely Lillian and her father, the Dean. Love at first sight on his part is mingled with awe at the graces of the highly born and indignation at the social contrast between himself and these privileged beings. Locke has a cousin, son of a newly rich and selfish father. He goes up to Cambridge to see his cousin, hoping to secure help in the publication of his poems. Here he admires the dogged Anglo-Saxon qualities displayed by Cambridge oarsmen, feels something of the potentialities of the ruling classes, but is angered by their irresponsibility and sense of caste. A visit to the Dean at the cathedral town of D—— results in aid towards the publication of his poems, but only at the price of treason to his order, for he is induced to soften some of his most revolutionary expressions. In a mood of regret at this treason, he accepts a mission from the Chartists to attend a farm labourers' meeting in East Anglia. Here his temper and unfortunate coincidences involve him in actual rioting and burning. Though he really was trying to calm the mob, he is caught, tried, and condemned to jail. Meanwhile his cousin—a mean fellow made meaner by an interested devotion to Puseyism—successfully courts Lillian. Locke, released from prison, returns to his trade. While trying to obtain the release of a farmer's son caught in a sweater's den, and held by perpetual debt to the sweater in a virtual prison, he is stricken with the typhus. He is nursed back to health by Eleanor, another member of the Dean's family, whom, in his infatuation with Lillian, he had misjudged. Eleanor is the perfect Christian Socialist. The premature death of her husband, an aristocrat with a profound sense of his obligation to his fellows, only deepened her devotion. She converts Locke—at great length—from his crude Chartist belief in the rights of man to a true appreciation of the revolutionary character of Christ's teachings. Meanwhile his cousin has ordered a wedding-coat from a sweating tailor. The workman who made the coat, destitute and unable to buy blankets, uses the garment as he works on it to keep his family warm. There is typhus in the household. Germs cling to the coat, and by an act of a just God not uninterested in melodrama, the cousin catches the typhus, communicates it to his bride, and both die. Locke, overwhelmed with grief, yet survives through his new faith. He decides to emigrate to Texas with a fellow workman, there to work out the principles of Christian Socialism. But Kingsley has not yet had enough of pathos. The industrial revolution must kill completely. Locke's confinement in the noxious atmosphere of the tailoring-shop has injured his lungs. He dies of tuberculosis on the way to Texas.

Most of Kingsley's Christian Socialism—and a great deal else—is to be found in this impassioned tract—his feeling that disease and poverty are unnecessary, the product of ignorance and social conditions, his love of sentiment, his bad taste, his hatred of religious asceticism, his interest in sanitation, his patriarchal devotion to his parishioners, even the strange mental leap by which he turned his uxoriousness into a theology. We must, however, attempt to put this chaos of emotion into some kind of order. Kingsley's Christian Socialism is far from a system. We shall most easily find out what underlies it if we make use of a method of analysis almost too obviously dictated by common sense. We shall see what in it is Christian, and what Socialism.

Of one cardinal principle Kingsley was always certain. Christianity is not an ascetic fleeing from the world of the senses. " The body the temple of the living God. . . . There has always seemed to me something impious in the neglect of personal health, strength, and beauty, which the religious, and sometimes clergymen of this day, affect."[1] At the base of our moral code must be a frank acceptance of the fact that man is an animal. There is no opposition between the flesh and the spirit properly understood. Not even the Christian doctrine of another world may be taken as casting upon the world of the senses the reproach of impermanence. " There was a butcher's nephew playing cricket in Bramshill last week, whom I would have walked ten miles to see, in spite of the hideous English dress. One looked forward with delight to what he would be ' in the

---

[1] *Letters and Memories*, vol. i., p. 83.

resurrection.' "[1] Kingsley held, though he did not publish, the very heterodox belief that the delights of marriage are continued in heaven.[2]

This acceptance of the flesh does not mean that all human desires should be requited. Kingsley was far from believing in the natural goodness of man. His doctrine here is a trifle muddled, but seems to run somewhat as follows: Man is a free agent. He can " not only disobey the laws of his being, he can also choose between them, to an extent which science widens every day, and so become, what he was meant to be, an artificial being; artificial in his manufactures, habits, society, polity—what not ? "[3] Nature is cruel and inhuman; she " kills and kills and kills " until man learns that she is only to be conquered by obeying her.[4] (We have insisted that Kingsley was a trifle muddled.) For the higher law of Nature is really the law of God. That law has come down to us in the form of Christian morals. As to ultimate realities, we are all ignorant, the theologian as well as the scientist. All we have is " mystery and morals."[5] It is this moral law which distinguishes for us between legitimate and illegitimate gratifications. Fornication, for instance, if natural in the lower sense, is unnatural in the higher sense. Monogamic marriage, however, is dictated by the moral law. Through this institution, our desires are disciplined into virtues. The moral law has not been revealed to us en bloc. From its central core of immutable truths it is constantly growing, aided by science. Between science and Christian morality there is no conflict. Kingsley welcomed the discoveries of Darwin. Though obscurantists may oppose his theories, the true Christians " find that now they have got rid of an interfering God—a master-magician, as I call it— they have to choose between the absolute empire of accident, and a living, immanent, ever-working God."[6]

For, though we are immensely guided by our reason through science in determining our conduct, moral action is

---

[1] *Letters and Memories*, vol. i., p. 341.   [2] *Ibid.*, vol. ii., p. 95.
[3] Inaugural Lecture, *The Roman and the Teuton* (1864), p. xxxii.
[4] *Letters and Memories*, vol. ii., p. 85.   [5] *Ibid.*, vol. i., p. 467.
[6] *Ibid.*, vol. ii., p. 171.

in the last resort the product of a specifically human quality, best defined—though it is incapable of being put into words —as love. " Love—truth—all are parts of that awful power of knowing, at a single glance, from and to all eternity, what a thing is in its essence, its properties, and its relations to the whole universe through all time."[1] We distinguish between what is worth while and what is not worth while, not by any petty reasoned calculus of pleasures and pains, but by this gift of judgment. " For mankind is ruled and guided, in the long run, not by practical considerations, not by self-interest, not by compromises; but by theories and principles, and those of the most abstruse, delicate, supernatural and. literally unspeakable kind; which, whether they be according to reason or not, are so little according to logic—that is, to speakable reason—that they cannot be put into speech. Men act, whether singly or in masses, by impulses and instincts for which they give reasons quite incompetent, often quite irrelevant; but which they have caught from each other, as they catch fever or smallpox."[2]

Nature and morality are thus allied in true Christianity, the Christianity of the Protestant Church as established in England. Roman Catholicism no doubt had its historical uses. But its sacerdotal tyranny and its ascetic foundations go against the grain of those instincts we know by more than knowledge to be true.[3] The Calvinism of English nonconformity is almost equally a denial of such instincts.[4] True Christianity is strong, masculine, progressive, stern but not cruel, abounding in the love that creates, the Christianity of God the Father, not of the weak Virgin. It is the Christianity of the cricket field, not of the cloister, nor indeed of the factory.

Kingsley, then, meant by Christianity the whole complex of values which his character had compounded from his experience. What he meant by Socialism follows as simply from these values. Men in the England of the 'forties were

---

[1] *Letters and Memories*, vol. i., p. 66.
[2] *Historical Lectures and Essays* (1889), p. 209.
[3] *Letters and Memories*, vol. i., p. 260 ; *Alton Locke*, chap. xiii.
[4] *Alton Locke*, chap. ii.

F

not living, and could not live, the good life. " What is flogging, or hanging, King Ryence's paletot, or the tanneries of Meudon, to the slavery, starvation, waste of life, year-long imprisonment in dungeons narrower and fouler than those of the Inquisition, which goes on among thousands of free English clothes-makers at this day ? "[1] As early as 1844 he wrote, " The refined man to me is he who cannot rest in peace with a coal mine or a factory, or a Dorsetshire peasant's house near him, in the state in which they are."[2] Here then was a definite situation, an evil thing which had to be destroyed. What were Englishmen doing about it ? Some were brutes enough not to be disturbed by it. Others were turning their backs on it and seeking an anodyne in Puseyism or the Church of Rome. Others were actually justifying it in the name of economic law. The Manchester school was the enemy that must first be destroyed. " Of all narrow, conceited, hypocritical, and anarchic and atheistic schemes of the universe, the Manchester one is exactly the worst." These men say all men should be freed from artificial restraints. They talk of independence for the workers, when what they mean is " that the men shall be independent of everyone but themselves—independent of legislators, parsons, advisers, gentlemen, noblemen, and every one that tries to help them by moral agents; but the slaves of the capitalists, bound to them by a servitude increasing instead of lightening with their numbers."[3]

The economists not only outrage human feelings, but err as scientists—though these are but two ways of saying the same thing. They maintain that " there are laws of Nature concerning economy, therefore you must leave them alone to do what they like with society. As if you were to say, you get cholera by law of Nature, therefore submit to cholera." As a matter of fact, political economy is still in a purely analytical and descriptive stage. " To be a true science, it must pass on into the synthetic stage, and learn how, by using the laws which it has discovered, and counteracting

---

[1] " Cheap Clothes and Nasty," reprinted in T. Hughes's edition of *Alton Locke* (1876), p. lxiii.
[2] *Letters and Memories*, vol. i., p. 121.   [3] *Ibid.*, vol. i., pp. 312-314.

them by others when necessary, to produce new forms of society. As yet political economy has produced nothing. It has merely said '*Laissez-faire*!'."[1]

The fundamental error of the economists is that they have no conception of a society. For them, a society is a collection of selfish atoms in perpetual conflict. But "selfishness can collect, not unite, a herd of cowardly wild cattle, that they may feed together, breed together, keep off the wolf and bear together. But when one of your wild cattle falls sick, what becomes of the corporate feelings of the herd then ?. . . Your Bible talks of society, not as a herd, but as a living tree, an organic individual body, a holy brotherhood, and kingdom of God."[2] It is society that effects the miracle of morality whereby a man is actually, behaves actually, better than anything discernible in him as a human atom would lead us to believe possible. Why, a mere village lad who enlists in the army becomes " member of a body in which if one member suffers, all suffer with it; if one member be honoured, all rejoice with it. A body, which has a life of its own, and a government of its own, a duty of its own, a history of its own. . . . He [the lad] does not now merely serve himself and his own selfish lusts: he serves the Queen. His nature is not changed, but the thought that he is the member of an honourable body *has raised him above his nature*."[3]

The problem nowadays is to recover this spirit of social discipline. We cannot turn backwards and repudiate the industrial revolution. On the contrary " it is the new commercial aristocracy; it is the scientific go-a-head-ism of the day which must save us, and which we must save."[4] Salvation lies, as it has always lain, in the Bible. English parsons " have used the Bible as if it was a mere special constable's handbook—an opium-dose for keeping beasts of burden patient while they were being overloaded—a mere book to keep the poor in order."[5] Actually the Bible is a charter for

---

[1] *Letters and Memories*, vol. ii., p. 36.   [2] *Yeast*, chap. xiv.
[3] Sermon on " Public Spirit," *Sermons for the Times* (1898), p. 297. The italics are mine.   [4] *Letters and Memories*, vol. i., p. 143.
[5] " Letters to the Chartists," *Politics for the People*, 27th May 1848.

the true society. From the inexhaustible well of " the Poor
Man's Book," Kingsley draws but a few drops: " he that
will not work, neither shall he eat. . . ." "Behold the hire of
your labourers which have reaped down your fields, which is
by you kept back by fraud, crieth . . ." and so on.[1] Our
worldlings forget that their lives make a mere pretence of
their belief in " the miracle of Pentecost, and the religion
that was taught by the carpenter's Son, and preached across
the world by fishermen."[2]

The Bible does not, however, preach the French doctrine
of the rights of man. The Chartists are justified in rebelling
against the injustice of modern society. But they are wrong
in claiming merely the same empty freedom which their
opponents possess. " Englishmen! Saxons! Workers of the
great, cool-headed, strong-handed nation of England, the
workshop of the world, the leader of freedom for seven
hundred years, men say you have common-sense! then do
not humbug yourselves into meaning ' licence,' when you
cry ' liberty.' "[3] We must distinguish between false freedom,
where a man is free to do as he likes, and true freedom, where
a man is free to do what he ought.[4] " True Socialism, true
liberty, brotherhood, and true equality (not the carnal, dead-
level equality of the Communist, but the spiritual equality of
the Christian idea which gives every man an equal chance of
developing and using God's gifts, and rewards every man
according to his work . . .) is only to be found in loyalty
and obedience to Christ."[5] That is, a Christian Socialist
society is an hierarchical society, where a man's place is
determined by his moral value, not by his capacity to cheat
and grab. It is a democratic society in the only possible
sense in which democracy is realizable here on earth—
every member by an act of faith feels that he has the place
allotted him by God.

[1] " Letters to the Chartists," *Politics for the People*, 17th June 1848.
[2] *Alton Locke*, chap. v.
[3] Poster addressed to Chartists in April 1848, reprinted in *Letters and Memories*, vol. i., p. 157.
[4] *Alton Locke*, ed. by T. Hughes (1876), p. xxxiii.
[5] *Letters and Memories*, vol. ii., p. 248.

Now all this is familiar enough, and to many will seem nonsense enough. Kingsley never accomplished what greater men have failed to do, the bringing to ground of such high abstractions as liberty and equality. But at least he has concrete notions of some of the things that must be done to realize the Kingdom of God on earth. In general, it may be said that the past of England was nearer to this Kingdom than the present. The Church, the gentry, and the old English commoner, the workman, were knit together by habits which were genuine *human* relationships. These habits may be revived against the new and inhuman relationship of employer and employed. If England is to be saved, the real battle will be between " the Church, the gentlemen, and the workman against the shopkeepers and the Manchester school." A true democracy in England " is impossible without a Church and a Queen, and as I believe, without a gentry."[1] Kingsley's programme is singularly like that of Tory Democracy.

The first step to be taken by this alliance will be to use the law-making power to prevent the obvious abuses of the industrial revolution. Universal suffrage, not itself a right or even a good, is to be welcomed as an aid to getting such legislation through Parliament. We must have no nonsense about "vested interests." The landlords of unspeakably dirty tenements never had a right to erect them. There is little use in exhorting them to improve these tenements, and less in urging the poor tenants to try and do so. The only remedy lies in the law. Public health can be improved only by drastic sweeping away of simpler obstacles, such as inadequate houses, by the compulsory installation of proper drainage, and finally by a campaign of education among the poor.[2] Kingsley was not to be disturbed by the reproach of paternalism. In his own parish of Eversley he played the benevolent despot in much the way Owen played it at New Lanark. He added to the duties of a conscientious parish clergyman those of teacher, doctor, lawyer, journalist, and man-of-all-work for his parishioners. Kingsley, in fact,

---

[1] *Letters and Memories*, vol. i., p. 315.   [2] *Ibid.*, vol. i., pp. 217-219.

was one of the first of the social-service parsons (a word, incidentally, that never offended him), who have since so multiplied these adjuncts of religion as to quite obscure its theological base.

Kingsley, however paternal his acts at Eversley, and however little fear he had of legislative action in itself, was far from repudiating, even in his most Socialistic period, the whole idea of competition. The economists were right enough in considering independence and self-help essential, especially to Nc̱se-Saxon civilization. Competition was all right, if it was the right kind. Here again we must look to the cricket field. The solution to the problem of retaining the moral stimulus of competition in industry, while preventing the chaos of Manchesterism, lies in workmen's associations. With Ludlow and Maurice, Kingsley played a large part in the Society for Promoting Working Men's Associations. Their ideal was pretty close to that of modern guild Socialism. A given trade was to be, in the end, completely organized in a co-operative corporation. Competition between trades for the patronage of the consumer would prevent the dry-rot of monopoly.[1] In a letter to Ludlow, of 1850, concerning a projected periodical to further association, he sketches a complete programme: " 1. Politics according to the Kingdom of God. 2. Art and Amusements for the People. 3. Opening the Universities to the People, and Education in general. 4. Attacking Straussism and Infidelity.[2] 5. Sanitary Reform. 6. Association: (α) Agitation on Partnership Laws. (β) Stores and Distribution. (γ) Agricultural Schemes. . . . The five former subjects *are* connected with Socialism; i.e. with a live and practical Church."[3]

Kingsley's Socialism began to evaporate rather early. By 1855 he could write that he would not have his children " insolent and scoffing Radicals." " I shall teach them," he

---

[1] " Cheap Clothes and Nasty," in T. Hughes's edition of *Alton Locke*, p. lxxxvii.

[2] " Who will denounce Strauss as a vile aristocrat, robbing the poor man of his Saviour—of the ground of all democracy, all freedom, all association—of the Charter itself ? " *Letters and Memories*, vol. i., p. 234.

[3] *Ibid.*, vol. i., p. 240.

continues, " that there are plenty of good people in the world, that public opinion has pretty surely an undercurrent of the water of life, below all its froth and garbage, and that in a Christian country like this, where, with all our faults, a man (sooner or later) has fair play and a fair hearing, the esteem of good men, and the blessings of the poor, will be a pretty sure sign that they have the blessing of God also."[1] And in 1856 he wrote to a Sheffield workman: " Emigrate; but never *strike* . . . but now, I see little before the English workman but to abide as he is, and endure."[2] It is difficult to escape concluding that Kingsley's youthful rebelliousness had its source in a feeling that he was cheated of his proper place in society. His early letters to his wife, with their romantic confession of his intent to roam the western plains of the United States and half-savage mixture of Byron and Daniel Boone, give unmistakable evidence of the kind of psychological maladjustment it is the fashion with some to detect in all revolutionaries. His success as a novelist, preacher, and lecturer made him feel that a society not unjust to Charles Kingsley was perhaps not so unjust to other men.

He did not lapse into complete conformity, and certainly not into silence. He continued to agitate for sanitary reform.[3] He urged local governments to insist on better housing conditions and better drainage. He would have hygiene taught to boys and girls alike, though he foresees an embarrassing transition before a supply of female teachers is secured—for of course Englishwomen cannot willingly learn the facts of hygiene from men.[4] It is of course especially important that English mothers know enough of medicine and sanitation to ensure healthy children. In particular, they must abandon the present abominable fashion of tight lacing. God—with whom, as Frederic Harrison pointed out, Kingsley was on singularly intimate terms, even for the time—does not like corsets.[5]

Kingsley, indeed, was no man to content himself with mere submersion in the daily round of living. He had to

[1] *Letters and Memories*, vol. i., p. 460.   [2] *Ibid.*, vol. i., p. 477.
[3] See the volume *Health and Education* (1874).
[4] *Ibid.*, p. 15.   [5] *Ibid.*, p. 48.

describe the universe to himself in terms of a corporate faith. When he abandoned Christian Socialism he took refuge in an amazing form of nationalism, which again we must insist is a bit too personal to be wholly Victorian, though it certainly throws light on the Victorian state of mind. He was deeply moved by his Teutonic inheritance. His first lecture on *The Roman and the Teuton*, which he delivered from the heights of a Regius professorship at Cambridge, is called " The Troll Garden." It is a parable on the downfall of the Roman Empire. The vicious, clever Romans are living in a magic garden, protected by walls. The Germans, children in frankness, purity, affectionateness, come upon the garden from their forest depths, climb into it, are corrupted by the vices of the Romans, but ultimately destroy the garden and build up a new and better one. These Germans were great boys: " very noble boys; very often very naughty boys."[1] But they had the essential virtues; energy, beautiful bodies, honesty, courage, and a peculiar respect for female virtue. The Franks, indeed, were an unfortunate exception. They were " false, vain, capricious, selfish, taking part with the Romans whenever their interest or vanity was at stake —the worst of all Teutons."[2] They were, in short, the ancestors of the modern French.[3]

The English are the true heirs of Tacitus' Germans. Even Alton Locke at Cambridge felt that " the true English stuff came out there . . . the stuff which has held Gibraltar, and conquered at Waterloo—which has created a Birmingham and a Manchester, and colonized every quarter of the globe— that grim, earnest, stubborn energy, which, since the days of the old Romans, the English possess alone of all the nations of the earth."[4] Nor is God to be left out of the matter. " For as surely as there is an English view of everything, so surely God intends us to take that view; and He who gave us our English character intends us to develop its

---

[1] *The Roman and the Teuton*, p. 6.   [2] *Ibid.*, p. 8.

[3] This nonsense, coming from a Regius professor, scandalized many who were quite as patriotic as Kingsley. See a review in the Conservative *Saturday Review*, 9th April 1864.

[4] *Alton Locke*, chap. xii. The old Romans were not so bad after all.

peculiarities."[1] Only, indeed, by casting off Rome " have we risen to be the most mighty, and, with all our sins, perhaps the most righteous and pure of nations."[2] So great a nation cannot avoid an imperial destiny. " We have at least brought the British Constitution with us out of the bogs and moors of Jutland, along with our smock-frocks and leather gaiters, brown bills and stone axes; and it has done us good service, and will do, *till we have carried it right round the world.*"[3] Small wonder that Kingsley welcomed the Crimean War, that he preached with deep emotion at Aldershot; nor is it strange that he saw God's hand in the punishment of France in 1870. He did not live to see the disconcerting quarrel of 1914 between the Teutonic nations.

Kingsley's achievements were by no means slight. For one thing, he helped translate Carlyle to the multitude. Certain passages of the novels, indeed, ape Carlyle's style. The sight of a butler left Locke " wondering at the strange fact that free men, with free wills, do sell themselves, by the hundred thousand, to perform menial offices for other men, not for love, but for money; becoming, to define them strictly, bell-answering animals; and are honest, happy, contented, in such a life."[4] Kingsley actually found in Carlyle, "not a dark but a bright view of life."[5] He himself is at times but a eupeptic Carlyle. His attacks on the industrial system sank into the English mind precisely because they were inspired by a facile optimism which never really questioned fundamentals. *Alton Locke,* like Mr. U. Sinclair's *Jungle,* really stirred the ultimate consumer, not to soul-searching discontent with society, but to an immediate discomfort. Kingsley was unquestionably an element in the downfall of *laissez-faire.*

Yet there seems singularly little transmissible, little genuinely common, in Kingsley's own faith. His Christianity was too comfortable to himself to do service in this world. Kingsley was a man of extremely simple and

---

[1] *Literary and General Essays and Lectures,* p. 261.
[2] *Letters and Memories,* vol. i., p. 203.
[3] *The Roman and the Teuton,* p. 276. The italics are mine.
[4] *Alton Locke,* chap. xiv.   [5] *Letters and Memories,* vol. i., p. 119.

F*

extremely intense desires. His energies were quite readily contained by a happy family life, an active cure of souls and bodies, an opportunity for exercise in the open air. His intellect was even more simply satisfied by a crude collection of generalizations like that of Nordic supremacy. His emotions gave him no trouble at all; he could always weep. But the great mass of men are still baulked by poverty from attaining the degree of physical comfort upon which Kingsley could base his spiritual contentment. There is no use telling them, as Kingsley told the Sheffield workman, to " endure," to console themselves with equality before God—especially when you assert, as Kingsley did, that God means his children to be healthy, well fed, beautiful, active, and contented. Traditional Christianity, which in spite of Kingsley was pessimistic, contemptuous of the flesh, offering consolation in the next world for the sufferings of this world, was a faith a poor man could hold. Kingsley's faith was not. His God, his virtue, his England, made too many promises to the flesh—promises unfulfilled to the common man. For the uncommon man, his faith was even more inadequate. Taste and intellect alike recoil from the simplicities of a universe on the pattern of Eversley.

4. DISRAELI[1]

" My mind," wrote Disraeli, " is a Continental mind. It is a revolutionary mind."[2] This is at first sight a curious claim to be set up by a man who ranks with Burke as one of

---

[1] Much of Disraeli's theoretical writings, including the important *Vindication of the English Constitution* (1835), has been conveniently collected under the title *Whigs and Whiggism* (ed. by W. Hutcheson, 1914). Of his novels, *Coningsby* (1844) and *Sybil* (1845) together give a pretty complete account of the Tory Democracy of the 'forties. His *Speeches* (ed. T. E. Kebbel, 2 vols., 1882) and of course the letters in Moneypenny and Buckle's *Life* are essential to a rounding-out of his contribution to political thought. See Moneypenny, W. F., and Buckle, G. E., *Life of Benjamin Disraeli* (6 vols., 1910-1920); Bagehot, W., *Works* (1915), vol. ix.; Cazamian, L., *Le roman social en Angleterre* (1904); Stephen, L., *Hours in a Library* (1892), vol. ii.; Somervell, D. C., *Disraeli and Gladstone* (1922).

[2] Quoted in Moneypenny, W. F., and Buckle, G. E., *Life of Benjamin Disraeli* (1910-1920), vol. i., p. 236.

the founders of conservative doctrine in modern England. Yet it has a certain justification. Disraeli's mind had the capacity for adapting itself to the outside world which is one of the essentials for moulding that world. His was not a revolutionary mind in the sense that Bentham's was. He never was tempted to use it to spin a consistent system of political values superior to, and outside of, the political world he knew so well. In the sense in which Godwin's *Political Justice* is revolutionary, no product of Disraeli's mind was ever revolutionary. But the outside world sometimes runs away from the habits of mind by which men make themselves comfortable in it. The England of the industrial revolution had quite definitely so run away. The ordinary uncritical intellect is helpless in such a situation. The purely speculative intellect is always helpless in this world. Now Disraeli's mind was neither uncritical nor purely speculative. What it sought for almost instinctively was adjustment between values arrived at by thought and conditions of life imposed by the outside world.

What Disraeli really possessed to an extraordinary degree, and what really lies behind the remark just quoted, was the intellectual detachment of the true mime. The mimetic instinct is commonly associated with the power to reproduce purely external characteristics; with Disraeli, it involved the capacity to reproduce the inner essence. Sometimes this shows itself in more or less successful imitation. The *Revolutionary Epick* is Shelleyan as the pamphlet on *Old England* is Carlylean. Sometimes, however, Disraeli goes beyond mere imitation, and attains absorption. He thus absorbed, and made his own, the work of men as different as Bolingbroke, Burke, and Coleridge. Thus he absorbed the hopes and enthusiasms of men like Lord John Manners. And thus he incurred the reproach of insincerity which still adheres to his reputation. Insincere his career was, but only as all great acting is insincere. No great actor would consent to limit himself to a single part. The universe is far too complex for such limitation. Disraeli had none of that vegetable adhesion to immediacies which makes most men seem sincere.

This amounts really to the commonplace assertion that Disraeli was an artist. Now, however possible it may be for the determined philosopher to convince himself that art and morals are ultimately one, most of us here below do commonly regard them as different. The moralist seeks to dam the stream of life in which the artist is content to flow. Both indeed attempt to create an order. But the order of the moralist would fix itself in a law, while the order of the artist is an attempted evasion of law. Both are aware of that fundamental dichotomy of human nature to which Thomas Hardy gave expression when he wrote that thought is a disease of the flesh. Both, indeed, have their remedies. But the remedy of the moralist—if a somewhat childish expression may be forgiven—is unavoidably homœopathic. However Epicurean a respect he may show for the flesh, his ultimate aim is the conquest of flesh by thought. Not so with the artist, though he be ever so intellectually gifted. He may not, with the extreme romantics, surrender entirely to the flesh. But he never willingly gives up the colourful uncertainties and curious interplay of the appetites. The remedy, if remedy there be, for the conflict between thought and flesh, he always brings back to the flesh. At bottom, perhaps, he despairs of a remedy. Art is never optimistic. Therefore it is always conservative.

Disraeli felt deeply that this world is not a comfortable place. " It is civilization that makes us awkward, for it gives us an uncertain position. . . . The Bedouin and the Red Indian never lose their presence of mind."[1] A chance remark, no doubt, and certainly no basis for assimilating its author to Rousseau. But it does show how Disraeli felt that with all man's social and scientific achievements he was singularly lost in the universe he seemed in part at least to have built up for himself. Now Disraeli was an intensely ambitious man. He wanted power and position quite simply, for the pleasure it gave him. He was an extremely clever man, with an artist's love of the phrase for its own sake. He was indeed quite dangerously clever in comparison with the

[1] *Sybil*, book iii., chap. v.

men he led. He was not a scrupulously honest man, and he had never been disciplined to the code of the English public school. A critic who is divided from him by all the imponderables of taste and morals, as was Bagehot for instance, may draw up an indictment that is indeed unanswerable. But only a very Whiggish critic would deny Disraeli what we have been trying to establish for him, a conservatism consistently developed out of his personality. We must try to concentrate, not on the accidents of his mannerisms, but on the fundamentals of this conservatism.

True to his deepest convictions that man is inescapably rooted in the irrational substratum of life, Disraeli always distrusted the instrument of thought. It is a paradox hardly worth noticing that only the greatest of thinkers achieve this distrust of thought. Disraeli attacked the utilitarians in much the same terms, and for much the same reasons, as Burke had attacked the French *philosophes*. " The schoolmen are revived in the nineteenth century, and are going to settle the State with their withering definitions, their fruitless logomachies, and barren dialectics."[1] But the State is the creation of generations of men who have built into it their whole lives, not just their ideas. If you start on the assumption that you can devise in your own head a system of government better than the existing one you run into a double difficulty. In the first place, in so far as your ideas prove workable, you cheat yourself by spinning out a system whose terminology merely disguises its impotence. Any government that has endured at all, for example, is founded on " the greatest happiness of the greatest number."[2] In the second place, in so far as you do succeed in inventing new standards by which to guide and test human actions, you upset human devotion to the old standards without ensuring human obedience to your new ones. For ideas are in themselves singularly devoid of driving force with most men.[3] The reality of change in the conditions of human life is certainly an inescapable fact in nineteenth-century England. But such

---

[1] " Vindication of the English Constitution," *Whigs and Whiggism,* p. 119.
[2] *Ibid.,* p. 115.   [3] *Ibid.,* p. 120.

changes are far more subtle and far-reaching than anything thought can encompass. No felicific calculus will fit them into an orderly scheme.

For men are uneasy and contentious animals. Even the stupidest of them, though he is not to be moved by a disinterested perception of an abstract truth, is capable of learning from the utilitarians that he should follow his desires against the inconvenient dictates of an older law. Liberty to the philosopher may have a positive content of rights and duties; to the man in the street it too often means the sweeping away of all the restraints civilization has put upon him. At some such unlucky state England has now arrived. Between the fabric of her settled institutions and the energies of her citizens there exists a dangerous tension. Now the way out of this difficulty is not to plot out an entirely new path for these energies, which is the radical solution, but first to inquire how this tension came about, and then to contrive such an adjustment that the energies shall strengthen, rather than weaken, the fabric. For we know——those of us at least whose tempers are chastened by a saving faith in earthly contingency——that the energies are self-destructive without the fabric. Imagination is the grace that saves us from our reason.

The tension has been brought about by two centuries of Whiggish rule in England. Disraeli's love for the dramatic perhaps distorted his picture of the villainy of the Whigs. Certainly to many sober Liberals his reading of English history is a shocking distortion. But real history, as Croce insists, is always contemporary history. Disraeli never failed to breathe into his historical generalizations an actuality far above antiquarian respect for truth. Nothing is more fundamental to his political thought than his reading of the immediate past.

The legitimate province of thought in politics is the investigation of what we must call loosely the " national character." In a study of the past of a people, wise men " separating the essential character of their history from that which is purely adventitious, . . . discover certain principles of ancestral conduct, which they acknowledge as the causes

that these [good] institutions have flourished and descended
to them; and in their future career, and all changes,
reforms, and alterations, that they may deem expedient,
they resolve that these principles shall be their guides and
their instructors. . . . This I apprehend to be the greatest
amount of theory that ever enters into those political institutions which from their permanency are alone entitled to the
consideration of a philosophical statesman."[1] Disraeli is here
asserting, with a careful avoidance of metaphysical terminology, something like what Coleridge meant by the English
constitution. There is what common sense would call " an
English way of doing things," and what philosophers would
call an idea of the English constitution. When Englishmen
so live that their actions conform to this idea, they are in a
state of social equilibrium. There is then no tension between
the individual and the society. But when their actions do not
so conform, such a tension does arise. The individual pulls
one way, society another. But you cannot alter such a society,
unless indeed you destroy it. The national character is
always seeking to impose itself upon the rebels. The result
is a constant disequilibrium.

Englishmen were first notably false to their national
character—that is, to their past—in the sixteenth century,
when they permitted the spoliation of the national Church
for the benefit of the ancestors of the present Whig aristocracy. They erred further when in the seventeenth century
they martyred Charles I., the exponent of a fair and essentially popular system of direct taxation, and accepted, under
the characteristically Whig disguise of popular rights and
representative government, the unjust system of indirect
taxation. But the culmination of this betrayal of the past, the
final capping of the perverted Whig system, came with the
Glorious Revolution of 1688. That revolution definitely
established the Venetian oligarchy of the great Whig families
by destroying the power of the Crown and substituting an
irresponsible Parliament corruptly chosen by the Whigs
themselves. This oligarchy kept itself in power by insisting
that the Crown was the natural enemy of the people, and

---

[1] " Vindication of the English Constitution," *Whigs and Whiggism*, p. 120.

that they were its friends. They maintained a whole series of
political generalizations based on what they called the rights
and liberties of Englishmen. They appeared as the defenders
of liberal principles. But " liberal opinions are the opinions
of those who would be free from certain constraints and
regulations, from a certain dependence and duty which are
deemed necessary for the general or popular welfare.
Liberal opinions are very convenient opinions for the rich
and powerful. They ensure enjoyment and are opposed to
self-sacrifice."[1] Under cover of this verbal prestidigitation
by which their privileges were made to appear the rights of
all, the Whigs, and their new recruits the manufacturers,
have exploited their fellow Englishmen. They have destroyed the social bond, and made possible the horrors of
laissez-faire. Thanks to them, a once-united England is
divided into two nations " between whom there is no intercourse and no sympathy; who are as ignorant of each other's
habits, thoughts, and feelings, as if they were dwellers in
different zones, or inhabitants of different planets; who are
formed by a different breeding, are fed by a different food,
are ordered by different manners, and are not governed
by the same laws "—the rich and the poor.[2]
This artificial " union of oligarchical wealth and mob
poverty "[3] cannot endure. Indeed, the people have never loved
their Whig masters, though misguided Londoners have
shouted for Fox and Sheridan. The arch-Whig Walpole was
never popular. " The Whig party has ever been odious to
the English people, and in spite of all their devices and
combinations, it may ever be observed that, in the long run,
the English nation declares against them. Even now [1835]
after their recent and most comprehensive *coup d'état*, they
are only maintained in power by the votes of the Irish and
the Scotch members."[4] There is then, in the present crisis, an
excellent opportunity for those elements in English political
life which have always opposed the Whigs, and which may

[1] *Speeches* (ed. T. E. Kebbel), vol. i., p. 178.
[2] *Sybil*, book ii., chap. v.
[3] " The Spirit of Whiggism," *Whigs and Whiggism*, p. 350.
[4] " Vindication of the English Constitution," *Ibid.*, p. 215.

be credited with a truer feeling for the right working of the
English constitution, to attain power by appealing to the
English people. What have the Tories done towards making
good their opportunity?

They have, under the leadership of Sir Robert Peel, done
just the wrong thing. The Tories indeed began to stray
under the administration of Lord Liverpool. " The peace
came. . . . The people . . . found themselves without guides.
. . . Commerce requested a code; trade required a currency; the unenfranchised subject solicited his equal
privilege; suffering labour clamoured for its rights; a new
race demanded education. What did the ministry do? They
fell into a panic. . . . They determined to put down the
multitude. They thought they were imitating Mr. Pitt
because they mistook disorganization for sedition."[1] Thus,
although with Canning and Huskisson the Tories came
nearer to true leadership than under the pure negations of
Liverpool, they failed to put themselves at the head of the
country, and suffered the Whigs to do in 1832 what they
themselves should have done earlier—and better. But by
the middle 'thirties it was clear that the Whigs could not use
their power. Here was the great Tory opportunity. Their
old obstructionist policy had been discredited with the failure
of Wellington to stop the Reform Bill. A new leader could
make them again the party of Bolingbroke. But all Peel did
was to attempt to cast off some of the odium attaching to the
Tory party from the days of Liverpool and Wellington by
rechristening it the Conservative party. Actually, Conservatism had nothing new to offer—nor nothing genuinely old.
" The Tamworth Manifesto of 1834 was an attempt to
construct a party without principles; its basis therefore
was necessarily latitudinarianism; and its inevitable consequence has been political infidelity."[2] And again, " There
was indeed a considerable shouting about what they called
conservative principles; but the awkward question naturally
arose, what will you conserve? The prerogatives of the

[1] *Coningsby*, book ii., chap. i. This chapter, together with *Sybil*, book i.,
chap. iii., forms a *locus classicus* for Disraeli's use of history.
[2] *Coningsby*, book ii., chap. v.

crown, provided they are not exercised; the independence of the House of Lords, provided it is not asserted; the ecclesiastical estate, provided it is regulated by a commission of laymen. Everything in short that is established, as long as it is a phrase and not a fact."[1] Conservatism, in short, " discards prescription, shrinks from principle, disavows progress; having rejected all respect for antiquity, it offers no redress for the present, and makes no preparation for the future."[2] Already in the early 'forties it is clear that Peel is meditating the final treason of the repeal of the Corn Laws. The new Conservatives are doing the work of the old Whigs; they are furthering industrial anarchy and social injustice under the name of a false freedom.

To re-establish social equilibrium in England something more is needed than utilitarian principles, Whig selfishness, and Conservative phrases. A new party, which will also be an old party, is needed. This is the party of Young England. From the maturity of 1870, Disraeli reviewed his platform of the 'forties: " To change back the oligarchy into a generous aristocracy round a real throne; to infuse life and vigour into the Church, as the trainer of the nation . . .; to establish a commercial code on the principles successfully negotiated by Lord Bolingbroke at Utrecht, and which, though baffled at the time by a Whig Parliament, were subsequently and triumphantly vindicated by his political pupil and heir, Mr. Pitt; to govern Ireland according to the policy of Charles I., and not of Oliver Cromwell; to emancipate the political constituency of 1832 from its sectarian bondage and contracted sympathies; to elevate the physical as well as the moral condition of the people, by establishing that labour required regulation as much as property; and all this rather by the use of ancient forms and the restoration of the past than by political revolutions founded on abstract ideas."[3] This, in outline, is the Tory democracy of Disraeli's prime, and his chief contribution to political theory. We must analyse it at greater length.

---

[1] *Coningsby*, book ii., chap. v.   [2] *Ibid.*
[3] General Preface to the *Novels*, edition of 1870.

At its base, as we have seen, lies a Burkean distrust of the abstract principle of individual liberty, a Burkean respect for the frame of civil society which protects the helpless, erring individual from himself. Where Disraeli differs chiefly from Burke is in his conviction that such a frame of civil society in England has been all but lost, and must be restored. Now the essential part of that frame is the alliance among the Crown, the gentry, and the common people. In this alliance, the place of the Crown is clear. If the parliamentary system is not to degenerate into mere bickerings between factions, the strongest of which will inevitably turn its power to its own selfish uses, a strong head lifted above party concerns is necessary. England's great kings, from the Normans through the Stuarts, have always been the protectors of the people. The Crown is no mere symbol, let alone a useless survival of the past. It is the head of the English nation in a very literal sense. Its prerogative is not to be diminished without throwing England open to the envious spirit of Whiggery and French republicanism.

The second element in the alliance, a real aristocracy, is also an English heritage, though it has, in the upper reaches where it should be strongest, betrayed its trust. Aristocracy is a fact. At Wodgate, that horrible industrial town which had grown up outside the good restraints of English parochial government, the fact of natural aristocracy was at its clearest. There the master workmen formed " a real aristocracy; it is privileged, but it does something for its privileges. . . . It possesses indeed in its way complete knowledge; and it imparts in its manner a certain quantity of it to those whom it guides. Thus it is an aristocracy that leads, and therefore a fact."[1] Of old England has possessed in her country gentlemen a class freed from the ignoble economic struggle and devoted to the good of the people. They have had the wisdom to give up titular nobility; they are no petty chevaliers of continental fashion, crowding each other in the race for court honours, living off the country. They, " instead of meanly submitting to fiscal immunities, support upon their broad and cultivated

---

[1] *Sybil*, book iii., chap. iv.

lands all the burthens of the State." They form a class " of whom it is difficult to decide whether their moral excellence or their political utility be most eminent, conspicuous, and inspiring."[1] The new Toryism must build upon these men, encourage them to live up to their standards. They must imitate Lord Henry Sydney in *Coningsby* ; " An indefinite yet strong sympathy with the peasantry of the realm had been one of the characteristic sensibilities of Lord Henry at Eton. Yet a schoolboy, he had busied himself with their pastimes and the details of their cottage economy. As he advanced in life, the horizon of his views expanded with his intelligence and his experience, and . . . on the very threshold of his career he devoted his time and thought, labour and life, to one vast and noble purpose, the elevation of the condition of the great body of the people."[2]

As to the people, they ask nothing better than to obey such leaders. Englishmen, left to themselves, have a strong sense of hierarchy. They take comfort and assurance from the knowledge that their betters are their shepherds. But you must beware of disturbing their confidence. This the Whigs, and especially the new industrial Whigs, have done in two ways. First, they have ceased to care for the people; they have allowed the people to become the " labouring classes," worse yet, the " poor." Second, they have borrowed the French vocabulary of the rights of man, or merely translated that vocabulary into utilitarian language. They have created a distrust of the very principle of aristocracy. " The evil is not so much that they have created a distrust in things; that might be removed by superior argument and superior learning. The evil is that they have created a distrust in persons, and that is a sentiment which once engendered is not easily removed, even by reason and erudition."[3] Indeed, the whole scheme of education which has been brought forward in modern times is calculated to undermine the instinct of obedience which is the source of

[1] " Vindication of the English Constitution," *Whigs and Whiggism*, p. 160.
[2] *Coningsby*, book ix., chap. i.
[3] *Speeches*, vol. ii., p. 559. This was said of the authors of *Essays and Reviews*, but it is obviously applicable here.

English strength. The new education is based on mechanics, not on life. It denies the mysteriously organic and personal bond which holds together the hierarchical state. The present leaders of England—the old Whigs and the new rich—are educating the people to revolt. These leaders " might make money, they might make railroads; but when the age of passion came, when those interests were in motion, and those feelings stirring, which would shake society to its centre, then . . . they would see whether the people had received the same sort of education which had been advocated and supported by William of Wykeham."[1]

This alliance of Crown, aristocracy, and people is cemented in the Established Church. The Church of England has been plundered in the past by Tudor monarchs and by rapacious Whigs. Gentlemen of Liberal opinions, impatient of her restraints, would plunder her to-day by disestablishment. But she has never been attacked by the people, of whom she is the natural protector.[2] This Church is no creature of the State, no Erastian moral police force, but an independent corporation living in happy alliance with the State. The Church has prevented society from degenerating into a mechanism, which means the death of society. " Our Church, always catholic and expansive in its character, has ever felt that the human mind was a manifold quality, and that some men must be governed by enthusiasm, and some controlled by ceremony. Happy the land where there is an institution which prevents enthusiasm from degenerating into extravagance, and ceremony from being degraded into superstition."[3] The Church to-day need only be true to her traditions to maintain her proper place in English society. She should assert what Coleridge called her Nationality by educating the people, by a moderate extension of the episcopate, by permitting a greater infusion of lay government in concerns not purely spiritual, by maintaining the parish and its complex life, and especially the right of visitation, by increasing the stipend of the parish

[1] Quoted in Moneypenny and Buckle, *Life*, vol. ii., p. 62.
[2] *Speeches*, vol. i., p. 177.   [3] *Ibid.*, vol. ii., p. 558.

clergy, and, above all, by maintaining a decent Christian
zeal against unbelief and superstition alike.[1]

The Church and State so conceived will maintain that
precious heritage of self-government which is the envy of
other countries. Now self-government is not egalitarian
democracy, it implies conditions just the opposite from the
centralized bureaucratic state of the French Revolution.
" The principle of the first equality, base, terrestrial, Gallic,
and grovelling, is that no one should be privileged; the
principle of English equality is that everyone should be
privileged."[2] For the Englishman who has his proper place
in society is privileged. He is protected by a whole inter-
locking system of natural groups from the tyranny of the
one or the many. " Without our Crown, our Church, our
Universities, our great municipal and commercial Corporations, our Magistracy and its dependent scheme of provincial polity, the inhabitants of England, instead of being
a nation, would present only a mass of individuals governed
by a metropolis."[3] Here, too, the Whigs and the Radicals
threaten destruction. The proposed municipal reforms of
1834 showed that " it is their evident determination to
assimilate the institutions of this country to those of France
—free and favoured France. Instead of the county and the
borough we shall soon have the *arrondissement* and the
commune. The préfet and the gendarmerie follow, of course."[4]
Not even representative government is safe from the falsity
of Whig professions. The real tendency of these gentlemen,
though they pay lip-service to parliamentary government,
is to encourage the actual transaction of affairs by paid
commissioners and select committees—by bureaucrats, in
short.[5] But if you stifle the natural organizations of men in
groups, if you suppress groups whose interests have been
harmonized and disciplined by time, you do but invite the
proliferation of groups with narrow and selfish purposes,

---

[1] *Speeches*, vol. ii., pp. 572-580.
[2] " Vindication of the English Constitution," *Whigs and Whiggism*, p. 229.
[3] *Ibid.*, p. 215.
[4] " Peers and People," *Ibid.*, p. 49.
[5] *Speeches*, vol. i., p. 178.

groups operating *ad hoc.* The completely unified State is the easy victim of agitation. See already around you Roman Catholic Associations, Political Unions, Anti-Corn Law Leagues.[1] Such a State will, indeed, not be stationary. But the changes it will undergo will be artificial, hurried, unadapted to its profounder life. They will not be progress, but " the epilepsy of decay."[2]

Now the great protector of this natural English State is the landed interest. By landed interest Disraeli is careful to indicate that he means, not merely the landed proprietors, but the church, the judicial fabric, the towns and rural populations[3] of which the landed gentry are but the active leaders. This landed interest, properly understood, provides the element essential to prevent the dissolution of society through the undue expansion of its productive powers. For it is a fact that the industrial wealth of England has been gained by men working under a system which, however adequate for the one purpose of producing a maximum of consumer's goods, is wholly inadequate as a rule of life. Economic laws are, properly speaking, not laws at all, for they have no moral basis. Economic practice—in industry, at least—divorces the idea of property from that of duty. Now landed property in England has always carried with it definite obligations. " Why, when the Conqueror carved out parts of the land, and introduced the feudal system, he said to the recipient, ' You shall have that estate, but you shall do something for it: you shall feed the poor; you shall endow the Church; you shall defend the land in case of war; and you shall execute justice and maintain truth to the poor for nothing'."[4] This is a fact, created by and consecrated by history. It is all very well to say that something of this spirit should be infused into the new industrialists. Some of them, like the good Traffords of *Sybil,* have indeed been true overlords of their workpeople. But you cannot make the whole class of industrial capitalists alive to their duty by preaching at them. Spirit is no

---

[1] *Coningsby,* book ii., chap i.
[2] " Coalition " (1853), *Whigs and Whiggism,* p. 431.
[3] *Speeches,* vol. i., p. 48.   [4] *Ibid.,* vol. i., p. 50.

abstraction to be spread abroad by mere words. Virtue here as elsewhere adheres to things concrete. This is the real reason for Disraeli's defence of the Corn Laws, and it is scant justice to him to hold that his break with Peel was but a clever piece of Parliamentary tactics. If the Corn Laws go, your whole agricultural polity goes and your broad " landed interest " is destroyed. Small competing land-owners, peasants after the French model, will supplant the country gentleman. The one bulwark of society, the one class which already practises its obligations instead of talking about them, will be destroyed.[1]

Of this fact the English people are beginning to be aware. The Chartists are hostile above all to the middle class, whom they feel to be their despoilers. This middle class, by the Whig *coup d'état* of 1832, has become the ruling class. But since it " was not bound up with the great mass of the people by the performance of social duties, and attained political station without the conditions which should be annexed to its possession," since, in short, it has power without responsibility, it has merely clamoured for cheap government, for centralized and efficient government, the " monarchy of the middle classes."[2] " To acquire, to accumulate, to plunder each other by virtue of philosophic phrases, to propose a Utopia to consist only of WEALTH and TOIL, this has been the breathless business of enfranchised England for the last twelve years [since 1832] until we are startled from our voracious strife by the wail of intolerable serfage."[3] Chartism is the despairing cry of a people forced to live in the degrading conditions of the new manufacturing towns. It is a cry, not for abstract rights, in spite of the wording of the Charter, but for bread and spiritual leadership. The English masses are eager for that alliance with the gentlemen of England which we have discerned to be one of the principles of her natural constitution.

The new England to be created by this alliance will not, of course, abandon what is good in the industrial revolution.

---

[1] *Speeches*, vol. i., p. 53.
[2] Moneypenny and Buckle, *Life*, vol. ii., p. 82-83.
[3] *Sybil*, book i., chap. v.

In spite of some highly coloured passages in the novels, Disraeli was no sentimental mediævalist. He does not hate the machine as Ruskin and Morris hated it. All that is needed is to redress the balance disturbed by the triumph of the industrial middle classes in 1832. Factory and sanitation acts will then take the first steps in the improvement of the condition of the labouring classes. Institutions and the example of a revived gentry will achieve what mere sentiment would never do, the conversion of the new industrialists to a feudal and English sense of duty. Already the aspiration of the manufacturer to be " large acred " is an encouraging sign that this conversion will be achieved, even though the Corn Laws go.[1]

But the new England will not rest content with a comfortable solution of her domestic duties. The incredible energies which have produced the industrial revolution are not destined to end in the tame security of a somewhat bigger Denmark. Once the two nations of *Sybil* have become one, that nation must embark on an even greater career. It is sometimes suggested that the Congress of Berlin was but a sorry ending for *Sybil*. Disraeli himself surely did not so regard it. The young pamphleteer of 1833 had written: " Great spirits may yet arise to guide the groaning helm through the world of troubled waters—spirits whose proud destiny it may still be at the same time to maintain the glory of the Empire, and to secure the happiness of the People."[2] Disraeli was an Imperialist from the start. He opposed Free Trade, not merely because the abrogation of the Corn Laws threatened the landed interest, but because the positive doctrine of Free Trade implied an internationalism which was too impractical to succeed, and which, if by a miracle it did succeed, would produce a flat, stale world where great spirits would have no place. Imperial England was as surely dictated by the national character as were the Factory Acts. Only by absorption in some such great common effort as the maintenance and increase of the Empire could the average

[1] *Sybil*, book ii., chap. vii.
[2] " What is He ? " *Whigs and Whiggism*, p. 22.

Englishman draw full satisfaction from his life as a citizen. Little England is the euthanasia of the old England.

There can be no doubt as to the immediate and great effects of Disraeli's ideas in English politics. Many political thinkers, from Plato on, have indeed held some form of what we may call Tory democracy. Ashley and other contemporaries of Disraeli perhaps translated its principles more definitely into legislation than did Disraeli. But Disraeli's influence on the temper of modern English Toryism can hardly be exaggerated. We may discern two major directions in which it operated.

In the first place, Disraeli did obtain in a measure that hold upon the lower classes postulated in the programme of Young England. The Reform Bill of 1867 did indeed consecrate an alliance between the Tories and the common people which has always scandalized the Liberal. " The Tories and the Residuum, to use the phrase of a later day," wrote Morley, " made that alliance which Cobden called unholy, but which rests on the natural affinities of bigotry and ignorance."[1] The following analogy is imperfect, both as to time and place; but it is an interesting problem why the ideas of the modern French traditionalists, which in many respects are very similar indeed to those of Disraeli, have never had any hold at all on the French masses, but have remained the property of a cultured, if noisy, few. The full answer would of course involve complicated considerations deriving from the history of the two countries. But one part of the answer is certainly that Disraeli possessed the common touch which not even M. Daudet, let alone M. Maurras, possesses. He had the gift, rare among aristocratic thinkers, of manipulating Parliamentary majorities, and of creating a party with a broad base outside of Parliament. The Primrose League was indeed a scandal to hardheaded positivism; but it cut clean across class lines. It was not wholly what Young England would have wished for, but it came amazingly close to being so.

In the second place, Disraeli caught and retained the devotion of the intellectuals who have given a definite tone

[1] *Life of Cobden*, p. 123.

to English Toryism. To this day, English Toryism has remained a sentimentalism tempered by epigram. Disraeli's work is full of what we are bound to call bad taste. His aristocrats are singularly unconvincing to a commoner. His racial theories, his consciousness of his Jewish inheritance, seem at best red herrings drawn across the trail of his thought. Yet no one would call his work dull. It is alive with the play of intellect. Disraeli threw off dozens of phrases which satisfy and spur the mind as do the phrases of a La Rochefoucauld. It has a singular attraction for the young men of lively sensibilities and livelier intellects who are the peculiar product of English higher education. Here again a comparison suggests itself with another modern nation. American Toryism has always been dull and stuffy, singularly lacking in intellectual graces. Bright young men in America either turn from politics in contempt, or take the Radical, not the Tory, side. Here, too, the whole history of the two countries must be brought in to explain the difference between them. The past of the United States is not quite romantic enough to give the imagination hold; *Sybil* without a ruined abbey would be impossible. America, as has often been remarked, is a Whig product. Yet surely no one can neglect Disraeli's influence in forging the Tory legend in England. He has helped to make many a young Englishman satisfied to remain loyal to things that are, rather than to seek new loyalties in new institutions.

For, in spite of its insistence that the England of the industrialists was not a good England, in spite of its claim to be a radical remaking of Eldonian Toryism, Disraeli's political philosophy is essentially conformist. Disraeli's mind was in some sense revolutionary, but his temperament was not. He helped rescue England from *laissez-faire*, but so, too, did Owen and J. S. Mill. Young England became inevitably the Primrose League. For Tory democracy, like Christian Socialism, is a contradiction in terms. One half despairs, the other half hopes. One half distrusts the human animal, the other half trusts him. Eventually one half is bound to triumph over the other. Disraeli the Tory was always stronger than Disraeli the democrat. The compromise of his later years was simply the Victorian compromise. The alliance between Crown, Church, aristocracy, and people was consummated in the unabiding achievements of household suffrage, Eastern Roumelia, and *Endymion*.

5. NEWMAN[1]

Newman is not, in the strictest sense, a political thinker. He has left behind no formal treatise on civil government. He modestly disclaimed any special knowledge or any special capacity in political affairs.[2] The State, even when most perfectly organized, can but make its members more comfortable here on earth; and earthly comfort or discomfort weighs little with a soul facing eternity. Yet Newman was very far from turning his back on this world. His work is political in a proper sense: first, because even the Church must realize its mission on earth and in time, and therefore is faced with the problem of its own political organization; second, because the Church as a political body must have relations with the State, and therefore must work out a satisfactory theory by which to regulate these relations; and thirdly, because the moral life of the individual on earth is all-important as a prelude to his immortal life, and therefore the social life in which his moral worth is tested must be a concern of the Christian thinker. Newman is never very far from the central problem of the place of man in society. As much as Mill or Disraeli, he is concerned that Englishmen

---

[1] Newman's political ideas are not to be found completely in any one treatise. Most important in forming an idea of his place as a *politique et moraliste* are the *Apologia pro Vita Sua* (1864); the *Grammar of Assent* (1870); the collection published as *Discussions and Arguments* (1872); and the *Essay on the Development of Christian Doctrine* (1845). Most of these are easily accessible in modern reprints. The letters in Mozley, A., *Letters and Correspondence of J. H. Newman during his Life in the English Church* (1891), and in Ward, W., *The Life of John Henry Cardinal Newman* (1913), are essential. The critical literature is very abundant. See Brilioth, Y., *The Anglican Revival* (1925); Thureau-Dangin, P., *La renaissance catholique en Angleterre* (1905-1906); Laski, H. J., *The Problem of Sovereignty* (1917), pp. 69-210; Ward, W., *Last Lectures* (1918).

[2] *Sermons Preached on Various Occasions*, p. 303.

should live better lives. He has, it is true, a very different notion of what that better life should be.

So different, indeed, is that notion that one is tempted to regard him as wholly in revolt against his age, as no index at all of the common English mind. If at first he is one of the guides of the Oxford movement, and one of the firmest supporters of that view of the Church of England as a *societas perfecta* which has helped discredit the Leviathan state, his conversion to Rome definitely separated him from this Anglo-Catholic group. He did not, as we shall see, follow that group into either of the political positions assumed by its members. He did not adopt a high Tory sentimental nationalism and wish the Stuarts back; nor did he embrace the cause of the poor as the cause of God and the Virgin, and surround the Red Flag with incense and candles. He continued, humbly and proudly, to be John Henry Newman, of no party but God's.

Now if Newman does so stand in isolation against his age, we can at least learn from him what his age was not. He was, in the first place, singularly open-minded. Leslie Stephen, indeed, with the assurance of a devout member of the Ethical Society, called him a sceptic. But this scepticism, however disturbing to others, never disturbed Newman himself. For Newman, unlike Mill, had no devouring social conscience. He felt acutely the intimate link between himself and God. He saw himself alone and naked in the universe, save for a presence of whose immediacy he was continually aware. Now no amount of thinking gave him any sense, so to speak, of being clothed. He could not convince himself that ratiocinative logic would ever provide an order which would take the place of the order which he felt to be God. But precisely because thinking could not disturb his security, he felt all the freer to think. Since he held to truth by a far more secure hold than mere words, he could afford to be critical of words. Words, symbols, even institutions, he realized well enough were mediately from God. In them most men found that assurance which is necessary to life on earth. But let such men as Kingsley content themselves with resounding and logically meaningless generalizations

like " the cause of Protestantism is the cause of liberty, of
civilization, of truth; the cause of man and God."[1] Let
other men, obsessed with the problem of making the
universe more friendly to the senses, use logic to spin out
schemes of social reform. He, Newman, was the dupe
neither of sentiment nor of logic. Secure in faith, he could
give his mind free play; and unfold, in the *Grammar of
Assent*, a doctrine so upsetting to most Catholics as that of
pragmatism.

Newman's asceticism is a complement and almost a condition of his open-mindedness. It separates him from his
fellow Victorians even more than the latter quality. He
really felt what so few modern men can bring themselves to
feel, that the flesh is utterly corrupt, that there is no use
trying to satisfy the senses, that bodily health is meaningless.
" Miserable as were the superstitions of the Dark Ages,
revolting as are the tortures now in use among the heathen
of the East, better, far better, is it to torture the body all
one's day, and to make this life a hell upon earth, than to
remain in brief tranquillity here, till the pit at length opens
under us, and awakens us to an eternal fruitless consciousness and remorse."[2] Man is essentially corrupt.[3]
Modern talk of " progress," since it assumes the perfectability of man, is mere slang.[4] Newman is a complete Christian in his pessimism. Man cannot improve his nature by
taking thought. He cannot do much with social institutions, save to make conditions here below less unfavourable
for the Christian life. He can, and must, take refuge in God.

But if the conditions of man's social and political life cannot be greatly improved, if indeed it is hardly important that
they should be improved, they may indeed so deteriorate as
to lessen his chances of salvation. God has made the Church
as an instrument to rescue man from the consequences of the

[1] Kingsley, C., *Literary and General Lectures and Essays* (1898), p. 189.
[2] *Parochial and Plain Sermons*, vol. i., p. xxiv.
[3] To his mother, 13th March 1829, *Letters and Correspondence* (ed. by A. Mozley), vol. i., p. 179.
[4] Quoted in Ward, W., *Life of John Henry Cardinal Newman* (1913), vol. ii., p. 81.

Fall. A good life is possible here below, but it is the life of submission to a power ordained by God and given corporate form in the Church Militant. This Church is an unmistakable and tangible thing, with its own laws and constitution, its own ritual, and above all with its own history and traditions. We know and recognize, as humble, ordinary human beings, much as we know and recognize any historically formed organism, such as the English nation, what that Church is. There is no excuse for the Protestant who substitutes his own judgment (which he mistakenly calls his conscience) for the living Church. Protestantism is a denial of God's rule. But in the nineteenth century Protestantism has taken on another and even more dangerous form, which is Liberalism.

Newman's attitude to what he called Liberalism must be the starting-point of any analysis of his position in politics. He uses the word in a sense far wider than that commonly given it. It is for him synonymous with the whole spirit of an age which was denying the fact of Christian rule. " By Liberalism I mean false liberty of thought, or the exercise of thought upon matters, in which, from the constitution of the human mind, thought cannot be brought to any successful issue, and therefore is out of place."[1] These matters, in which we know by faith that the human mind is powerless, are the dogmas of the Church. In general, we may say that these matters are the ultimate evaluations, or ends, of human conduct. Thought must be quite free to pursue its own immediate concerns, the measuring of the facts of the external world. Science is perfectly legitimate and perfectly free. Even Galileo was justified—though rash, and inconsiderate of his weaker brethren—for the heliocentric theory is not contrary to *evaluating* dogmas. A certain latitude must be left to those lower values we call taste. But thought alone cannot arrive at ultimate ethical judgments. When it attempts to do so, it does but discredit Christian ethics, and weaken their hold on men. It merely sets up a metaphysics of its own, with no more sanction than any other heathen belief. Such a metaphysics notably is that stemming from

---

[1] *Apologia pro Vita Sua* (1924), note A., p. 288.

Bacon and Locke, which sets up a mechanical universe governed by a rigid law of cause and effect which our deepest experience contradicts, and to which the ever-recurring fact of miracles give the lie.

Newman gives concrete illustrations of the erroneous beliefs to which Liberalism gives rise. One is that " no revealed doctrines or precepts may reasonably stand in the way of scientific conclusions. Therefore, e.g. Political Economy may reverse our Lord's declarations about poverty and riches, or a system of Ethics may teach that the highest condition of body is ordinarily essential to the highest state of mind."[1] Or again, " there is a right of Private Judgment: that is, there is no existing authority on earth competent to interfere with the liberty of individuals in reasoning and judging for themselves about the Bible and its contents, as they severally please. Therefore, e.g. religious establishments requiring subscription are Anti-christian." Other Liberal heresies are the beliefs that " there is no such thing as a national or state conscience," that " utility and expedience are the measure of political duty," that " the Civil Power may dispose of Church property without sacrilege," that " the people are the legitimate source of power." Finally, Liberalism holds that " virtue is the child of knowledge, and vice of ignorance. Therefore, e.g. education, periodical literature, railroad travelling, ventilation, drainage, and the arts of life, when fully carried out, serve to make a population moral and happy."[2]

Newman consistently opposed the revolutionary movements of his day, in all of which he saw the hand of Liberalism. " The French are an awful people," he wrote in 1830. " How the world is set upon calling evil good, and good evil! This Revolution seems to me the triumph of irreligion."[3] Somewhat later he wrote: Popes are " Conservatives in the right sense of the word; that is, they cannot bear anarchy, they think revolution an evil, they pray for the peace of the world and the prosperity of all Christian

---

[1] *Apologia pro Vita Sua,* note A., p. 295.
[2] *Ibid.,* pp. 295-296.
[3] *Letters and Correspondence,* vol. i., p. 240.

States, and they effectively support the cause of order and good government. The name of Religion is but another name for law on the one hand, freedom on the other; and at this very time, who are its professed enemies but Socialists, Red Republicans, Anarchists, and Rebels?"[1] Perhaps because he himself was always deeply conscious of the egocentric predicament, he regarded all rebellion as the wilful assertion of the blind self. He learned that during the plague certain individuals were burying the bedding of the afflicted, instead of burning it, as they had been ordered to do. " Is not this the very spirit of Whiggery," he wrote, "—opposition for its own sake, striving against the truth because it happens to be commanded us: as if wisdom were less wise because it is powerful."[2]

The root errors of Liberalism, then, are two: it holds that logic, as worked successfully in mathematics and the physical sciences, can be applied to all the operations of the human consciousness, and, therefore, it repudiates the Christian polity; it holds that men are fundamentally good, and, therefore, it repudiates external authority and justifies rebellion.

Now the truth is that the human mind does not arrive at the values which it accepts as the truths of taste and morals by the methods of formal logic; it arrives at these values by what we shall call the Illative sense. This sense—which is close to what Aristotle called φρόνησις—is most apparent perhaps in our æsthetic judgments. It operates on all the elements of a given experience. Compared with ratiocination, it is as the winding, colourful, varying river to the straight and regular canal. It is the full human being in action, of which logic does but provide the logarithm. Through it we attain to real, as opposed to mere notional, assent. Through it, by the slow building up of the strands of experience, we may attain a certitude which is to the knowledge arrived at by logic as the cable is to the simple iron bar. It is this certitude which sanctions our concrete

---

[1] *Historical Sketches* (1856), vol. iii., p. 131.
[2] Quoted in Brémond, H., *The Mystery of Newman* (1907), p. 24.

G

judgments. Now this Illative sense varies immensely with individuals. Some possess it in music, others in legal pleading, others in handicraft. Unlike logic, "it supplies no common measure between mind and mind, as being nothing else than a personal gift or acquisition."[1] Therefore, men are not guided by this sense in the same way to assent to the truths of Christianity, for instance. Some men possess it so inadequately that they cannot be guided to these truths at all. But if we look fairly at the whole history of Christendom, we do see that most men arrive somehow, by various routes, at the values summed up in Christianity. *Securus judicat orbis terrarum.* In despite of Liberalism, there *is* a Christian polity.

The second error of Liberalism is the assertion of the natural goodness of man. Revelation—which operates directly, without need of the Illative sense as an intermediary—and the Illative sense itself, operating through experience, alike teach us the falsity of this doctrine. There is in man a primary tendency to evil, the mark of the Fall. La Mennais, for instance, went astray when he turned from the Church to the masses, fancying " that the multitude of men were at bottom actually good Christians."[2] So all Liberals go astray when they trust the individual to guide himself. The remedy for the viciousness of man is the remedy provided by Christ's sacrifice—the Christian Church. Only in the Church will be found the authority without which liberty is an illusion.

Newman is as certain as any mediæval Churchman that the Church is the ultimate force which makes any society possible. So little did he trust the State to provide a full sanction for moral conduct, that, as we shall see, he was willing enough to let the State proceed, within definite limits, along Liberal lines. He recognized, indeed, that sentimental Nationalism was capable of giving the State a hold over the emotions of its members, that the nation-State did rest on the Illative sense, that it was a true corpora-

---

[1] *Grammar of Assent* (1870), p. 362.
[2] *Essays, Critical and Historical* (1919), vol. i., p. 153.

tion, that, indeed, it might substitute itself for the Christian polity. But he profoundly distrusted Nationalism and the nation-State. Its authority was incomplete, unhistorical, and its disciplinary powers inadequate for wicked men. It was particular and not universal. Its spirit was " the apostate spirit."[1]

It is an obvious postulate from the necessity and the perfection of the authority of the Church that it should be independent of the State. Newman's insistence that the Church is an organism, a *societas perfecta*, not bound to the State in any relation involving dependence and command, is too well known to occupy us for long. He fought the long struggle of the Oxford movement to emancipate what he regarded as the Church of the Apostles from the Erastian bonds in which she was held. He abandoned her when he was finally convinced that her bondage was so complete as to give the lie to her claim to be apostolic. " We see in the English Church, I will not merely say no descent from the first ages, and no relationship to the Church in other lands, but we see no body politic of any kind; we see nothing more or less than an establishment, a department of Government, or a function or operation of the State—without a substance —a mere collection of officials depending on and living in the supreme civil power."[2]

The Church of England, then, is not the true Church. She is not the body politic in which men can find salvation in another world, and discipline in this. Only in the Church of Rome can these requisites be found. We may here, since we are concerned with the history of political thought, omit those aspects of the true Church which are concerned primarily with the salvation of men's souls, and consider those aspects in which she provides a discipline for men on earth. In the first place, the Church provides in dogmatic truth a necessary anchor for fickle, rebellious men. Without dogma, such are the multiplicities and contradictions of human desires, you can never fix passion in institutions.

[1] *Sermons preached on various occasions* (1921), p. 304.
[2] *Difficulties of Anglicans*, lecture i., quoted in Thureau-Dangin, P., *La renaissance catholique en Angleterre*, vol. i., p. 421.

(The nation-State, for instance, can have no dogmas, but only crude theories of race.) " From the age of fifteen, dogma has been one fundamental principle of my religion . . . religion, as a mere sentiment, is to me a dream and a mockery."[1] Dogmas have concrete reality; they literally *embody* human consciousness. They have thus a regulative action over human lives which the conclusions of logic cannot have. " Many a man will live and die upon a dogma; no man will be a martyr for a conclusion."[2]

In the second place, the Roman Church possesses an authority capable of, and indeed habituated to, enforcing these dogmas. This authority is hierarchically organized in accordance with the fact of human inequality. It has, in the Pope, an infallible head. It possesses a long and faultless line of organic descent from Christ Himself. It is an authority that knows how to rule, that is free from false humanitarian sympathies. " In this world no one rules by mere love; if you are but amiable you are no hero."[3] It is an authority which can and does brook no nonsense about private judgment. The trouble with the modern State as an authority is that it has almost wholly abdicated in favour of private judgment. It has ceased to be a *res publica*.[4] Newman himself had a passionate desire for the self-abnegation of submission—a desire the cant of his age liked to consider feminine. " I loved to act as feeling myself in my Bishop's sight, as if it were the sight of God. It was one of my special supports and safeguards against myself. . . . What to me was *jure divino* was the voice of my Bishop in his own person."[5] He valued this willingness to submit as strongly as he deprecated the spirit of self-assertion. With Hurrell Froude in the Mediterranean he met " an American who was a pompous man, and yet we contracted a kind of affection for him. He was an Episcopalian, and had better principles far than one commonly meets with in England, and a docile mind."[6] The American turned out, indeed, to be a Metho-

---

[1] *Apologia*, p. 49.   [2] *Discussions and Arguments* (1924), p. 93.
[3] *Historical Sketches*, vol. iii., p. 85.   [4] *Ibid.*, vol. i., p. 173.
[5] *Apologia*, p. 50.
[6] *Letters and Correspondence*, vol. i., p. 310.

dist Episcopalian, but presumably retained the docility that
seems to be a national heritage.

Authority, then, is the one safety of man on earth. The
Church has a sounder and fuller authority than any other
body, and this is the true charter of her independence. But
no valid authority is to be rejected, for in this world of
Liberalism there is too little such. Custom, law, and traditional wisdom, as incorporated even in secular institutions,
lend valuable support to weak men. Newman summed up
his own conservatism when he described Keble's devotion
to authority. " Conscience is an authority; the Bible is an
authority; such is the Church; such is Antiquity; such are
the words of the wise, such are hereditary lessons; such are
ethical truths; such are historical memories, such are legal saws
and state maxims; such are proverbs; such are sentiments,
presages, and prepossessions." With Keble he hated as
destructive of authority " heresy, insubordination, resistance to things established, claims of independence, dis-
loyalty, innovation, a critical, censorious spirit."[1]

The error of modern reformers lies not in their desires,
and certainly not in their energies, which are good. Much
even of their programme is good. Their error lies in their
incompleteness, in their repudiation of the Church. " Let
Benthamism reign, if men have no aspirations. . . . The
ascendancy of faith may be impracticable, but the reign of
knowledge is incomprehensible. The problem for statesmen of this age is how to educate the masses, and literature
and science cannot give the solution."[2] For literature and
science are external disciplines; they assume that goodness
follows " upon a passive exposure to influences over which
we have no control." They " may change the fashionable
excess, but cannot allay the principle of sinning. Stop
cigars, they will take to drinking-parties; stop drinking,
they gamble; stop gambling, and a worse license follows."[3]
But once the proper supremacy of religion is admitted, the

---

[1] *Apologia*, p. 290.

[2] *Grammar of Assent*, p. 92, quoting from his own writings of 1841 on the
Tamworth Reading-Room.

[3] *Discussions and Arguments*, pp. 266-273.

modern English State is seen to have many excellent qualities. Newman sympathized with certain practical aspects of Liberalism to a greater degree than his principles as hitherto outlined would seem to admit.

In his Biglietto speech on assuming the rank of Cardinal, he admits that the ethics of English Liberalism are good, that its " natural laws of society," as seen in its economic thought, have in their proper sphere a genuine validity.[1] In *Who's to Blame* he develops the view that there are two essential elements in a State, power and liberty. "The seat of power is the Government; the seat of liberty is the Constitution."[2] Now there is no such thing as pure power, as an absolute despotism. The despot is limited by his fears, by the dagger or the bow-string. The absolute monarch is limited by complicated rules of etiquette. All societies thus have constitutions, which do but embody old habits, idiosyncrasies, varieties sometimes trivial, sometimes absurd, but for those who hold them " first principles, watchwords, common property, natural ties, a cause to fight for, an occasion of self-sacrifice."[3] The English constitution is a precious possession of the English people. Its great virtue is that it limits the power of the central government. For " the more a State secures to itself of rule and centralization, the more it can do for its subjects externally ; and the more it grants to them of liberty and self-government, the less it can do against them internally."[4] That is, Newman is willing to admit a great deal of *laissez-faire* in politics. The State, as a purely disciplinary force, is to be distrusted, for its discipline is always that of the master, never that of the father. Discipline in the Church, freedom in the State— that is the best we can achieve here on earth. Newman is ironically contented with his England. " It has not the climate; it has not the faith; it has not the grace and sweetness, the festive cheerfulness, the moral radiance, of some foreign cities and people; but nowhere else surely can you

[1] Ward, W., *op. cit.*, vol. ii., p. 461.
[2] *Discussions and Arguments*, p. 318.
[3] *Ibid.*, p. 315.   [4] *Ibid.*, p. 326.

have so much your own way, nowhere can you find ready
to your hand so many of your wants and wishes."[1]

Newman, almost alone among the thinkers of his generation, and certainly alone among the thinkers we are studying
in this chapter, was not preoccupied with the condition-of-
England question. The immediate outward results of the
industrial revolution seem to have troubled him but little.
The social implications of the philosophy we have sketched
would seem to involve resignation in the face of the evils of
poverty. Newman was not indifferent to the ugliness about
him. He certainly preferred the Oxford of his youth to the
Birmingham of his maturity. But he had not, it must be
repeated, a social conscience in the obvious sense of the
phrase. Mere ugliness could not move to revolt a man for
whom revolt was a denial of Christian rule. Newman was
either too self-centred or too detached—the critic may
choose the word he prefers—to try to remake the world
in his own image, as did Carlyle and Ruskin.

Yet his interest for the historian of thought is not limited
to his bare doctrine of submission to the authority of a
Christian polity. Newman's mind was far too active to
permit him to assume the nature of that polity was clear
even to himself, let alone to others. And his mind was far
too good not to throw off extremely interesting ideas in its
effort to probe into the reality he felt must exist behind the
routine of life. With an analysis of two of these ideas we
shall conclude this study of Newman. Like all generalizations,
these ideas might be held by men with very different immediate desires, and so accommodate themselves to very different
specific programmes of action. But again, like all generalizations, they do have, in the long run, a certain limited
moulding power over the desires of men who accept them.

The first of these ideas is that of development. Now it
is far from true that until Darwin men envisaged the universe as static rather than dynamic. The fact of change is
too obvious not to have been translated into some conception
of evolutionary growth as long ago as the time of Thales.
But it is true that neither the universe of the Schoolmen nor

---

[1] *Discussions and Arguments,* p. 353.

that of Newton included any rational explanation of the fact of growth and decay. Newman is not by any means a direct precursor of Darwin. But he did see that the eighteenth century had no answer to give to the question why certain institutions survived and others perished, why all were subject to change. More specifically, he was faced with the problem of the place in time of his own true Church. That Church, he must hold as an article of faith, is eternal. But he was far too intelligent to persuade himself that the Church of Pius IX. was identical with the Church of St. Paul. No, "in a higher world it is otherwise, but here below to live is to change, and to be perfect is to have changed often."[1] The *Essay on the Development of Christian Doctrine* is an interesting attempt to turn the tables on the critics of the Catholic Church by showing that, far from maintaining an obstinate and impossible resistance to all change, that Church has, by its very survival, proved that it has reconciled permanence and change in the only way they can be reconciled on earth, by the maintenance of an organic life.

Now the life we have to study is the life of an idea which incorporates itself variously in institutions, and which thus mediately makes itself a part of human life. A given doctrine, once enunciated, is not just passively received, but becomes an active principle in diverse minds. " Such is the doctrine of the divine right of kings, or of the rights of man, or of the anti-social bearings of a priesthood, or utilitarianism, or free trade . . . doctrines which are of a nature to attract and influence, and have so far a *prima facie* reality, that they may be looked at on many sides and strike various minds very variously."[2] In time, such a doctrine " will have grown into an ethical code, or into a system of government, or into a theology, or into a ritual, according to its capabilities: and this body of thought, thus laboriously gained, will after all be little more than the proper representative of one idea, being in substance what that idea meant from the first, its complete image as seen in a com-

[1] *An Essay on the Development of Christian Doctrine* (1845), p. 40.
[2] *Ibid.*, p. 36.

bination of diversified aspects, with the suggestions and corrections of many minds, and the illustration of many experiences."[1]

This history of an idea in action Newman calls its development. He is careful to avoid the reproach of over-intellectualism. He admits that ideas do not operate in a vacuum, that no metaphysical dialectic can trace their development *a priori*. An idea " not only modifies, but is modified, or at least influenced, by the state of things in which it is carried out, and is dependent in various ways on the circumstances which surround it. . . . It may be impeded or swayed, or even absorbed by counter energetic ideas."[2] Sometimes the idea is posterior to the event, as Hooker's theory of the Church and State follows the Elizabethan Revolution; at other times, ideas more clearly mould events. Locke's theories were a real guide to the era of the glorious Revolution. But, however closely the actual process needs to be studied, we must eventually ask ourselves what is a legitimate development, and what is an illegitimate one. Or, to use more neutral terms, we must distinguish between development and corruption.[3]

Now corruption is a breaking-up of life, preparatory to its termination. A stone can be crushed, but not corrupted. Corruption, like development, is a process limited to that which has life. But the life we are studying is that of an idea, not that of a simple organism. We cannot, therefore, have any simple and indisputable criterion of the difference between the corruption and the development of an idea. We must appeal to the Illative sense, and not to logic, for this criterion. Newman outlines seven " notes," no one of which is rigidly applicable as a chemical formula might be, but which taken together do, he thinks, serve as a test to distinguish between corruption and development in those high matters where logic is helpless.[4]

The first note is that of preservation of type. The modern Tory holds doctrines resembling those of the primitive Whig; yet the Whig and Tory characters have each a

[1] *An Essay on the Development of Christian Doctrine*, p. 38.
[2] *Ibid.*, p. 39.   [3] *Ibid.*, p. 170.   [4] *Ibid.*, part ii.

discriminating type. From the republic of Cato to the principate of Augustus, there was little superficial change; yet there was a deviation from type which meant corruption of the republican idea. The second note is continuity of principles. Principles are abstract and general, and grow up later than doctrines, which relate directly to facts. But their very generality implies permanence and universality. Pagans may have, but heretics cannot have, the same principles as Catholics. The third note is power of assimilation. Life means growth, and growth means the absorption, sometimes very difficult, of foreign bodies. Only mathematical and other abstract creations may pretend to be external and self-dependent. " An eclectic, conservative, assimilating, healing, moulding process, a unitive power, is of the essence . . . of a faithful development."[1] The stronger an organism or an idea, the less it needs safeguards against innovation. " Vows are the wise defence of unstable virtue, and general rules the refuge of feeble authority."[2] The fourth note is logical sequence. But this is not the sequence of logic as commonly understood; it is the sequence of that logic of taste and judgment Newman later called the Illative sense. The fifth note is anticipation of its future, the flashes of insight which occur to certain minds and enable them to be wiser than their generation. The sixth note is conservative action upon its past. Growth is a matter of difficult balance, and is equally impeded by repudiating the past and by adhering closely to it. Finally, there is the note of chronic vigour. Corruption is but the first stage of dissolution and death, and cannot be of long standing. What *is* of long standing, therefore, cannot be corrupt. The very violence and swiftness of revolutions is a mark of corruption. The healthy organism is not subject to revolutions.

The Catholic Church emerges triumphantly from the test of these notes. Naturally enough, for Newman devised the test in view of her triumphant emergence. But others might apply the test with quite other results. There still

[1] *An Essay on the Development of Christian Doctrine*, p. 186.
[2] *Ibid.*, p. 189.

remains Newman's guiding idea: Ideas, incorporated in institutions, live and die; they follow a process to which the methods of physical science afford no final key; there is, indeed, no final key to the process but the process itself; the human mind, however, by using all its capacities, not merely its logical gift, can arrive at some appreciation of the values incorporated in the process, can estimate approximately what will further and what will hinder it, and thus, in a measure, guide it. We are not quite helpless if we realize that the Word is life.

We are thus brought to the second idea we have chosen to isolate in Newman's work. This is his notion of law, or, if the phrase is preferred, of the order of Nature. His own generation held pretty firmly to the belief that the order of Nature, of which man is a part, is ruled by invariable laws, of which the Newtonian law of gravitation may be taken as an example. Even the nineteenth-century idealistic reaction to eighteenth-century mechanism had not ventured to question the applicability of mechanist theories to the order of Nature. Now Newman denied altogether that we have any experience of a universe where cause follows effect in an invariably predictable sequence. He admitted the utility of scientific method; but " still let us not by our words imply that we are appealing to experience, when really we are only accounting, and that by hypothesis, for the absence of experience."[1] If we consult experience, we realize that " all laws are general; none are invariable."[2] A scientific law is but an approximation, subject to constant revision, or it is not at all scientific. We must not confuse the human desire to find permanence outside experience—which is a legitimate, and at bottom religious, desire—with the operations of the pure intellect. That is just what we have done. Men's religious instincts have perversely fastened themselves upon the hypotheses of science as if these hypotheses were the fruit of a complete relationship between the thinker and that about which he thinks. They have made a dogma of a law of cause and effect which is really but a statistical approximation.

---

[1] *Grammar of Assent*, p. 70.   [2] *Ibid.*, p. 202.

The affiliation of these ideas with what became later to be called Pragmatism is too clear to need further emphasis. The *Grammar of Assent* was a strange book to have come from a Catholic priest. Science, even in the hands of the economists, was at least a rule, an order to which men could be disciplined. Tradition, too, is a rule and a discipline. Newman, repudiating science and tradition alike, in their simpler forms, threw himself ultimately on God and good taste. Now if you are willing to take God directly on the authority of the Church, and thus accept *en bloc* a system of values externally dictated to you, you have what seems to an unbeliever, at least, historical Catholicism. But good taste, even if optimistically reinforced by the *securus judicat orbis terrarum*, seems a dangerous ally of a Catholic God. At bottom, men do demand a sterner master than Newman's Illative sense. In spite of many of his words which support authoritarianism—and which we have attempted to reproduce as strongly as possible—Newman is a free and adventurous soul, a romantic ally of the liberal spirit he distrusted.

6. CARLYLE[1]

It has been suggested that Carlyle is partly to blame for the war of 1914.[2] It would be less venturesome to assert that the war is largely to blame for the present discredit of

[1] Carlyle's political thought, though it crops out in everything he wrote, is best studied in *Sartor Resartus* (1831), *Past and Present* (1843), *Heroes and Hero-Worship* (1841), *Chartism* (1839), and *Latter-Day Pamphlets* (1850). These have all been reprinted ; and they can be found in the centenary edition of the *Works* (30 vols., Chapman and Hall). Carlyle's literary reputation is no doubt responsible for the enormous body of writing about him. See Froude, J. A., *Carlyle : a History of the First Forty Years of his Life* (1890), and *Carlyle : a History of his Life in London* (1884) ; Wilson, D. A., *Carlyle till Married* (1923), and subsequent volumes : *Carlyle to the French Revolution, Carlyle on Cromwell and Others, Carlyle at his Zenith, Carlyle to Threescore and Ten* ; Robertson, J. M., *Modern Humanists* (1895) and *Modern Humanists Reconsidered* (1927) ; MacCunn, J., *Six Radical Thinkers* (1907) ; Roe, F. W., *The Social Philosophy of Carlyle and Ruskin* (1922) ; Stephen, L., *Hours in a Library*, vol. iii. (1892).

[2] Young, N., *Carlyle, His Rise and Fall* (1927), p. 8. p. 366

Carlyle. He is still an immediate concern of the biographers and the seekers of the Ph.D. in English letters, but he is no longer read by the younger generation, and he is certainly no longer a prophet. The worshipper of Frederick the Great was bound to share in the war revulsion against things Prussian. The preacher could not survive in a generation that seems to distrust most kinds of preaching. Yet Carlyle was unquestionably listened to by his contemporaries. Hardly a biography or a collection of letters but has some reference to him. The still active interest of scholars in his work is a tribute to this past reputation. The common opinion which sets him up against Mill as one of the two divergent forces of his day is not unsound. We may well conclude a chapter on the political thought of Chartist England with Carlyle.

The bareness, the scantiness, to which Carlyle's political thought is easily reducible is at first pause astonishing. It is not merely that he repeats himself endlessly. Self-plagiary is almost a prerogative of great thinkers. It is rather that, when the critic sets about the task of finding out what political order Carlyle was attempting to create, what, in short, his programme was, the result is so slight. Mill, in the *Representative Government* and *Liberty*, throws out a dozen specific suggestions to one of Carlyle's. Even Kingsley, with his Working Men's Associations, his sanitary reforms, his Church of social service, can embody his hopes in a plan. Carlyle is too busy in the pulpit to descend to the workshop. This hater of words has a more than Christian faith in the Word.

This reproach of absence of constructive suggestions has often been made to Carlyle. It is certainly an unjust reproach. For the major clue to Carlyle's thought is that for him all programmes are useless, mere Morrison's Pills. No plan will save a man's soul; and if a man's soul is saved, all plans and any plans will work well. Carlyle was a preacher, and little else. Now preaching is, for those who undergo it, a form of amusement. The preacher's congregation, like the actor's audience, submits with delight to a vicarious experience. The preacher himself is hardly more directly concerned with the concrete lives of his hearers than is the actor or the cricketer with the lives of those who watch him. He satisfies their immediate emotional needs best when he most skilfully manipulates the medium in which he is working. He is not, of course, without concern for actual human conduct. But the preacher, as opposed to the simple moralist, is always engaged in the *dramatization* of human conduct. He wants to attain that emotional and momentary oneness with his hearers which is the aim of the artist. He does not want to dissect them, to understand them, and thus eventually to mould their actions.

The trouble with most preaching is that it loses its force when put in print. It depends too much on the voice and gestures, on the living personality of the orator. Here Carlyle achieves a miracle rare in letters. His sermons read better than they could possibly have sounded. On cold paper his words attain an intensity, a persuasive fire that any pulpit orator might envy. His extraordinary and happily inimitable style may be a poor instrument of thought, but it does what hardly another style has ever done—it gives the written word the dramatic illusion of speech.

Carlyle, however, is a preacher, not an actor. He never had any of Disraeli's capacity for assuming and working out the most varied *rôles*. His work is one long and rather monotonous soliloquy, delivered with the obvious contempt for his audience which was one of the secrets of his hold over them. It is, indeed, the soliloquy of a suffering man, and, in spite of his many inconsistencies, a sincere man. There is no use here in repeating the commonplace gibe of his enemies, that Carlyle, to be true to himself, should have suffered in silence. Neither dyspepsia nor Calvinism are ills that feed on silent forbearance. Carlyle's suffering was bound to be lyrical and dramatic. Here a curious and let us hope not overdrawn parallel suggests itself with the work of Cobbett. Both men were personally uncomfortable in their England; both men despaired of the England created by the new industry, and both appealed from this corruption to something fine and Anglo-Saxon which might yet be rescued from corruption; and both have come to be esteemed, not as political thinkers and moralists, but as men of letters.[1]

The parallel is not laboured, for both Cobbett and Carlyle were conservatives of the flesh; both lacked that intellectual resilience which welcomes experimentation and innovation. Both, at bottom, distrusted the planning intellect. But Carlyle's is the conservatism of the diseased flesh, Cobbett's of the healthy flesh. "*Schadenfreude*, 'mischief-joy,' the Germans call it," wrote Carlyle of his emotions at Disraeli's alliance with the masses in 1867, "but really it is *justice*-joy withal."[2] Carlyle distrusted the simple human animal as much as he did the complex, beer and cottage comfort as much as claret and industrial efficiency. His conservatism is weighted down with a sense of sin. No good life is possible here on earth for men unwilling to be unhappy. "Was it thy aim and life-purpose . . . to be what men call ' happy,' in this world, or in any other world? I answer for thee deliberately, No. The whole spiritual secret of the new epoch lies in this, that thou canst answer . . . No! "[3] His imagination has a sadistic touch. He found it incredible that other men should be insensitive or stupid enough to be contented where he was unhappy.

Now the final trick of Carlyle's temperament, the last step by which he secured himself in his pulpit, was his alliance with God. He worked out, from his background of poetic imagination, Scottish peasant inheritance, Calvinism, dyspepsia, and what we must call in cant terms sense of personal inferiority, a definite and very personal set of values. These values he resolutely called Facts. The relation between demand and supply, for instance, was no Fact, but a petty theory of the economists. That you cannot " grind me out Virtue from the husks of Pleasure "[4] (Carlyle was no

---

[1] As early as 1897, H. D. Traill could write that Carlyle " is neither political prophet nor ethical doctor, but simply a great master of literature who lives for posterity by the art which he despised." Introduction to the centenary edition of Carlyle's *Works*, vol. i., p. viii.

[2] *Shooting Niagara* (1867), chap. iii.

[3] *Past and Present* (Chapman and Hall, 1893), p. 175.

[4] *Sartor Resartus*, book ii., chap. vii.

man to reject even such a minor ally as Capitalization), was
not a consoling fancy, but a Fact. And Facts are the decrees
of God. " Certainly it were a fond imagination to expect
that any preaching of mine could abate Mammonism. . . .
But there is one Preacher who does preach with effect, and
gradually persuade all persons: his name is Destiny, is
Divine Providence, and his Sermon the inflexible Course
of Things."[1]

This alliance saved Carlyle from the common necessity of
attempting to test the truth of his statements by reference
to what many men fondly hold to be a world external to their
desires. Carlyle was completely incapable of conceiving such
a thing as an hypothesis. What he knew he knew once and
for all by a revelation superior to cavilling logic. He was
thus free to use all the artifices of the preacher, to carry on
his soliloquy with no regard for anything save its effect on
his hearers, and its value as a catharsis for himself. No man
ever used the argument from analogy with a more complete
indifference to its logical limitations. You would not sail a
ship around Cape Horn by taking a ballot among the sailors
as to her course. Therefore the ballot is no solution for
English political difficulties in 1850.[2] Teufelsdröckh would
as soon hold that an acorn could be nursed into a cabbage, or
a cabbage seed into an oak, as admit that men are the
products of their environment.[3] Carlyle is willing to take
full advantage or rather unfair advantage of the emotional
overtones of words. " A false man found a religion ? Why,
a false man cannot build a brick house! "[4] Surely, if words
are more than playthings, if this universe is at all the serious
matter Carlyle thought it, this is nonsense. For, although
poets and preachers may be granted pretty complete freedom in an imperfect world, there is perhaps a limit, set
jointly by common sense and logic, to this use of words
without regard to their simple meaning. In this instance,
" false," though it obviously has no simple meaning, is used

[1] *Past and Present*, p. 251.
[2] *Latter-Day Pamphlets, Works* (centenary edition), vol. xx., p. 15.
[3] *Sartor Resartus*, book ii., chap. ii.
[4] *Heroes and Hero-Worship* (Chapman and Hall, 1873), p. 41.

CHARTISM

to suggest the possession of one or more moral defects;
" brick house," however, has an inescapable concrete meaning. Now a man is qualified to build a brick house by
training in and capacity for masonry, architecture, car-
pentry. A man may be disqualified for such a task by lack
of such training and capacity, and by any one of a number
of physical disabilities—blindness, for instance. He may be
partially disqualified by what are commonly considered
moral failings—laziness, for instance, though here adequate
supervision, or even fear of consequences, may get the house
built. But the list of moral obliquities, from occasional
drunkenness to permanent adultery, which would not in
themselves disqualify a man from building a brick house is
enormous and exhaustive. Carlyle was safe enough in
asserting that a false man cannot found a religion, but he
should not have brought in the brick house.

Nor is Carlyle troubled by mere logical inconsistency.
" As for me, I honour in these loud-babbling days, all the
Silent rather." The silent Romans are far greater than the
prattling Greeks.[1] And yet " Speech is the gaseous element
out of which most kinds of Practice and Performance,
especially all kinds of moral Performance, condense themselves, and take shape; as the one is, so will the other be."[2]
A pardonable inconsistency, perhaps, since it justifies
Carlyle's very articulate life, and his failure to attain to any
Performance beyond the creation of a row of books. Again
" Man's philosophies are usually the ' supplement of his
practice '; some ornamental Logic-varnish, some outer skin
of Articulate Intelligence, with which he strives to render his
dumb Instinctive Doings presentable when they are done."[3]
And yet, " not only all common Speech, but Science,
Poetry itself is no other, if thou consider it, than a right
Naming."[4] Carlyle once wrote " no man is, or can hence-
forth be, the brass-collar thrall of any man; you will have
to bind him by other, far nobler and cunninger methods."[5]
If later the defender of Governor Eyre did suggest a revival

---

[1] *Past and Present*, p. 138.   [2] *Ibid.*, p. 180.   [3] *Ibid.*, p. 161.
[4] *Sartor Resartus*, book ii., chap. i.
[5] *Past and Present*, p. 215.

of negro slavery in Jamaica,[1] this is perhaps but the legitimate acquisition of wisdom with age.

Yet if Carlyle has no neat political platform, he certainly applies his measuring-rod of values to the stuff of politics. It is possible to outline what he considered desirable political aims. His most fundamental postulate is the famous " laborare est orare." In this miserable world, man must work to live. Not to work is to attempt to cheat God. Therefore any human society which numbers a large class of drones within it is condemned by God's law to disappear. The French Revolution was a divine punishment upon the idle courtier nobility of old France. Of course this formula demands a definition of work. Work is first of all wrestling with material things—the work of farmer and artisan; it is also the work of the soldier and the policeman; it is finally the work of moral and artistic leadership, that of the teacher, the man of letters, the statesman and the priest. But the results of the work must be good, or the worker cannot be justified. Much of the work that has gone into the industrial revolution is misdirected, and counts for no more than idleness. The hatter who paraded a colossal hat through the streets " has not attempted to *make* better hats, as he was appointed by the Universe to do . . . but his whole industry is turned to *persuade* us that he has made such! "[2] So, too, the work of lawyers, clergymen, statesmen, so far as it is directed to upholding an unjust order, is no work at all.[3]

Modern England, then, supports in idleness a nobility and a gentry which have ceased to perform the mediæval labours of an Abbot Samson; it maintains an increasingly large number of *rentiers*, who live on the industry of others; and it directs much of its actual labour to unworthy ends. It cannot long so continue to defy the order of the universe. Already Chartism is an unmistakable warning, a warning that must be heeded, though the remedy Chartism proposes is no true remedy, but a Morrison's pill.

---

[1] " The Nigger Question," *Works* (Centenary edition), vol. xxix., p. 348.
[2] *Past and Present*, p. 122.　　　[3] *Ibid.*, p. 224.

CHARTISM

Now the root of the trouble is this, that Englishmen have ceased to obey their superiors. They have embraced, under the name of *laissez-faire*, the doctrines of anarchy. They assume that each man can, if left to himself, work out his own contribution to society. Life thus becomes a mad scramble, in which cunning, brutal, selfish men win wealth and esteem, and, since men are imitative, hero-worshipping animals, set the tone for society. But life, though God wills that it should be a struggle, is not this mad scramble of modern England.

Carlyle is here faced with a difficulty which he never solved. He insists over and over again that the process of Nature is a struggle from which the fittest inevitably emerge. " All fighting, as we noticed long ago, is the dusty conflict of strengths, each thinking itself the strongest, or, in other words, the justest;—of Mights which do in the long-run, and forever will in this just Universe in the long-run, mean Rights."[1] And again, " In this great Duel, Nature herself is umpire, and can do no wrong: the thing which is deepest-rooted in Nature, what we call *truest*, that thing and not the other will be found growing at last."[2] This, it is clear, is just what the Manchester men were saying, what the political Darwinists were later to say. But Carlyle could not trust the evidence of his senses as to the course of the struggle. Surely Plugson of Undershot was not, in the long run, the elect of God and Nature ?

No, there is an order discernible in the struggle, an order which enables us to distinguish true labour, or life, from false labour, or death. " All works, each in their degree, are a making of Madness sane."[3] In the chaos which surrounds us, in the impulses which drive us to action, we are not without a guide so superior to the process that the very process itself sometimes seems an illusion. " The Universe itself is a Monarchy and a Hierarchy."[4] Permanence is not an illusion, but the reality we poor human

[1] *Past and Present*, p. 164. Carlyle is as fond as any economist of the phrase " in the long-run."
[2] *Heroes and Hero-Worship*, p. 56.
[3] *Past and Present*, p. 177.   [4] *Latter-Day Pamphlets*, p. 19.

171

beings are striving for. " Happy is he who has found a master. . . . In all human relations *permanency* is what I advocate; *nomadism*, continual change, is what I perceive to be prohibitory of any good whatsoever."[1] In the England where men buy in the cheapest and sell in the dearest markets even human labour, there is no hierarchy, and no permanence. It lacks " the basis from which all organization hitherto has grown up among men, and all henceforth will have to grow: The principle of Permanent Contract instead of Temporary."[2] Carlyle rescues himself from the unpleasant consequences of the theory that the best emerges victorious from the free competition of human beings only by an inconsistent denial that the modern competition is on a fair basis. And this denial is surely inconsistent with the omnipotence of Providence, Destiny, or whatever other deterministic Abstraction Carlyle found at hand.

He takes ultimate refuge in a Platonic Republic, but a Republic with the stamp of Craigenputtock on it, and not that of the Academy. The remedy for the evils of modern liberty lies in true liberty. " The true liberty of a man, you would say, consisted in his finding out, or being forced to find out the right path, and to walk thereon. . . . You do not allow a palpable madman to leap over precipices [the argument from analogy again]; you violate his liberty, you that are wise. . . . Every stupid, every cowardly and foolish man is but a less palpable madman: his true liberty were that a wiser man . . . could . . . lay hold of him when he was going wrong, and order and compel him to go a little righter."[3] And surely most men are stupid, cowardly, and foolish—the " rotten multitudinous canaille, who seem to inherit all the world and its forces and steel weapons and culinary and stage properties "?[4]

Liberty for John Jones, then, must consist in obedience to his superiors. This is a liberty easily attained, for John Jones wants nothing better than to obey his superiors. " He is a social being in virtue of this necessity; nay he could not

---

[1] " The Nigger Question," *Works*, vol. xxix., p. 367.
[2] *Past and Present*, p. 237. [3] *Ibid.*, p. 182.
[4] *Reminiscences*, vol. ii., p. 170.

be gregarious otherwise. He obeys those whom he esteems better than himself, wiser; and will forever obey such; and even be ready and delighted to do it."[1] The problem really comes down to selecting and placing in power your superiors —the Platonic problem of the guardians. These superiors will enjoy complete liberty; that is, they will obey God, Providence, Destiny and the Law of Nature immediately, not mediately as must the lower classes. Carlyle is not wholly clear as to the constitution and composition of his class of guardians. " Aristocracy and Priesthood, a Governing class and a Teaching class; these two, sometimes separate, and endeavouring to harmonize themselves, sometimes conjoined as one, and the King a Pontiff-King:—there did no Society exist without these two vital elements, there will none exist."[2] This is one formula. At another time Carlyle is willing, following St. Simon, to admit the " Captains of Industry " to his ruling class. The Plugsons are at least strong and silent; with a little more divine light, a little more military iron, instead of commercial pliancy—they " must be real captains even to shooting their recalcitrant troops "[3]—they may at last prove themselves worthy of ruling England. But they must change their *nomadic* labourers to *permanent* labourers, they must clean England of its soot and dirt, its cheap and nasty goods, its ramshackle buildings. They must build forever, instead of tearing down and rebuilding every seventy-five years.[4] In the end, Carlyle makes the drill-sergeant—at least " no humbug "—his aristocrat, and advocates the full exploitation of the disciplinary value of military drill in all the walks of life.[5]

Carlyle's State would at first sight appear to be a bureaucratic State. " I could conceive an Emigration Service, a Teaching Service, considerable varieties of United and Separate Services, of the due thousands strong, all effective as this Fighting Service is."[6] He thinks the appointment of Cabinet officials by the Crown without regard to

---

[1] *Past and Present*, p. 207.   [2] *Latter-Day Pamphlets*, p. 207
[3] *Ibid.*, p. 28.   [4] *Shooting Niagara*, chap. ii.
[5] *Ibid.* chap. ix.   [6] *Past and Present*, p. 225.

their ability to get into Parliament would provide doers rather than talkers.[1] He would set up a ministry of education, a new Colonial Office to send out a new kind of colonial governor. Yet he is sure that "attorneyism"—that is, bureaucracy—is the curse of European governments, and rejoices that the English democracy is strong enough to prevent the introduction of Continental methods of government in England.[2] Yet beyond asserting that there *is* a difference between his aristocratic administrators and mere bureaucrats, he does not help us much to ensure a supply of one rather than the other.

At least one sort of social action is immediately necessary. Carlyle did not limit himself to generalities against *laissez-faire* and cash payment. Legislative interference between masters and workers is indispensable—nay, with the introduction of factory inspectors it has already begun. Legislation must regulate hours and conditions of labour. Parliament must draw up and enforce through inspection a factory code providing for smoke abatement, baths and other sanitary apparatus, wholesome air, moderate temperature, ceilings at least twenty feet high. It must similarly regulate housing conditions. The State must provide a compulsory system of education, not divorced from religion. It must establish, in co-operation with the colonies, aids to emigration.[3] Do not worry about the theoretical justification for State interference. It lies in every human heart, in the obvious fact of human solidarity. Men are brothers and sisters, not mere warring atoms. A Scotch widow, left free to starve in a slum according to economic law, contracts the typhus and kills seventeen other human beings, thus proving her sisterhood.[4]

There is, however, an aspect of Carlyle's political thought we have not yet touched. Men may be fools and cowards, in the mass, but as a mass they possess a mystic power of growth and expansion. That is why, though crude democ-

[1] "The New Downing Street," *Latter-Day Pamphlets.*   [2] *Ibid.*
[3] *Past and Present*, book iv., chap. iii. ; *Chartism*, chap. x.
[4] *Past and Present*, pp. 128-129.

racy is impossible, a mere cancelling of all into zero, some form of Parliamentary Government is desirable. " Votes of men are worth collecting, if convenient. True, their opinions are generally of little wisdom, and can on occasion reach to all conceivable and inconceivable degrees of folly; but their instincts, where these can be deciphered, are wise and human; these, hidden under the noisy utterance of what they call their opinions, are the unspoken sense of man's heart, and well deserve attending to."[1] Through parliaments, true governors will discern what this dumb, wise people really want, not what they think; and what they want is sure to be dictated by the silent voice of Nature.

Now if the philosopher thus takes stock, not of the surface of political societies, but of their deep mystic force, he will discern that the Anglo-Saxon race is closest of all races to this mute wisdom. Their present greatness is the prevailing, through all the noise of their Sir Jabesh Windbags, of their capacity for growth. Contrast the silent English with those jabbering apes, the French. Why, at the very historic roots of the race, this superiority is evident. Who would not prefer the Norse mythology in its " genuine, very great and manlike broad simplicity and rusticity " to the mannered falsity and corruption of the Greek mythology ?[2] Who can doubt that the history of Ireland shows the inferiority of the Milesian to the Saxon ?[3]

For the great struggle which is decreed by Nature to be the law of human existence is not the internecine struggle of Englishman with Englishman for personal economic prevailing, but the struggle of race with race. Here, and nowhere else, is it fully true that Might is Right. There are no unjust and enduring conquests. The conquering race —Roman, Norman—is the superior race.[4] The Anglo-Saxons have inherited the earth, " Sugar Islands, Spice Islands, Indias, Canadas—these, by the real decree of Heaven, were ours; and nobody would or could believe it,

---

[1] " Parliaments," *Latter-Day Pamphlets,* p. 240.
[2] *Heroes and Hero-Worship,* p. 18.
[3] *Chartism,* chap. iv.   [4] *Ibid.,* chap. v.

till it was tried by cannon law, and *so* proved."[1] They remain, in spite of all, "a stubborn, taciturn, sulky, indomitable rock-made race of men; as the figure they cut in all quarters, in the cane-brake of Arkansas, in the Ghauts of the Himmalayha, no less than in London City, in Warwick or Lancaster County, does still abundantly manifest."[2] Carlyle was not acquainted with the State of Arkansas, or he might have been obliged to admit that environment can alter even Anglo-Saxon race characteristics. He does indeed refer to the American people in another place as " eighteen millions of the greatest *bores* ever seen in this world before."[3] Still, this is perhaps hardly an alteration in his previous definition of Anglo-Saxon qualities.

Carlyle is thus one of the founders of modern British Imperialism. Long before other political Darwinists he applied the principle of the struggle for life to the struggle between states. We need not here attempt to criticize his identification of state and race, nor his doctrine of race survival. It is sufficient to note that his imperialism was one of the secrets of his influence. However much good liberal Englishmen were shocked by some of his later writings, by his appeal to the drill-sergeant, by his assurance that Might —even Prussian Might—makes Right, they were willing to accept his confidence in the virtues of Anglo-Saxons. His attacks on *laissez-faire* gained the ear of still other Englishmen, all the more easily because they counselled a spiritual remedy rather than an inconvenient Socialism. His style, his prophetic air, his alliance with God, his contempt for mere dull logic, all gave him a hold over his fellows. Poor Mill, with all his efforts to embrace a multiform reality with his mind, could never attain to the mystic graces, could never live down the terrestrial limitations of Benthamism. Carlyle had these graces, and through them captured the attention of the thousands who are impatient of grubbing thought, who seek in submission to the equivocal charm of words a

---

[1] " The New Downing Street," *Latter-Day Pamphlets,* p. 46.
[2] *Chartism*, chap. viii.
[3] " The Present Time," *Latter-Day Pamphlets,* p. 21.

vicarious assurance that all is well with the world. His achievements were ultimately conservative.

Yet his thought has none of the true conservative richness. He admired the Middle Ages as the rule of permanence and strength. But he has none of Burke's imaginative devotion to a society enriched by tradition, a society whose oddities and seeming perversions are really precious stays against the devastating pressure of the anarchic forces of fallen men. Though he preached submission and renunciation, he has not the profound Christian assurance that the meek shall inherit the earth. He had little appreciation of the slowness of the historical process. He had, indeed, the impatience of the true radical, an impatience sprung from a personal maladjustment. But he lacked the true radical's trust in his fellow men. Carlyle was a radical in the skin of a conservative—a porcupine in the shell of a tortoise. Naturally the quills grew inward, and forced him to cry out. He cried out eloquently, but not with great significance for his fellows. Carlyle did not help remake England.

CHAPTER IV

THE PROSPEROUS VICTORIANS

The forty-odd years which follow the turn of the nineteenth century have a reality less illusory than most historical periods, a reality fixed for us in the epithet Victorian. In these years of relative prosperity, of freedom from great and pressing social struggles, art and morals, two of the most characteristic efforts of the human spirit to find fixity in flow attained a momentary completeness of corporate form. Dissenters and heretics there no doubt were in abundance. And any attempt to recapture in words the reality of this corporate form must partially fail. But to doubt its existence is to surrender to a meaningless scepticism.

English prosperity was an unquestionable fact. The problem of poverty was still unsolved. The machine had not brought riches to all. But the very worst conditions of the English poor, the conditions against which Cobbett had revolted, had been improved by Factory Acts and sanitary legislation. With the definite failure of Chartism, working-class agitation subsided into a temporary acquiescence in a capitalistic organization of society. Troubles indeed there were. The Civil War in America brought suffering to thousands in the cotton trade. Economic science had certainly failed to solve the problem of the business cycle. Yet when one compares the calm atmosphere in which the Reform Bill of 1867 was passed with the tension and bitterness of 1832, the contrast is striking. The element of fear was singularly lacking in Victorian England. A country which enjoyed the great industrial supremacy of the England of the Exhibition of 1851 could afford even the leap in the dark of household suffrage. The English workman was too sensible, too English, in fact, to want much that he did not already have.

England's international position, too, was very strong. The Crimean War was but an interlude. The great Continental struggles which culminated in the war of 1870 seemed at the time to have cost her nothing, seemed, indeed, but to have made her own position firmer. England was no oppressed nationality, but a strong, free State, endowed with a constitution the envy of the world, and with a geographical position that secured her from the curse of militarism. There was indeed the Empire, a Sepoy rebellion and a frontier war or two. But the Empire, with the aid of economic wisdom, could take care of itself.

Victorian civilization seemed real enough and secure enough to permit free play for political speculation. There is abundant variety in the political thought of the time. For the Victorians were not entirely the complacent people our modern smartness sometimes makes them out to be. The very absence of bitter social conflicts helped to emancipate the intellect. There was no need to fear the worst from an idea. There were no Jacobin clubs in England. Moreover, was not England's present greatness the fruit of English freedom ? Had not innovation proved its uses in English industrial expansion ? However true it may be that men are custom-ridden, intolerant animals, the ideas of Mill's essay *On Liberty* had certainly penetrated into a number of quite ordinary heads. Men had grown used to expecting novelty, to tolerating a degree of eccentricity in innovators. Victorian notions of indefinite progress may have been uncritical enough, they may even at bottom be inconsistent with social equilibrium, but they were undoubtedly widely held. They accustomed men to a greater degree of questioning, to a greater willingness to speculate in political matters, than had existed, at least in so widespread a degree, at any other time. We need not, then, look for any general agreement among the thinkers we are to study. The age of Victoria may have been an age of faith; but it was an age of conflicting faiths.

As the century drew near its end, there cropped up real and tangible difficulties which destroyed the Victorian compromise. The Irish question took on a form too acute for the existing party system to fit into its habitual loyalties. The Socialist movement began to make an impression on the consciousness of the English working man. With the formation of a Labour Party, the old subordination of the English masses to the leadership of the ruling class was

ENGLISH POLITICAL THOUGHT

menaced as it never had been before, save during the brief
Chartist agitation. The moment the English workman
ceased to be " deferential " a great deal of Victorian thought,
that of Bagehot as well as of Disraeli, lost its validity. Moreover, the political rise of Germany and the increasing industrial achievement of such countries as Germany and the
United States, threatened English supremacy and nullified
the basic assumptions of Cobdenism. By the end of the
century we are faced with new problems, new political
alignments, a new spirit. We are, in fact, entering upon
contemporary problems beyond the scope of this book.

I. BAGEHOT[1]

" My dear Mamma,
    " I will now attempt the life of St. Augustine of Hippo.
This bulwark of orthodoxy was born at Tagaste, a town in
Africa. . . ."[2]
    At the age of twelve, Walter Bagehot was an essayist, and
an essayist he remained. He has the lively curiosity, the
faculty for throwing out seminal ideas, the ability to reflect
his environment with only a slight and pleasing distortion
through the medium of his personality, the paradoxical
combination of a bustling ruminativeness, characteristic of
the masters of his genre. Through all his work there run
certain leading ideas, which take on the rich colours of
circumstances, and appear and reappear clothed in different
guises of fact. Even his tricks of exposition are those of the
portraitist striving to fix in salient lines the character of his
subject. His favourite beginning is, " There are two or

---

[1] For Bagehot's political thought the essential documents are *The English
Constitution* (1867) and *Physics and Politics* (1872). These are included in
the *Works*, edited by Mrs. R. Barrington (10 vols., 1915). The youthful
Letters on the coup d'état (1851) (vol. i. of the *Works*) and much of the more
purely literary essays are full of interest for the historian of political thought.
Critical writing on Bagehot is surprisingly slight in volume. See Barrington,
Mrs. R., *Life of Walter Bagehot*, published as vol. x of the *Works*; Hutton,
W. R., *Memoir of Walter Bagehot*, prefixed to vol. i. of the *Works*; Stephen,
L., *Studies of a Biographer* (1910).
[2] Barrington, Mrs. R., *Life of Walter Bagehot*, in *Works*, vol. x., p. 83.

three kinds " of poetry, of democracy, or what not. All this does not imply that Bagehot was not an original thinker. On the contrary, he excels in the pregnant phrase which may start his reader on a whole new train of thought. " You may talk of the tyranny of Nero and Tiberius; but the real tyranny is the tyranny of your next-door neighbour."[1] But he was not a system-building man, like Bentham or Owen. Even in *Physics and Politics* he takes from the biological and anthropological achievements of the time a grand leading idea, and applies it to his subject with a proper feeling for the twistings and turnings of human nature in politics; but he does not pursue this idea to its bitter and logical end, and he does not construct any grand system well-armoured against the attacks of an impertinent reality. He regarded himself as too good an Englishman to attempt to construct such a system. We may content ourselves by saying that he was too good an essayist.

At any rate, many of his ideas do ring true to his age, and hence a little false to ours. He held firmly to the notion that one great source of the strength of the English nation was the deferential character of the average Englishman. Thanks to the Englishman's innate respect for rank, the apparently democratic changes of the nineteenth century have not altered the position of the ruling classes. This is fortunate, because ". . . a deferential community, even though its lowest classes are not intelligent, is far more suited to a Cabinet government than any kind of democratic country, because it is more suited to political excellence. The highest classes can rule in it; and the highest classes . . . have more political ability than the lower classes."[2] The great weakness of the philosophical radicals was their failure to take into account this deferential character in Englishmen. " To preach that the numerical majority ought to rule to a numerical majority which does not wish to rule is painful."[3] This has a far-off sound in the England of the Clydesiders and Mr. Jack Jones. It is true that Bagehot himself saw

---

[1] *Works*, vol. ii., p. 181 (Essay on Peel).
[2] *Ibid.*, vol. v., p. 350 (The English Constitution).
[3] *Ibid.*, vol. v., p. 96 (Essay on Grote).

signs that this deference was dying out. " In communities where the masses are ignorant but respectful, if you once permit the ignorant class to begin to rule you may bid farewell to deference for ever."[1] The Liberal Bagehot was horrified at the reform proposed by the Tory Disraeli in 1867. Any uniform franchise is bound to rest on the uniformity of the lowest. He would go back to the days before 1832, and have a great variety of franchises, a few on the " scot-and-lot " basis to give some representation to the workers, but most on a basis calculated to prevent the swamping of the upper classes by the lower.[2]

Still another of Bagehot's favourite ideas was that of the peculiar capacity of the Anglo-Saxon race. He held this doctrine with a moderation, and defended it with a grace, which robs it of the offensiveness it holds for certain minds. For one thing, he eschewed the support of Odin and the rest of the Nordic trappings dear to Carlyle and Kingsley. But he held it, and, especially in the form in which he applied it to America, it has to-day a quaint inapplicability that tempts one to doubt whether it ever held true. If the Americans, he wrote, " had not a regard for law, such as no great people have yet evinced, and infinitely surpassing ours—the multiplicity of authorities in the American Constitution would long ago have brought it to a bad end. . . . The men of Massachusetts could, I believe, work *any* Constitution."[3] And again, " America is not a country sensitive to taxes. . . . Certainly she is far less sensitive than England."[4] Bagehot pursues his distinction between rigid and flexible constitutions—a distinction we must now regard as of but slight direct validity—to the conclusion that it is almost impossible to alter the " Washington constitution."[5]

As applied more particularly to England, Bagehot considers that Anglo-Saxon political superiority rests partly on the deferential nature of Englishmen, partly on their happy

[1] *Works*, vol. v., p. 351 (The English Constitution).
[2] *Ibid.*, vol. iii. (Parliamentary Reform) ; vol. vii., p. 65 (Lord Althorp).
[3] *Ibid.*, vol. v., p. 321 (The English Constitution).
[4] *Ibid.*, vol. v., p. 153 (The English Constitution).
[5] *Ibid.*, vol. vii., p. 74 (The Chances for a Long Conservative Régime).

stupidity. The business of life is dull, and it takes dull men
to live well. " An irritable, far-seeing originality is commonly a vice in business."[1] " By the sound work of old-
fashioned generations—by the singular painstaking of the
slumberers in churchyards—by dull care—by stupid industry,
a certain social fabric somehow exists; people contrive
to go out to their work, and to find work to employ them
actually until the evening, body and soul are kept together,
and this is what mankind have to show for their six thousand
years of toil and trouble."[2] The trouble with the French is
that they are not stupid enough to govern themselves. They
are an impatient people, interested in ideas, devoted to the
fascinating possibilities of to-morrow instead of to the routine
obligations of to-day. Your Englishman, however, is not to
be led away by the lure of the intellect. He hates clever
people and clever controversy. He is saved for this earth
by a dull, animal attachment to the routine of sense-
experience.[3] Now this again is an interesting, plausible, and
widely held idea, though the youthful Bagehot delights in
making it as paradoxical as possible. The trouble is that it
isn't true. If one were to be wrecked on a desert island with
an unfortunate limitation of reading matter to a choice of
Hansard, the *Journel Officiel*, or the *Congressional Record*,
one could hardly do other than choose *Hansard* unless,
indeed, one were drawn to the *Congressional Record* by a
special taste for low comedy. The English are extremely
fond of clever controversy, and Bagehot himself played up
to that fondness.

Again, Bagehot's notions of morality bear the definite
stamp of his age. It is not merely that he has his share of
what we are now apt to dismiss as Victorian prudery, so that
he can write that " another most palpable defect—especially
palpable nowadays—in *Tristram Shandy* is its indecency,"[4]
whereas the indecency of that irritating bit of prosing is
almost its sole preservative against time. It is rather that he

---

[1] *Works*, vol. v., p. 90 (Essay on Lord Clarendon).
[2] *Ibid.*, vol. i., p. 84 (Letters on the *coup d'état*).
[3] *Ibid.*, vol. i., pp. 100-124 (Letters on the *coup d'état*).
[4] *Ibid.*, vol. iv., p. 242 (Sterne and Thackeray).

endows what he elsewhere called the " cake of custom," at least in the form in which he knew and practised it, with a mystic sanction which emancipated it from time and accident. He characteristically derives religion from morality. " Our only ground for accepting an ethical and retributive religion is the inward consciousness that virtue being virtue must prosper, that vice being vice must fail. From these axioms we infer, not logically, but practically, that there is a continuous eternity, in which what we expect will be seen, that there is a Providence who will apportion what is good, and punish what is evil. . . . Our religion cannot by any possibility swallow up morality, because it is dependent for its origin—for its continuance—on that morality."[1] The way of life which we thus know to be moral is the sober life of the middle classes. God is against the aristocrat. The life we see depicted by men like Grammont, the life of the old French aristocracy, is " a life . . . such as God has never suffered men to lead on this earth long, which He has always crushed out by calamity and revolution."[2] Bolingbroke failed because " as is usual in England, grave decorum and obvious morals had a substantial influence, and against these Bolingbroke offended."[3]

Finally, there is more than a touch of complacency in Bagehot's acceptance of the rule of his " quiet " middle class. " In England . . . the sovereign authority is the diffused respectable higher middle-class, which, on the whole, is predominant in the House of Commons."[4] The aristocracy " live in the fear of the middle classes—of the grocer and the merchant. They dare not frame a society of enjoyment as the French aristocracy once formed it."[5] As to the lower classes " no movement will really carry the working-class, which does not find many influential representatives among the sober, quiet, wealthy members of the middle-class."[6]

---

[1] *Works*, vol. iv., p. 93 (The Ignorance of Man).
[2] *Ibid.*, vol. iv., p. 244 (Sterne and Thackeray).
[3] *Ibid.*, vol. iv., p. 139 (Bolingbroke as Statesman).
[4] *Ibid.*, vol. iii., p. 371 (The Present Crisis, 1861).
[5] *Ibid.*, vol. v., p. 239 (The English Constitution).
[6] *Economist*, 14th January, 1871.

England is happily a stable society, a society that works and lives, but does not attempt the impossible. It will not listen to false prophets like Dickens. Now Dickens, though by nature a sentimental radical, began by attacking removable ills. " He has ended by describing the natural evils and inevitable pains of the present state of being, in such a manner as must tend to excite discontent and repining." He has taught some to speak " in what really is, if they knew it, a tone of objection to the necessary constitution of human society."[1] But England will have none of him, at least as a social reformer. It has already calmed the troubles of the previous generation. " The world of the ' Six Acts,' of the frequent executions, of the Draconian criminal law, is so far removed from us that we cannot comprehend its having ever existed."[2] Well may we say that " there is no worse trade than agitation at this time [1866.] A man can hardly get an audience if he wishes to complain of anything."[3]

Bagehot, then, affords an excellent introduction to the political ideas of his time. He was a superior person, but not superior to his age. He was liberal, but not a liberal immersed in the party struggle and held to party loyalties. One of our tasks must be the clothing of the abstraction, liberalism, in something recognizably concrete and temporal, like the novels of Trollope or the buildings of Sir Gilbert Scott. For this purpose, Bagehot is the best of material.

He has many of the characteristics we must associate with the liberal temperament. Hardly a robust person, he had yet what is commonly called an excellent disposition, cheerful, sunny, and open. Domestic troubles occasioned by his mother's madness did not unduly darken his life. He was no shallow optimist, no superficial dweller in a world mediately or immediately his own. But an optimist he was, undeterred from hope by any depths of personal suffering. He had no sentimental faith in the goodness of his fellows, and he was certainly no rationalist to be led, as Godwin was led, to run

[1] *Works*, vol. iii., p. 101 (Essay on Dickens).
[2] *Ibid.*, vol. iii., p. 99 (Essay on Dickens).
[3] *Ibid.*, vol. v., p. 274 (The English Constitution).

H

the idea of liberty down into anarchy. But he held very strongly an idea which is perhaps as instrumental in making its holder a liberal as any more direct impulsion of temperament or circumstances—the idea that truth, truth moral, æsthetic, and scientific, can only be arrived at through a process of trial and error. Now this process demands freedom for experimentation, which in the last resort means some degree of individual freedom. No man, and no group of men, is wise enough to censor, and certainly not to persecute. " At heart they [the censors] think that they are wiser than the mass of mankind, just as they are wiser than their children, and would regulate the studies of both unhesitatingly. But experience shows that no man is on all points so wise as the mass of men are after a good discussion, and that if the ideas of the very wisest were by miracle to be fixed on the race, the certain result would be to stereotype monstrous error."[1] Granted free discussion, truth has the full advantage over error, in the long run at least. If you attempt to protect truth by State action, or by Church action, you give it no advantage at all. " The truth has the best of the proof, and therefore wins most of the judgments. The process is slow, far more tedious than the worst Chancery suit. Time in it is reckoned, not by days, but by years, or rather by centuries."[2]

Not only is it clear that what we may attain of truth must be arrived at by a process of trial and error, but truth itself is not a fixed, attainable summit. The notion of evolution —a notion very much in the air, and one that Bagehot willingly adopted—in itself precludes the possibility of regarding truth as fixed. This notion is reinforced by one of our fundamental instincts, the revulsion from uniformity. " If it be said that people are all alike, that the world is a plain with no natural valleys and no natural hills, the picturesqueness of existence is destroyed, and, what is worse, the instinctive emulation by which the dweller in the valley is stimulated to climb the hill is annihilated and becomes

---

[1] *Works*, vol. vi., p. 225 (The Metaphysical Basis of Toleration).
[1] *Ibid.*, vol. vi., p. 223 (The Metaphysical Basis of Toleration).

impossible."[1] It is this instinct that drives us to unjust, but inevitable and precious, revolt against the preceding generation. The nineteenth century is no doubt unfair to the eighteenth; but were it not, were it to accept eighteenth-century standards, its stronger spirits would soon stereotype the world. Bagehot has to the full the Liberal distrust of the stereotype.

Bagehot's liberalism, like Mill's, is primarily an idea. He can, however, on occasion feel something of that deep and irrational hatred for the strong and successful, that love for the weak over whom the strong have climbed to success, which is perhaps the surest mark of the Liberal temperament. Notably in his indignant reply to Carlyle on the Eyre case he is the emotional Liberal. Eyre, in Jamaica, led " a six weeks' carnival, proclaiming martial law, hanging, slaying, flogging, using God's own image for target practice at four hundred yards." Bagehot almost attains the ironic writhing, under sympathy for the oppressed, one finds in the *Masque of Anarchy*. " Even the squires, unless they are bitten by Mr. Bright, looking on these Jamaica transactions by the light of Quarter Sessions, feel that Game itself would not tempt them to commit such acts of naked injustice."[2]

Finally, Bagehot was a liberal because he was a gentleman in Victorian England. It is easy enough to cherish doubts as to the merits of the English ruling classes in modern times, to feel that if Waterloo was won on the playing-fields of Eton, so, too, were Morant Bay and Amritsar. Yet at his best, the Victorian gentleman attained a moral security that carried with it a certain detachment, a disdain for moral tyranny and persecution. At his best, he was so sure of the validity of his code that he would not attempt to force it on others. Evil there is in the world, and evil must be resisted. But you must not fight fire with fire, evil with further evil. Self-discipline is the mark of a gentleman, and surely this is a gentleman's world ? You may educate the lower orders, you may influence them by your

[1] *Works*, vol. iv., p. 262 (Sterne and Thackeray).
[2] *Ibid.*, vol. ix., pp. 42, 44 (Mr. Carlyle on Mr. Eyre).
187

example, but you will not use the power of the Government to regulate their lives, or the lives of the recalcitrant members of your own order. Drunkenness is beastly, but temperance by prohibitory legislation is altogether outside the code. This attitude may seem to the modern reformer selfish, and even Laodicean, but it was re-enforced in practice by the strictness of Victorian personal morality. It is, however, an attitude of tolerance; and when on it are grafted, as with Bagehot, philosophical ideas favourable to individual liberty, the result is a sympathy for the nonconformist, the eccentric, the rebel.

Bagehot, however, is very far from being a doctrinaire individualist. He does not believe that the new is always better than the old. He does not hold that the individual is all and the State nothing. On the contrary, he has a deep sense of the seamlessness of the fabric of society, of the slowness of growth of institutions, of the impotence of man's intellect before the overpowering complexity of civil society. If these be the marks of a Conservative, he was a far better Conservative than Carlyle. Although, in *Physics and Politics*, he found scientific justification for this Conservative side of his thought, its proper origin, like that of his Liberalism, lies in the equipment of his mind. Traces of it are certainly to be found as early as the *Letters on the coup d'état* of 1851.

With some men—perhaps with most—Conservatism has its source in fear—from fear imaginatively rooted in the shocking contrast between men's desires and their attainments, down to the stupid fear of dispossession felt by the possessor. Bagehot's Conservatism, even more than his Liberalism, is an idea. It was not, indeed, an abstract idea, for he was too good an essayist to cherish any such; but an idea got from an artist's experience of the world, and not from an introspective survey of his own difficulties. The idea has various facets, but it appears chiefly as an assertion of the relatively late appearance, and therefore of the relative impotence, of thought in the biological process. There are passages in Bagehot's work which show that at moments he distrusted the instrument of thought, that he

THE PROSPEROUS VICTORIANS

feared its triumph would destroy the colour of life.[1] But
he is never guilty of an inconsistency common among
panicky Conservatives. He does not assert the incapacity
of thought to move men in politics and at the same time
attack rationalist schemes of reform as dangerous lures.
This convenient and, in the hands of a great man like Burke,
not insurmountable inconsistency does not greatly trouble
Bagehot. He did indeed write from Paris of the new
Montaguards, ready " like soldiers of the first Republic, to
use their arms savagely and well in defence of theories
broached by a Robespierre, a Blanqui, or a Barbès, gloomy
fanatics, *over*-principled ruffians."[2] But he later came to
feel that something deeper than thought makes fanatics,
that intellectual effort is usually a dissolvent of fanaticism,
that, at any rate, freedom of thought is the first requisite if
we are to make powerless the incomplete " rationalist "
thought of a Robespierre. *Physics and Politics* is rightly
enough counted as one of the sources of modern anti-
intellectualism in politics and in psychology. But it is anti-
intellectual in a reasonably objective sense. Bagehot finds
thought weak, but not damnable.

Physics and Politics—the title is misleading, for Bagehot
is concerned rather with biology than with physics—is a
very interesting book. It marks one of the first attempts of
political thought to find a new ally in the young, and, in
1872, lusty science of biology. The alliance of political
thought with Newtonian physics had suffered serious discredit in the revolution of the last century. Attempts to
renew the alliance, such as that of Fourier with his *attraction
passionelle*, were failures. Men wanted to explain society in
terms of decent predictability, but not of hard and fast
determinism. If political change could be assimilated to
organic growth, novelty could be reconciled to continuity.
Hence the popularity of *Physics and Politics*, of Spencer's
organic theory of the State, of a host of minor Darwinists
and Weissmannians in politics. Nature herself had gone

[1] *Works*, vol. ii., pp. 101 ff. (Essay on Macaulay). For example : " A
warmth of life is on the Hebrew, a chill of marble is on the Greek " (p. 105).
[2] *Ibid.*, vol. i., p. 81 (Letters on the *coup d'état*).

Victorian, and agreed to a perpetual compromise which meant perpetual progress.

Bagehot's work, however, is far superior to most political writings, which take their cue from another science. He is never dogmatic, never desirous of proving too much, even to himself. He merely examines, with due regard for the limitations of logic, some of the implications of the doctrine of the survival of the fittest applied to human society. Bagehot is not seriously troubled by the difficulties of assimilating a society to an organism. He is concerned with the nature and survival of what common sense calls a " national character," and which exists for every group. " A national character is but the successful parish character; just as the national speech is but the successful parish dialect, the dialect, that is, of the district which came to be more—in many cases but a little more—influential than other districts, and so set its yoke on books and on society."[1] This character of the group—national, parish, tribal—is a very real thing. The problem of its reality need trouble only the absurdly determined nominalist. You can, it is true, lay your hand on the individual, and you cannot lay it on the group. But, at least until very modern times, individuals were much more like than unlike; the commonwealth was more real than individual idiosyncrasies. Now what makes one individual like another is the principle of *unconscious imitation*, which is also the principle through which the survival of the fittest operated in primitive societies. Even to-day, man is an imitative animal. The reign of fashion shows how uncomfortable he is when he sees himself to be externally different from those around him. What is true of fashion in clothes is true, and was truer in the past, of all human activity. This imitative principle is unconscious, however, not consciously willed. It holds even in the activity we consider above all things conscious—thought, or if you prefer, belief. " In true metaphysics I believe that, contrary to common opinion, unbelief far oftener needs a reason, and *requires an effort*, than belief."[2]

---

[1] *Works*, vol. viii., p. 24 (Physics and Politics).
[2] *Ibid.*, p. 61.   The italics are mine.

Now as far back as we can trace men, they form groups of a kind. But modern anthropology has destroyed for ever the myth of a golden age. Savage life is more nearly what Hobbes thought it than what Rousseau thought it. Climate, geographical position, perhaps mere accident, will give a certain group the beginnings of a character which makes it, as a group, stronger. Then the principle of unconscious imitation will operate to weld that group together, to discipline it. In primitive societies, military strength, and military discipline, are the most valuable assets of a group. " The child most fit to be a good Spartan is most likely to survive a Spartan childhood. The habits of the tribe are enforced on the child; if he is able to catch and copy them he lives; if he cannot he dies."[1] So, too, religious beliefs come to increase the cohesive strength of the group, to aid it to survive. What we call morality—that honesty is the best policy, for instance—is obviously a useful thing for a group that can practise it. A society moral in this sense will, if nothing else, be a more productive society, and hence, if it maintain concurrently its military strength, a stronger society. The history of Rome brings out to the full the survival value of military discipline, religion, and morals.

Competition between groups, then, tends to the survival of the fittest, the strongest, and in certain marked peculiarities " the strongest tend to be the best." (Note the temperateness of this statement.) Within the group, the types of character most attractive and useful tend to prevail, and those types are on the whole the best. Both kinds of competition, external and internal, are subject to interference from outside forces. But both tend, left alone, to annihilate themselves, and to substitute stability for competition, a static for a dynamic society. The very principle of unconscious imitation which makes men political animals, and hence capable of improving their control over their environment, ends by establishing a " cake of custom " extremely difficult to break. Thus division of labour, in itself obviously useful, may harden into a caste system which makes adapta-

---

[1] *Works*, vol. viii., p. 68 (Physics and Politics).

tion to new conditions impossible. For men are obstinately conservative creatures, and they dislike originality. " They will admit it in theory, but in practice the old error—the error which arrested a hundred civilizations—returns again. Men are too fond of their own life, too credulous of the completeness of their own ideas, too angry at the pain of new thoughts, to be able to bear easily with a changing existence; or else, *having* new ideas, they want to enforce them on mankind—to make them heard, and admitted, and obeyed before, in simple competition with other ideas, they would ever be so naturally."[1]

What breaks the cake of custom is discussion. Most civilizations have been arrested at a point barely beyond barbarism. Græco-Roman civilization, however, and our own—which is descended from theirs—admitted government by discussion. Now discussion is in itself an admission that there are alternative actions possible, that the fixed rule of custom does not plainly and incontestably dictate a given course. It gives the innovating intellect a chance to play. Through the device of legal fictions, as Maine has shown, discussion may reconcile change with the obstinate devotion of men to the complex of customs on which unconscious imitation has fixed their loyalties. Moreover, discussion affords a cure for another vice of primitive societies—over-activity. The savage is always rushing from sleepy indolence to hasty and ill-considered action. This tendency survives even in modern business. Part of every mania (we would say " boom ") is caused by a " mere love of activity " as well as by a desire to get rich.[2] But if you want to stop immediate action, make it a condition that a considerable number of persons talk it over in public. Government by discussion is a valuable check to mere restless, expansive activity. Finally, trade and colonization are subsidiary activities which, along with discussion, tend to break the cake of custom, and throw men's minds open to new influences.[3]

A survey of the past of mankind makes it clear that certain groups of men have progressed. Bagehot admits that

---

[1] *Works*, vol. viii., p. 38 (Physics and Politics).
[2] *Ibid.*, p. 123.   [3] *Ibid.*, p. 114.

Manning, Huxley, and Ruskin, for example, would differ as to what is " higher " and what " lower," and hence as to the real nature of " progress." He himself is far from holding that progress is inevitable, or that the struggle for life must be understood by the politician as it is understood by the biologist. He is inclined to Spencer's position that increase in intellectual capacity, which is one of the marks of progress, involves decrease in other forms of human energy, and that notably it involves a decrease in reproductive power which may prove disastrous.[1] But on the whole his doctrine is optimistic. However much we may differ as to the value of machines, for instance, or however much we may prefer Homer to Tennyson, we must admit that there is a verifiable progress. Compare the English colonists and the Australian natives. The colonists can beat the natives at war, they have books, utensils, machines, a complex of aids to a varied life, and they possess the power of storing up against the future, of preserving their way of life against mere accident.[2]

Bagehot's writings contain many valuable observations on the actual framework of contemporary politics. Even the *English Constitution*, though like all such books it very definitely dates, is certainly more interesting, certainly more full of political wisdom, than the latest text-book manuals of actual government practice. We shall not, however, subject Bagehot's other political writings to the sort of analysis we have given to *Physics and Politics*, but select for discussion certain of his ideas which have permanent interest.

There are, says Bagehot, three social systems possible in the modern world, which are to be distinguished by their attitude towards the problem of social equality. There is the system of equality as practised in the United States and in France (a penetrating coupling, in which Bagehot rightly went beyond race to the common political ideas). There is the system of caste, or of irremovable inequalities. And there is the system of removable inequalities, which has on the

---

[1] *Works*, vol. viii., p. 129 (Physics and Politics).
[2] *Ibid.*, p. 134.

H*

whole been the heritage of English society.[1] This last system Bagehot naturally regards as best. Human beings are not equal in any of the qualities by which men can be measured. On the other hand, human heredity is too complex and unpredictable to allow us to suppose that those at the top of the social pyramid—or those at the bottom—will always breed true. The valuable element in the notion of equality, the element that conforms to what we know about the biological basis of society, is the principle of equality of opportunity. Doctrinaire equality of the French sort aims at a stereotyping as dangerous to progress as the old primitive methods of forming a cake of custom. The caste system has already arrested the progress of civilizations like that of India and the late Roman Empire. The middle way, the practical way, is to allow the highly gifted commoner to achieve social rank, to secure what Pareto was to call the " circulation des élites." This would seem to demand also the lowering in social rank of the inadequately gifted of high birth—a difficulty which Bagehot hardly meets.

Bagehot was one of the first to write fully and well on the distinction between what he called parliamentary and presidential governments—between the English system of cabinet government and the American system of congressional government. He rightly saw that an hereditary monarchy is not essential to cabinet government, and predicted that the new Third Republic could get along with an ornamental president instead of an ornamental king. If he predicted the immediate fall of the French Republic, it was for other reasons, chiefly the obvious but delusive fact of the failure of any French Government since 1789 to endure.[2] His analysis of the practical differences between the cabinet and the congressional system is penetrating, and has hardly been improved on since. He saw that the American system was based on an erroneous interpretation of the English Constitution current in the eighteenth century, the theory of the separation of powers. He saw that the American

---

[1] *Works*, vol. iv., pp. 261-262 (Sterne and Thackeray).
[2] *Economist*, 10th September 1870.

system was unwieldy, that it discouraged natural selection of men of ability as political leaders, that it really placed obstacles in the way of democratic government in that it made it difficult to organize responsible public opinion, that it artificially separated administrators and legislators. His preference for the English system is echoed to-day even in America. One system or the other he thought must inevitably be adopted by any State which hopes to endure. " No State can be first-rate which has not a government by discussion, and those are the only two existing species of that government."[1] He hardly foresaw the present attack on representative government.

Bagehot distinguishes in all good constitutions two parts, the *dignified* and the *efficient*.[2] Most men are still but a little above savages. Society is like a mountain, in which the lower geological strata are quite literally earlier, more primitive. It can hold together only by providing something common to such inferior people. Bagehot rather irreverently finds Queen Victoria to be this common something. " The use of the Queen, in a dignified capacity, is incalculable. . . . It is nice to trace how the actions of a retired widow and an unemployed youth [the Prince of Wales] become of such importance."[3] Thousands of Englishmen, and even more Englishwomen, think they are ruled by the Queen, and it is fortunate they do, for otherwise they could not be ruled at all. Nothing is more erroneous than the Benthamite notion that men are ruled by rational self-interest. " No orator ever made an impression by appealing to men as to their plainest physical wants, except when he could allege that those wants were caused by some one's tyranny. But thousands have made the greatest impression by appealing to some vague dream of glory, or empire, or nationality."[4] A good constitution, then, will provide decorative symbols, a ritual for which the crude emotional needs of the multitude can find satisfaction. Its dignified part will allow its efficient part to function under the care of the " upper ten thousand."

---

[1] *Works*, vol. v., p. 159 (The English Constitution).
[2] *Ibid.*, p. 162.   [3] *Ibid.*, p. 182.   [4] *Ibid.*, p. 164.

But this efficiency is rather that of the amateur than that of the professional. You need professionals—a bureaucracy, in fact—for the mere machine work. But a government of bureaucrats cannot last. In spite of its recent victories, the Prussian Government will find that it lacks power to adapt itself to new conditions as long as it places its trust in its bureaucracy.[1] Here again England is lucky in her government of amateurs. The ultimate weakness of the bureaucrat is his confined and petty outlook. " The summits . . . of the various kinds of business are, like the tops of mountains, much more alike than the parts below—the bare principles are much the same; it is only the rich, variegated details of the lower strata [the place of the bureaucracy] that so contrast with one another. But it needs travelling to know that the summits *are* the same. Those who live on one mountain believe *their* mountain is wholly unlike all others."[2]

We have seen that Bagehot held individual liberty to be unquestionably a political good. He realized, however, that in practice you must set a limit upon that liberty. He claimed to have no final formula for the solution of this central problem of political theory. But he does suggest certain rules of thumb which are more valuable than many more rigid solutions. First, as to freedom of speech. The very existence of a progressive society depends on this freedom. On the other hand, it cannot be unlimited. The test must simply be this: does the airing of a given idea threaten the very existence of a society ? If, in the opinion of those in power, it does so threaten destruction, it may be suppressed. Now it may be objected that this only pushes the difficulty a bit further. The line must be drawn somehow. But, says Bagehot, the line between sanity and insanity " has necessarily to be drawn, and it is as nice as anything can be."[3] Yet we do manage to draw it. Similarly it is hard to say whether a given idea is more than public order can bear safely, yet we must manage to make the decision. The important thing is that we bring to making this decision all the skill, all the knowledge, all the detachment which a good

---

[1] *Works*, vol. v., p. 298 (The English Constitution).   [2] *Ibid.*, p. 299.
[3] *Ibid.*, vol. vi., p. 226 (The Metaphysical Basis of Toleration).

doctor brings to the determination of the sanity of his patient. In the long run, the educated classes are the ones who decide between what can be said and what cannot. They must decide not according to their arbitrary likes and dislikes, but according to their knowledge. Naturally no specific decision is permanent. Society is always changing, and so are its needs. But to borrow another analogy from medicine, the human body is always changing, and yet we can distinguish between a fatal change and one that admits the continuance of life. So, too, with society. We must admit discussion, and hence change, up to the point which threatens the very existence of our society.

Again, the problem of individual liberty faces us in economic life. Bagehot states temperately the argument for *laissez-faire*. " That when no blinding passion prevents individuals from discerning what is their greatest pecuniary interest; when their pecuniary interest coincides with that of the nation at large; and when also the pecuniary interest of the nation is coincident with its highest interests and highest duties—the welfare of the nation will be better promoted by leaving every man to the exercise of his own unfettered discretion, than by laying down a general legislative rule for the observance of all."[1] This is already far from the dogmatic assertion of the right of the individual to do as he wishes with his own. Bagehot further admits that *laissez-faire* should not stand " opposed to the enforcement of a moral law throughout the *whole* sphere of human acts susceptible of attestation: to the legislative promotion of those industrial habits which conduce to the attainment of national morality or national happiness at a sacrifice of national wealth: to efforts at a national education, or a compulsory sanitary reform: to all national aid from England towards the starving peasantry of Ireland : to every measure for improving the condition of that peasantry which would not be the spontaneous choice of the profit-hunting capitalist." Economists must not lend colour to the suspicion that they " are perpetually assuming that the notion of Government interference is agreeable only to those whose hearts are

---

[1] *Works*, vol. viii, p. 146 (The Currency Monopoly).

more developed than their brains."[1] The conclusions of economics are but tools with which the cultivated politician can work. They are not in themselves capable of determining the ends of government. Even in economic matters, there is an exaggerated tendency to attack monopoly as if it were always an evil. On purely economic grounds, Bagehot defends government monopoly not only of metallic, but of paper, currency. Business men, even bankers, left to themselves, do *not* naturally do the right thing in regard to currency. A central authority must curb the business man's desire for a perpetually rising market.

Bagehot is no man to be summed up in a formula. His most abiding influence has lain in his work as a political psychologist, in which field his insistence on the *rôle* of unconscious imitation, on the vulgarization of ideas into symbols, on the weakness of pure logic in politics, on the ponderousness of any given society, is a permanent acquisition. Of even greater value, however, is the temperateness of all his judgments, his ability to attain concreteness without dogmatism, his successful display of the working of Newman's " Illative sense " applied to politics. And in this day of pretentious specialization in social studies, of social scientists who affect the graceless technical phraseology of the physical scientists, Bagehot's command of English prose is a valuable example. The day of the amateur whom he so much admired may be ended; but surely that of the artist is not ended ?

2. ACTON[2]

Lord Acton is not at first sight obvious choice for one seeking a representative English liberal among Victorian

---

[1] *Works*, vol. viii., pp. 147-148 (The Currency Monopoly).

[2] Acton's published work is slight in volume. The essentials of his political thought may be found in the collections published as *A History of Freedom and other Essays* (1909) and *Historical Essays and Studies* (1907). His *Correspondence* (ed. J. N. Figgis and R. V. Laurence, 1917) is indispensable. See Gooch, G. P., *History and Historians in the Nineteenth Century* (1913) : Brinton, Crane, " Lord Acton's Philosophy of History," *Harvard Theological Review*, June 1919.

thinkers. Born of an old Catholic family, he remained loyal throughout his life to a Church which seems to an outsider at least an uncompromising opponent of liberalism. Descended on his mother's side from a South German family, he was educated at Oscott and on the Continent, and thus excluded from the direct influence of the English public school and university. He was primarily an historian, trained in the rigidly conscientious German school, and prevented by an almost undue respect for research from successfully completing a great historical synthesis. Yet the very fact that he was not in all respects a typical English liberal makes his work all the more valuable to us. We cannot, as we must try to do, isolate the type unless we can test it by variations from type. Morley, for instance, is an almost dangerously simple liberal. With Acton, the liberal temperament is always struggling against an alien inheritance and an authoritarian loyalty, and in the struggle the fundamentals of the temperament emerge more clearly. Moreover, Acton is one of the influences that went to make up twentieth-century pluralism. Maitland is perhaps nearer the centre of that movement, especially in so far as it derives from formal jurisprudence, and no complete account of nineteenth-century political thought in England could omit him. But we are committed to a method of sampling, and Acton is a more complex sample than Maitland. Moreover, the ethical basis of pluralism is at least as clear in the work of Acton as in that of any other thinker.

Acton himself would hardly object to the statement that the starting-point of his political thought was a devotion to liberty. He was not perhaps a liberal in the strict party sense, though he did accept a peerage from Gladstone. But his whole life, first as an active supporter of the Liberal movement within his Church, and then, after the decree of Papal Infallibility had put an end to that movement, as the patient architect of his grand *History of Liberty*—a work for which we unfortunately have but the sketch—was spent in furthering the cause of liberty. " By liberty," he wrote in a famous definition, " I mean the assurance that every man shall be protected in doing what he believes his duty against the influence of authority and majorities, custom and opinion."[1] It is important to note what this definition omits from the notion of liberty. There is almost no trace in Acton of the utilitarian argument that liberty is the necessary basis of the method of trial and error by which human beings improve their control over Nature and over themselves, no trace of Bagehot's adaptation of that argument to the new theories of biology. Liberty is to Acton an end, not a means, an absolute, not a condition. It follows that he is not primarily interested in the kind of liberty preached by the economists. He admits the greatness of the achievements of Adam Smith, and the validity of the stand of the economists as long as they confine themselves to economics. But he objects to Buckle's idolatry of Adam Smith, and he considers the English school of economists to be wedded to an *a priori* determinism derived from the methods of French eighteenth-century thought.[2] But if he is indifferent to that optimistic strain of liberalism which sees in innovation an essential value of human life, he is hostile to that mystic strain which is embodied in the *Contrat Social*. He profoundly distrusts the metaphysical trick by which a man is said to be " forced to be free." He rarely permits himself the dangerous distinction between " true " freedom and " false " freedom, and leaves such a play on words to uncritical enthusiasts like Kingsley. It is not that he is an anarchist, not that he believes any man is free to do as he likes. But he insists that the necessary checks on individual freedom must be sought in the whole of human inheritance, in the State, the Church, the family, and in other groups, and not in any one central authority. Authority there must indeed be in this world, but the individual must be free to choose the authority to which he submits. The Rousseauist in action— the Jacobin—does but substitute one universal authority for another.

If you must hold that liberty is somehow obedience,

---

[1] " The History of Freedom in Antiquity," *The History of Freedom and other Essays* (1909), p. 3.

[2] See his account of Roscher in " German Schools of History," *Historical Essays and Studies* (1907), pp. 388-390.

Acton would maintain that you must make the qualification that this obedience is obedience to the moral law. Acton rescues himself from anarchism by an appeal to the common notion of morality. But morality is no closed system. Above all it is not the simple codification of a set of rather crude desires assimilated by a hasty dogmatism to the laws of physics and chemistry. Morality is at once less absolute and more absolute than the school of Bentham and the Continental liberals would have it. It is less absolute because it is based on all human experience, on all man's instincts and emotions, as well as on his calculations; on his art, his religion, his patriotism, his family affections, as well as on his economic interests. It is more absolute precisely because it is so based on a whole rather than on a partial experience. It has not the superficial completeness of logic, but the thorough, abiding completeness of faith. Our search for the moral law is never done, and it is a search which can—indeed must—make use of some of the methods employed in our search for a physical, or natural, law.[1] But the two searches are not identical.

They are not identical because, in the realm of natural science, the searcher must postulate determinism, and in the realm of morals he must postulate free will. Political liberty cannot be assimilated to scientific determinism. It follows that not to the scientist, but to the historian, is entrusted the task of discovering the content of the moral law. Now the historian is no mere annalist. The annalist " sees, not the connection, but the succession, of events. Facts are intelligible and instructive,—or, in other words, history exhibits truths as well as facts,—when they are seen not merely as they follow, but as they correspond; not merely as they have happened, but as they are paralleled."[2] The historian then will not merely narrate, not merely arrange facts in an order into which proper research will find they fall of their own accord, but will judge those facts by their conformity to what he knows of the moral law. For history, truly understood, " the record of truths revealed by expe-

---

[1] " Mr. Goldwin Smith's Irish History," *History of Freedom,* p. 233.
[2] *Ibid.,* p. 233-234.

rience, is eminently practical, as an instrument of action and a power that goes to the making of the future."[1]

The historian is thus the great mentor of political action. He sees in the past at once a limitation and a source of freedom for the present. But he must avoid the vulgar error—an error that has taken on a new respectability, thanks to German metaphysics—that historical explanation of a given phenomenon is a moral justification of that phenomenon. He must not assume that " die Weltgeschichte ist das Weltgericht," at least not in the Hegelian sense. He will be " objective " in that he will conscientiously strive to rid his mind of prejudice, in that he will balance evidence with the most honest care. But at bottom he has that within him which is somehow outside and above the process of history—his conscience. His conscience must dictate his judgments. He knows that persecution is an evil. Therefore he will condemn the Massacre of St. Bartholomew. He cannot excuse it as a product of " the spirit of the age."[2]

Now the moral law which thus speaks through the historian's conscience is no abstraction. It has affinities neither with Kantian metaphysics nor Baconian physics. It is simply a crystallization of human experience. " Opinions alter, manners change, creeds rise and fall, but the moral law is written on the tablets of eternity."[3] The strength of Christianity lies in this, that its ethics are the best to which men have yet attained. Acton once wrote to a correspondent: " You would imply that Christianity is a mere system of metaphysics which borrowed some ethics from elsewhere. It is rather a system of ethics which borrowed its metaphysics elsewhere."[4] Morality is not to be discerned by fine-spun philosophical arguments, not to be won through a mystic abdication of common sense. " It is the common, even vulgar code that I appeal to," he wrote. The Sermon on the Mount is enough. Once grant, as we must grant if human life is to have a meaning, that man is a free moral agent, that

[1] *Lectures on Modern History* (1906), p. 2.
[2] *History of Freedom*, pp. 101-149.
[3] *Lectures on Modern History*, p. 24.
[4] *Correspondence* (ed. Figgis and Laurence, 1917), p. 264.

the choice between good and evil is a real one, and you have at once a clue to history and a principle of present action.[1]

That clue and that principle may be summed up as liberty. For practical purposes, we may take the sacredness of human life as the ultimate test of a society. The historian, for instance, must condemn the Reign of Terror. " Our judgment of men, and parties, and systems, is determined by the lowest point they touch. Murder, as the conventional low-water mark, is invaluable as our basis of measurement. It is the historian's interest that it shall never be tampered with. If we have no scientific zero to start from, it is idle to censure corruption, mendacity, or treason to one's country or one's party, and morality and history go asunder."[2] Secure in this ultimate objective test that human life is always sacred, the historian may proceed with his task of tracing the gradual development of human freedom. For all history is really the history of freedom. " We have no thread through the enormous intricacy of modern politics except the idea of progress towards more perfect and assured freedom and the divine right of free men."[3]

Acton does not solve the insoluble problem of the relation between liberty and authority. His moral law is more nearly an absolute than he liked to think. But no working solution of the problem is possible without some standards accepted on faith. Let us take Acton's standards, and try to see how they may be used to guide our conduct as political animals.

Liberty, defined as the opportunity to follow conscience against the organized pressure of an external authority, has many enemies. In the past, religion has been the chief of those enemies, and even to-day religious persecution, in its subtler forms, is not unknown. Now a persecuting religion is a contradiction in terms. The truths of religion emancipate their holder from a blind obedience to evil instincts, to bad habits, to fear of authority. They incorporate and bring

---

[1] *History of Freedom*, p. xviii.

[2] " Morse Stephens's History of the French Revolution," *Historical Essays and Studies*, p. 494.

[3] Quoted in Gooch, G. P., *History and Historians in the Nineteenth Century* (1920), p. 387.

home to men in institutional form those rules which are
the essence of morality, indeed, but which without religion
are mere formulas. But a religion which kills, or simply
silences, men who will not voluntarily conform to its creed
ceases to be a religion and becomes a mere police. Persecution is always a useless thing, for belief is a spiritual force
and can never come from the outside, from sheer physical
pressure. Moreover, persecution is immoral not only because it reacts upon the persecutor and makes him careless
of law, brutal, bigoted, but because it may result in the suppression of truth. Toleration is vindicated by the fact that
truth can never suffer in open competition with falsity.
Give truth free rein, and it will by its very nature emerge
victorious. Falsehood, however, must always depend not on
moral but on physical force. The danger in persecution lies
in the fact that it may be employed on the side of the false.
Indeed, as soon as any great and good principle enlists the
aid of persecution it falsifies itself. Liberty of conscience is
the only guarantee for the triumph of moral principles in the
life of a community. When the Catholic Church made use
of persecution to stamp out heresy it was acting in a spirit
contrary to Catholicism.

Civil authority, however, is in modern society a greater
danger to liberty than religious. Absolute monarchy in
Europe was the child of the Renaissance and Reformation.
It is not in the nineteenth century a great danger in itself.
But it has left as an inheritance the doctrine of reason of
State, the Machiavellian worship of power, of mere crude
prevailing. Machiavelli's doctrines are not popular on paper,
but statesmen who are shocked by his principles are not
unwilling to put them into practice. Now though we must
believe that in the long run the truth will prevail, the
immediate pragmatism of the doctrine that might makes
right at any given moment is a repudiation of the moral law.
Through the weaknesses of ordinary men, politics is
inevitably a matter of compromise and rule of thumb. But
if we refuse to recognize any other rule at all in politics, if
we weakly let ourselves go with the current, we must end in
the absolute rule of whatever is most powerful in the State.

The greatest danger to liberty in the modern State, however, is not absolute monarchy, but absolute democracy. Democracy " no less than monarchy or aristocracy, sacrifices everything to maintain itself, and strives, with an energy and a plausibility that kings and nobles cannot attain, to override representation, to annul all ᵗhe forces of resistance and deviation, and to secure, by Plebiscite, Referendum, or Caucus, free play for the will of the majority."[1] The development of absolute democracy has been the joint work of France and America. In France the great revolution dissolved the protecting restraints upon power which had grown up even during the monarchy, and gave the Jacobins a chance to put into practice the authoritarian ideas of Rousseau. Under the cloak of the General Will, the rulers of the First Republic swept away all restraints against their own will. The despotism of Napoleon, the middle-class rule of Guizot, the recent alliance of Socialists and Jacobins, were all based on the notion that there must be no restrictions of the power of rulers representing the will of the people. In America, the republic was founded in the midst of struggles between Anglo-Saxon constitutional ideas represented by Hamilton, and French ideas represented by Jefferson. The present Civil War is perhaps the culminating point in this struggle. " A theory that identifies liberty with a single right, the right of doing all that you have the actual power to do [Jefferson], and a theory which secures liberty by certain unalterable rights, and founds it on truths which men did not invent and may not abjure [Hamilton], cannot both be formative principles in the same Constitution."[2] In the present war, the North is fighting for the centralized tyrannical rule of the majority, the South for individual liberty protected by federalism and by historically guaranteed rights.

Acton's view of the situation in America was over-simplified, if not worse. To maintain that the North was Jeffersonian and the South Hamiltonian is somewhat of a paradox. The truth is that neither side cared much for what Acton

---

[1] " May's Democracy in Europe," *History of Freedom*, p. 93.
[2] " The Civil War in America," *Historical Essays*, p. 132.

meant by liberty. But his main argument, that the doctrine of popular sovereignty was tending to realize itself in practice as a form of absolute rule, is clear and incontrovertible. Moreover, as Acton saw, the will of the majority cannot be ascertained, cannot indeed be said to exist. What actually happens is that through electoral manœuvring one party succeeds in establishing itself in power, and then justifies all its actions as embodying the mythical will of the majority.[1]

Finally, democracy has found an ally in nationalism, and the combination is almost irresistible against liberty. Nationalism, as the feeling of " a community . . . which imposes on its members a consistent similarity of character, interest, and opinion "[2] has been throughout history a characteristic of many European race groups. In itself, it is a valuable restraint on the power of a single ruler. But when fused with the doctrine of popular sovereignty—a fusion effected by the French Revolution—it strengthens the absolutist tendencies of modern democracy. If the State is to be one, it cannot permit the existence of community interests within itself; hence, racial, linguistic, provincial, and national differences within it must be abolished. Several nationalities cannot form a state, for state and nation must be co-extensive. In pursuance of this theory the Convention proceeded to attempt to eradicate all traces of local differences in France and sought to make the country a perfect ethnographic unity. This spirit is characteristic of the nationalist movements of the nineteenth century. They are not so much movements for national liberty as for national unity. Harsh intolerance of other race groups inhabiting the same territorial state is an invariable accompaniment. The dominant race strives forcibly to impose its language and civilization on weaker ones, as the Magyars did in Hungary and the Germans in Alsace-Lorraine and in Posen. The aim is to make men conform to a single pattern, to realize concretely the principle of equality.

---

[1] " May's Democracy in Europe," *History of Freedom*, p. 97.
[2] " Nationality," *History of Freedom*, p. 289.

Doctrinaire nationalism is thus as hostile to liberty as doctrinaire democracy. Both have a common origin in unhistorical *a priori* political thought. The perfect nation-state is an ideal entity, an abstraction, a body founded without regard for historic growth and racial diversity. Put to the test of contact with the world, such an ideal leads to absolutism of the worst kind. There is nothing between the individual and the State, and there can thus be no guarantee of private rights. " Whenever a single definite object is made the supreme end of the State, be it the advantage of a class, the safety or the power of the country, the greatest happiness of the greatest number, or the support of any speculative idea, the State becomes for the time inevitably absolute. Liberty alone demands for its realization the limitation of public authority."[1]

A state of mind which accepts politics as inevitably immoral (that is, which identifies right with immediate success), absolute democracy, and nationalism—these are the three chief obstacles to liberty in the modern world. Is there anything to offset them ? What support can the conscientious Liberal find against these enemies ?

In the first place, there is the English Constitution, and the English Liberalism which finds in the past its securest ally. The greatest error of Continental Liberalism has been its repudiation of the past, its attempt to construct society anew according to logical formulas. But precisely because compromise is the soul of politics,[2] history has seen the slow building-up of limitations on any given interest, limitations which prevent the usurpation of power by any single group. Out of the very weaknesses of men, complicated social arrangements arise to restrain their worst weakness, the lust for power. Acton agrees with Burke that civil society is an almost divine scheme for saving man from himself. The happy accidents of geography and history, perhaps even a natural endowment of political sense in the race, have given England a constitution which so balances power that abuse

---

[1] " Nationality," *History of Freedom*, p. 288.
[2] " Bright's History of England, 1837-1880," *Historical Essays*, p. 489.

of power is difficult. Even more important than the machinery of that constitution is the spirit that informs it. Englishmen nurtured under it have come to practise toleration, to put up with and even to value eccentricity, to realize that in practice the rights of man involve the rights of minorities.

It is in the root-principle involved in the rights of minorities that liberty finds its strongest ally in the modern world. When the State has come to be identified with the will of the majority, the only protection against tyranny lies in the limitation of the power of the State. The details of the English constitution are rooted in English soil, and cannot be transferred to another soil. Continental Liberals have copied the details instead of accepting its fundamental principle, the recognition and protection of minorities within the State. The modern theory " condemns, as a State within the State, every inner group and community, class or corporation, administering its own affairs; and, by proclaiming the abolition of privileges, it emancipates the subjects of every such authority in order to transfer them exclusively to its own. It recognizes liberty only in the individual, because it is only in the individual that liberty can be separated from authority, and the right of conditional obedience deprived of the security of a limited command."[1] In England the diversity of religious sects, the strength of local corporations, the opposition of landed and commercial interests, the number and strength of voluntary groups, have operated to provide innumerable transitions between the nakedness of the individual and the omnipotence of the State.

Liberty, then, implies diversity. But men, at least as political animals, cannot attain to diversity as individuals, but only as members of competing groups. The attempt to attain full diversity of individual life by destroying group life is bound to end in failure. The career open to talents as preached by *laissez-faire* economics, attractive though it may sound, is really destructive to talents, for it must end in the control of the machinery of the State by one kind of

---

[1] " The Protestant Theory of Persecution," *History of Freedom*, p. 151.

talent—the talent for making money. The masses, excluded from the new wealth of the capitalists, will turn against the middle classes the democratic theories by which these classes rose to power, and a despotic Socialist democracy will arise.[1] Individualism is the ruin of the individual.

Acton, then, has sketched the outlines of what we now call political pluralism. In the group the individual finds a liberty he loses in the unified State. In the rights of the group over against the State he finds necessary protection. Acton was not primarily interested in the kind of institution necessary to achieve this end, but he has left indications of a concrete programme. He welcomed in proportional representation a definite institution capable of embodying the principle of the rights of minorities in an organ of government hitherto most careless of such rights.[2] The modern party system has turned parliaments into mere machines for registering the dictates of power. Proportional representation may make parliaments what they should be, instruments of free discussion, clearing-houses for ideas, a means for balancing interests and securing mutual toleration.

Federalism is another institution which must be welcomed by Liberals. It affords, indeed, the only possible solution to the problems of nationalism. Austria, for example, has the opportunity of working out in a federal State a form of government higher than that of England. The variety of her national groups is in itself capable of being made a source of great richness. The fact that her nationalities are at very different stages of advancement, and that no single nation is so predominant as to overwhelm the other, makes Austria ready for the highest degree of organization which government is capable of receiving. These conditions, " supply the greatest variety of intellectual resource; the perpetual incentive to progress, which is afforded not merely by competition, but by the spectacle of a more advanced people; the most abundant elements of self-government, combined with the impossibility for the State to rule all by its own will; and the fullest security for the preservation of

---

[1] " May's Democracy in Europe," *History of Freedom*, p. 93.
[2] *Ibid.*, p. 97.

local customs and ancient rights."[1] This federalism must be a real one; it must limit the power of the imperial Parliament as jealously as that of the Crown, and must discharge many of the functions of government through provincial diets and a descending series of local authorities. Although he realized that the American Civil War meant increasing centralization in the State where the federal scheme had had its greatest test, Acton is not without hope for the future of federalism. " It is the only method of curbing, not only the majority but the power of the whole people, and it affords the strongest basis for a second chamber, which has been found the essential security for freedom in every genuine democracy."[2]

Finally, Acton has hopes that economic adjustment may yet bring with it political adjustment. No one has insisted more emphatically than he that political power is the handmaid of economic power. " This idea of the necessary balance of property," he wrote, " developed by Harrington, and adopted by Milton in his later pamphlets, appeared to Toland, and even to John Adams, as important as the invention of printing, or the discovery of the circulation of the blood."[3] Now the chief danger in modern democracy comes from the discrepancy between its political egalitarianism and its concentration of wealth in relatively few hands. May we not hope that political economy will some day achieve the objectivity, the rigorous certainty, of science ? " Whenever that shall be attained, when the battle between Economists and Socialists is ended, the evil force which Socialism imparts to democracy will be spent."[4] A scientific organization may do away with the patent evils of free competition

---

[1] " Nationality," *History of Freedom*, p. 296.
[2] " May's Democracy in Europe," *Ibid.*, p. 98. The difference between the pragmatic liberalism of Bagehot and the ethically idealistic liberalism of Acton comes out from a comparison of above remarks on federalism and Bagehot's. " The State of Delaware is *not* equal in power and influence to the State of New York, and you cannot make it so by giving it an equal veto in an Upper Chamber " (*Works*, vol. v., p. 228).
[3] *Ibid.*, p. 83.
[4] *Ibid.*, p. 98.

without surrendering the individual over to a centralized Socialist State.

In few Englishmen has the bare idea of liberty taken on a form more immediately emotional than with Acton. He loved freedom as Shelley did, as some direct bright object of the sense. But he was far from the romantic anarchism of Shelley. It is not only that his Burkian respect for the past, his feeling for the contingency of earthly things, his sense of the reality of corporate life and the loneliness of the individual, his conviction of the immanence of the moral law all served to qualify and soften his demand for individual freedom. It is even more that he had another, and a stronger love than his love of liberty. Why did not the author of the two essays on the *History of Freedom* follow his master Döllinger out of the Catholic Church in 1871 ? Surely the logic of liberty could not admit Papal Infallibility ? Yet, Acton submitted. The universality of the Catholic Church was a sacred mission. Better incur a temporary loss of part of the moral strength of the Church than wholly abandon that mission. The commission of a wrong may be justified on the ground that it will lead to a greater right. Acton had thus introduced into his moral life that very principle of relativity which he had so sternly rejected from his ethical theory.

Acton's submission suggests the reflection that an ethical devotion to the idea of liberty is in itself no firmer ground for absolute Liberalism than the more empirical ground of economic or biological theory. Even in his own life, Acton did not escape Rousseau's dilemma of forcing a man to be free. Principles, informed with emotion though they be, are always at the mercy of something deeper than principles. And yet Acton's words never ceased to defy, with a touch of theatricality that does but bring out the ultimate humanity of his dilemma, this compromising world. Eighteen years after the Vatican Council, he numbered himself among those who " believing that the doctrines of Laud are to those of Bradlaugh as heaven to hell, yet glorify the Providence that sent the primate to the Tower and the atheist to the House of Commons."[1]

---

[1] " Bright's History of England," *Historical Essays*, p. 474.

3. T. H. GREEN[1]

No one, not even the Mill who wrote so sympathetically of Socialism in his later years, marks better than Thomas Hill Green the change which came over English Liberalism in the latter half of the nineteenth century. Green himself wrote in 1881: "There is a noticeable difference between the present position of political reformers and that in which they stood a generation ago. Then they fought the fight of reform in the name of individual freedom against class privilege. Their opponents could not with any plausibility invoke the same name against them. Now, in appearance—though as I shall try to show, not in reality—the case is changed. The nature of the genuine political reformer is perhaps always the same. The passion for improving mankind, in its ultimate object, does not vary. . . . [It is] the same old cause of social good against class interests, for which, under altered names, liberals are fighting now as they fought fifty years ago."[2] The methods are different, but the goal is the same. Legal regulation of wages aims at freedom as much as did the abolition of the Corn Laws.

Green held that his idealist metaphysics provided the necessary basis for the transition from *laissez-faire* to State regulation, that through a proper philosophy the new freedom would be seen to be but the inevitable development of the old. Whether we agree with him or not will depend on our own estimate of the importance of metaphysics. At any rate his own generation was struck with the novelty of

---

[1] Green's political thought is almost wholly contained in *The Principles of Political Obligation*, printed in vol. ii. of the *Works* (3 vols., edited by R. L. Nettleship, 1888) and issued as a separate volume with a preface by Bernard Bosanquet (new impression, 1924). Some of the miscellanies in vol. iii. of the *Works* are useful illustrations of the concrete proposals in which he works out his idealism. See Nettleship, R. L., *Thomas Hill Green, A Memoir* (1906; and in vol. iii. of the *Works*); Hobhouse, L. T., *The Metaphysical Theory of the State* (1918); Chin, Y. L., *The Political Thought of T. H. Green* (1920); Ritchie, D. G., *The Principles of State Interference* (1891); MacCunn, J., *Six Radical Thinkers* (1907).

[2] "Liberal Legislation and Freedom of Contract," *Works*, vol. iii., p. 367.

his position. The idealist reaction to eighteenth-century empiricism had for most Englishmen a necessary alliance with conservatism in politics. German idealism, as interpreted by Coleridge and Carlyle, had seemed to sacrifice the individual to the State, to be irreconcilable with the common-sense notion of liberty, to be committed, in its final form, to the pessimistic despotism of Carlyle's later years. Mark Pattison thought that Green's attempt to be a liberal in politics and an idealist in philosophy indicated a hopeless confusion of mind.[1] The journal of an Oxford friend of Green's comments on him in 1862: " He is a philosophic radical, but of a very peculiar kind. Almost all his definite opinions might be endorsed by Bright or Cobden, but neither Bright nor Cobden could understand the process by which Green's opinions are obtained, nor the arguments by which they are defended. An idealist in philosophy, he argues for the most utilitarian of political schools on idealist principles; and attaching the greatest importance to national life, constantly expresses a contempt for so-called ' national honour ' and imperial greatness which might perhaps offend the nationalism even of Mr. Cobden."[2]

For those who seek the explanation of a man's political ideas in the relation between his personality and his environment, it is important to note that Green was a very earnest, rather inarticulate young man of sober evangelical background in the midst of a university of Tory traditions. M. Thibaudet has remarked that in the Third Republic, literature and the graces are definitely on the side of the Conservative Right. No such remark could be made of the England of Shaw, Wells, and Galsworthy. Nor is it true of contemporary Oxford. But in the Oxford of the middle nineteenth century one marked literary grace, cleverness, tended to take the Tory side. That combination of verbal facility and social distinction which we have before noted as characteristic of Disraeli's young England found the Oxford Union, and the Oxford common-room, very con-

---

[1] Quoted in Ritchie, D. R., *The Principles of State Interference*, p. 132.
[2] Quoted in Nettleship, R. L., *T. H. Green : A Memoir*, in *Works*, vol. iii., p. xx.

genial. Balliol was soon to witness under Jowett and Green himself the reconciliation of cleverness with evangelical fervour, of erudition with a sober Liberalism, of an Oxford common-room with the rest of England, and even with North Oxford. But in Green's undergraduate days, the bright young men were Tories and High Churchmen. That Green should be driven by a natural revulsion to take the other side in politics was only to be expected. Nettleship says in his *Memoir* that " anyone who knows the Union will not need to be told that a society which would applaud clap-trap, personalities, flippancy, and impertinence, to the echo, would hardly give a hearing to Green."[1] We need not be surprised that when, in 1858, Green brought forward in the Union a motion eulogizing John Bright he found himself in a minority of two![2] Thus the youthful Green was confirmed in his dislike of English social castes. He came to *feel* for the people, to colour his Liberalism with a little Byronic love of revolt, curious in a staid philosopher. He was very young when he wrote of a proposed volunteer rifle corps, " Fools talk at Oxford of its being desirable, in order that the gentry may keep down the chartists in the possible contingency of a rising. I should like to learn the use of the arm that I might be able to desert to the people, if it came to such a pass."[3] This ardour he no doubt lost with age, but he never ceased to feel that his mission was to win Oxford for England. To a surprising extent, that mission was successful.

At the very start of his political philosophy, Green comes to grips with the problem of freedom. He is too good an Englishman to dismiss with contempt the common-sense notion that, metaphysics put aside, a man is free when he does at any given moment what at that moment he wants to do. So, too, political freedom may be given the common-sense definition of the exemption of the individual in doing what he wants to do from the interference of any other individual or individuals. But Green is perfectly aware of the barrenness of such common-sense definitions. In what sense is the man who drinks himself to death a free man ?

---

[1] *Works*, vol. iii., p. xxi.   [2] *Ibid.*, p. xxiv.   [3] *Ibid.*

Must we not say that " it is one thing when the object in which self-satisfaction is sought is such as to prevent that self-satisfaction being found, because interfering with the realization of the seeker's possibilities or his progress towards perfection; it is another thing when it contributes to this end " ?[1] In the former case, he is free in the common-sense definition—he does what he wants to do. But in another sense he is not free, for his will to arrive at self-satisfaction is not adjusted to the law which determines where this self-satisfaction is to be found. The drunkard is a bondsman who is carrying out the will of another, not his own. It is true we are talking in a metaphor, and therefore dangerously. But by virtue of our human gift for self-objectification, a man can set himself over against certain elements even of his own consciousness, and thus establish in thought, let us say as between " I " and " my desire to drink," a relation borrowed from the relations of outward life, the relation between one who commands and one who obeys. " Hence, as in Plato, the terms ' freedom ' and ' bondage ' may be used to express a relation between the man on the one side, as distinguishing himself from all impulses that do not tend to his true good, and those impulses on the other. He is a ' slave ' when they are masters of him, ' free ' when master of them."[2]

The way is thus open for us, if we like, to say with Hegel that true freedom, as the condition in which the will is determined by an object adequate to itself, is realized in the State. Such a State may be regarded as " objective freedom," as incorporating the attainable perfection of a higher reason than is found in the individual. Submission to law as defined by the State is thus really liberty, and we can aptly employ Rousseau's paradoxical phrase about forcing a man to be free. With this position Green finds himself to a certain extent sympathetic. He accepts to the full the Aristotelian position that the State is " natural " and therefore moral,

---

[1] " On the Different Senses of ' Freedom ' as applied to Will and to the Moral Progress of Man," *Principles of Political Obligation* (1924), p. 2.
[2] *Ibid.*, pp. 3-4.

that the accumulated efforts of generations of men striving to translate their aspirations into reality, their *values* into *facts*, have built up a nexus of social relations which definitely embodies the good life, and to which, therefore, the good man will on the whole conform.[1] But he is shocked by the full collectivist implications of the Hegelian position, by its sacrifice of the individual to the State, by its easy adaptability to such unpleasant formulas as " whatever is, is right " and " might makes right." He insists that " we cannot significantly speak of freedom except with reference to individual persons; that only in them can freedom be realized; that therefore the realization of freedom in the State can only mean the attainment of freedom by individuals through influence which the State . . . supplies."[2] Surely in any given State such a realization of freedom has been most imperfect. " To an Athenian slave, who might be used to gratify a master's lust, it would have been a mockery to speak of the state as a realization of freedom; and perhaps it would not be much less so to speak of it as such to an untaught and underfed denizen of a London yard with gin-shops on the right hand and on the left."[3] Hegelian idealism too easily identifies aspiration with fact.

Yet we cannot wholly wish away this metaphorical use of the term " freedom," confusing though it has proved, since it does embody the effort of reflecting men to put into effective action the distinction between good and evil. Green's own way out of the confusion is perhaps not wholly clear to the empirical mind. Moral perfection—the whole system of values of which the best man has but an incomplete apprehension—is the work of *reason* (reason rather in the Coleridgian sense than in the eighteenth-century sense). *Will* is the simple fact of human consciousness—it is that specifically human attribute which distinguishes men from machines, which enables them, not indeed to act in defiance of the " natural laws " of the physical scientist, but to control their acts in conformity to these laws. Now in God,

---

[1] *Principles of Political Obligation,* pp. 6-8.
[2] *Ibid.,* p. 8.   [3] *Ibid.*

will and reason are actually one, and even in men they are alike expression of one self-realizing principle, and *tend* to unite. Civilization is the long and still unfinished process by which the impulse for self-satisfaction, which belongs to the will, and the idea, which belongs to the reason, undergo modifications which render their reconciliation *in the individual* (not in the collectivity) more attainable.[1] Their ultimate reconciliation would result in anarchy—that is, in the absence of external compulsion upon an individual whose will is identical with his reason.

But in the present world it is necessary to maintain the distinction between the ideal and the real. The ideal is the realm of moral obligation, the real that of political obligation. The two are not indeed to be considered as watertight compartments; they have no meaning unless it is realized that in all human activity their mutual interdependence is a constant fact. Broadly speaking, we may say that " those acts only should be matter of legal injunction or prohibition of which the performance or omission . . . is so necessary to the existence of a society in which the moral end stated can be realized, that it is better for them to be done or omitted from that unworthy motive which consists in fear or hope of legal consequences than not to be done at all."[2] That is, a strictly moral act is done as an end in itself, without regard for any enforcing agent outside the individual. At the other extreme is an act conforming to a law, but done through fear of the enforcing agent. That enforcing agent may be a government official acting according to a specific law; or it may be society at large, acting according to convention or tradition. The act itself, we must repeat, is moral in that it conforms to what reason points out as desirable. But it is incompletely moral in that it is not, in the very purest sense of the word, free.

We may, then—nay, we must, if we are to avoid the Hegelian deification of the State—distinguish logically between moral freedom and political freedom. The individual is politically free when, by an act of imaginative reason, he accepts the whole nexus of social relations as a necessary

---

[1] *Principles of Political Obligation*, p. 23. [2] *Ibid.*, p. 38.

J

guide, when he realizes that his own good must also be the common good. Incompletely, if you like, from the point of view of the ideal, but none the less genuinely for mortal beings, the State is founded upon will. Therefore what we know as self-government, or democracy, is for a people capable of it the highest form of government, a government towards which all peoples must strive. Fear, if only fear of the policeman, is even to-day a necessary concomitant of government; but the less fear enters into civil obedience, the better the government.

Accepting the State as a moral force, admitting the existence of the general will, we have now to consider two important related problems which cover the essentials of politics: what are the limits of the power of the group—that is, the power of the group acting socially through convention, as well as acting politically through law—over the individual; and how far can such power be used to promote pure morality?

The first problem may be put in this way: when may the individual be said to have the right to resist the group? Now " a right against society, in distinction from a right to be treated as member of society, is a contradiction in terms."[1] The trouble with the eighteenth century was that in the name of a misunderstood " Nature," it set the individual crudely in opposition to the State. There are indeed individual rights, and we may call them " innate " or " natural," but only in the Aristotelian sense that the State itself is natural. These rights "arise out of, and are necessary for the fulfilment of, a moral capacity without which a man would not be a man."[2] Stripped of their dogmatic assertiveness and their false philosophical origins, these rights are substantially what the last century thought them to be. In a parliamentary State like England, these rights are pretty substantially equivalent to the fabric of existing law. Therefore a modern Englishman has not a right to resist the law. In the first place, any existing social system incorporates the efforts of so many generations of men, is so thoroughly in accordance with the national character, that the presumption must be

---

[1] *Principles of Political Obligation*, p. 110.   [2] *Ibid.*, p. 47.

in its favour against even a very wise individual. Moreover, resistance to a single law is apt to end in resistance to the whole fabric of the law, in an attempt at complete revolution. If an Englishman is convinced that a law is a bad one, his duty is to agitate against it, to attempt by legal propaganda to secure its repeal. If he thinks a custom a bad one, he may refuse to conform to it, though he must never lose sight of the fact that his brethren may find it a necessary limitation. But there are four cases, none of which apply to modern England, where the individual has a right to resist. First, where the legality of a given command is doubtful. In the United States, for instance, the States rights question is so involved that there is nothing to amount to a real right in either the State or the federal side, and the good citizen may obey whichever authority his conscience directs him to obey. Second, where there is no means of agitating for the repeal or alteration of a law. Here resistance is not only a right, but a duty. Third, where the whole system of government is so perverted by private, selfish interests hostile to the public, that temporary anarchy brought on by revolution is preferable to the maintenance of the existing order. Fourth, where the authority commanding is so easily separated from the whole system of rights and order that the latter will not be affected by resistance to a particular law.[1] But the good man, who is also a humble man, will hesitate long before he resists the State. Revolutionists are forced to " go it blind," and incur consequences beyond the power of our intelligence to predict.

Our second problem is this: How far can the State, acting through concrete laws enforced by its police power, promote morality ? Now the essential point about Liberalism is that it aims at increasing moral freedom for the individual. The root idea even of *laissez-faire* Liberalism is sound: the individual must help himself. Paternalism, well-meant autocracy, is bad because it keeps him like a child in leading-strings, because it atrophies his moral strength. But the Manchester school, barred by their atomistic view of the

---

[1] *Principles of Political Obligation*, Lecture F., sections 101-112.

individual, have missed an important distinction. The State ought indeed to remove many of the historic restraints on free dealing between man and man, for such restraints, though rising partly perhaps from some confused idea of maintaining morality, have arisen much more from the power of class-interests.[1] But its purpose must be the *removing of obstacles to morality*; and such a removing may often mean positive legislative enactments enjoining specific performances—that is, legislation quite contrary to the programme of *laissez-faire*. For instance: an ignorant man cannot be morally autonomous, cannot to-day be a good citizen. But it is clear that not all parents will voluntarily make the sacrifices necessary to educate their children. Therefore a compulsory system of education, showing due respect for the preferences, ecclesiastical and otherwise, of the parents, must be set up by the State. Such a compulsion will not deaden spontaneity, for it is only felt as compulsion by those who have, in this respect, no spontaneity to interfere with. Again, there is the principle of freedom of contract. " The freedom to do as they like on the part of one set of men may involve the ultimate disqualification of many others, or of a succeeding generation, for the exercise of rights. This applies most obviously to such kinds of contract or traffic as affect the health and housing of the people, the growth of population relatively to the means of subsistence, and the accumulation or distribution of landed property."[2] The results of a contract freely entered into by weak or ignorant men may be such as to place insuperable obstacles in the way of their attaining moral freedom. Such for instance is the " contract " between the Irish landlord and his tenant. " To uphold the sanctity of contracts is doubtless a prime business of government, but it is no less its business to provide against contracts being made, which from the helplessness of one of the parties to them, instead of being a security for freedom, become an instrument of disguised oppression."[3]

The way is thus open to consider some of the practical

[1] *Principles of Political Obligation*, p. 210.   [2] *Ibid.*, p. 209.
[3] *Works*, vol. iii., p. 382.

problems of our present society. Recognizing that the
State has a positive, and not merely a negative, function, that
the current attitude which condemns all legislation beyond
the bare repression of crimes of violence is short-sighted and
wrong, we can ask ourselves what sort of legislation the good
citizen should promote.

In the first place, at least in England, he will work for
universal suffrage. Only through active participation in the
affairs of State does a man become a citizen, and capable of
improving himself. Parliament must cease to be a " rich
man's club," though it be necessary to provide for payment
of members.[1] It is true that a completely democratic
Parliament may be a tyrannical Parliament. From the
dangers of a centralized democracy on the French pattern,
England, however, has been hitherto singularly free. The
diversity of English group life must be preserved. " A state
presupposes other forms of community, with the rights that
arise out of them, and only exists as sustaining, securing, and
completing them."[2] Groups whose interests conflict too
obviously with those of society as a whole—the landed
interest founded on primogeniture, for instance—must be
restrained. But other groups, such as churches, trade
unions, benefit societies and the like must be allowed considerable freedom. Green welcomed the co-operative movement among workmen as promising to secure the benefits
of Socialism without the evils of a centralized bureaucracy.[3]

Education must be a primary concern of the English
liberal. Like Matthew Arnold, Green felt that the heart of
the problem lay in the education of the newly enriched
industrial classes. Nettleship writes that " his strongest
sympathies were with the education of the middle classes,
whom the universities were just beginning to touch. An
undercurrent of indignant pity for the intellectual condition
of these classes pervades his writings. He is oppressed with
' the monotonous level of commercial intelligence,' and with
the conviction that ' only by a special grace can anyone bred

[1] *Works*, vol. iii., p. cxix.
[2] *Principles of Political Obligation*, p. 139.
[3] *Works*, vol. iii., p. xlii.

amid the keen interests, the obvious profits, the quick returns of prosperous commerce, be drawn into the devious and difficult paths which lead to the knowledge that is its own reward.' . . . ' For a single man to be found having views about better education for the middle class, a hundred may be found having views about the education of the poor.' "[1] Yet the immediate necessities of the poor are so great that state action must first be enlisted to improve their physical condition. The middle classes, beyond physical want, are the ones upon whom a good system of education can work with immediate benefit. Green himself was for a short time a special commissioner employed by the Government in investigating secondary education, and his reports are still of interest. He wished to straighten out the tangle of endowed schools, charity schools, schools run for commercial profit, and establish a national system of secondary education, national standards, and national inspection. The curriculum, while not neglecting scientific knowledge, modern languages, and history, was to be at bottom classical. The middle-class thirst for the " practical," the demands of middle-class parents that their children learn something useful, was one of the limitations of the commercial spirit which education must correct. Green himself was one of the founders of the Oxford High School. Concomitantly with this system of secondary education, a higher education must be provided for the ablest youth of all classes. The monopoly of the gentry at Oxford and Cambridge must be destroyed. Open scholarships must be increased, and the snobbishness of the public school element broken down. Provincial universities must be established to supplement the work of the older universities.

In economic life, Liberalism must go a long way towards what an older generation would have called Socialism or Communism. We have had Factory Acts and sanitary legislation even during the reign of the Manchester school. If we take as our guiding rule that the State should interfere not to coddle the workman, not to encourage his vices by protecting them, as did the old Poor Law, but to remove

---

[1] *Works*, vol. iii., p. lvi.

obstacles to self-help, our path is fairly clear. " Every injury to the health of the individual is, so far as it goes, a public injury. It is an impediment to the general freedom; so much deduction from our power, as members of society, to make the best of ourselves. Society is, therefore, plainly within its right when it limits freedom of contract for the sale of labour, so far as is done by our laws for the sanitary regulation of factories, workshops, and mines."[1] Therefore, as Liberals, we shall encourage labour unions, co-operative societies, the various forms of social insurance (exacting a share of the premiums from the workman himself), regulation of the liquor trade, and similar measures. We shall, as privileged by our wealth and education, encourage wise private charities, even more, take part ourselves in the work of social service.

How far Green's temper, in spite of his metaphysics, was determined by the traditions of his party comes out in his attitude towards the other economic problem of English society, the land problem. Where Tory democrats like Disraeli welcomed the alliance of the old landed aristocracy and the new captains of industry, Green profoundly distrusted it. He is moved not at all by respect for the " old oaks " of the English aristocracy. Far from holding that the fundlords have corrupted the landlords, he thinks that the reverse is true. The urban proletariat descends from the serfs and semi-serfs of the feudal *régime*. There is nothing in capitalism itself that makes a proletariat inevitable. It is because the capitalist has assimilated himself to the feudal overlord that English industry has grown so lop-sided.[2] We must reform our land laws, break up the great estates, abolish primogeniture. The debased population of landless agricultural labourers is the source of our glutted labour market, and forms a constant obstacle to the work of the better trade unions. No individual benevolence can cure this evil. " It can only be cured by such legislation as will give the agricultural labourer some real interest in the soil."[3]

---

[1] *Works*, vol. iii., p. 373.
[2] *Principles of Political Obligation*, p. 228.
[3] *Works*, vol. iii, p. cxii.

We must, of course, go slowly. But we must at once guarantee to the tenant the full value of unexhausted improvements; we must limit, and finally abolish, entail; we must put land on the same footing as other property, and allow the natural play of economic law to split it up into small holdings; we may even, in the end, be obliged to limit the power of the landlord to withdraw land from cultivation for parks or forests. In Ireland, we must do more, and provide government aid for the cottier to enable him to set himself up as an owner of his land.[1]

Green's temperance programme is simply a part of his programme of labour legislation. But he himself held it to be so important, and it is so typical of the practical translation of his theories into a programme, that we may here consider it apart. Again, we must pay our tribute to the political psychologist by admitting that Green was the brother of a dipsomaniac. But even without this personal example, he could hardly have admitted the full play of freedom in the liquor trade. He had the courage to take up a position almost eccentric for an Oxford don, and was President of the Oxford Band of Hope Temperance Union. " It is idle," he wrote to Sir William Harcourt, " to say that education and comfortable habits will check the vice in time. The education of the families of the sober has no effect on the families of the drunken. Unless the vice is *first checked by a dead lift of the national conscience*," (an interesting phrase), " education and comfortable habits are impossible in those very families which are to be saved from drunkenness by them. Meanwhile an immense commercial interest is fattening upon the evil, and of course doing all it can do to disguise it."[2] His own remedy was a form of what used to be known in America as local option. He admitted that " to attempt a restraining law in advance of the social sentiment necessary to give real effect to it, is always a mistake."[3] He would not then attempt a national prohibitory law. But if Parliament would allow local units to close public houses within their own limits, he trusted that temperance agitation

[1] *Works*, vol. iii., pp. 381-382.   [2] *Ibid.*, p. cxvii. The italics are mine.
[3] *Ibid.*, p. 384.

would go on from local victory to local victory, and that Englishmen would limit, or even altogether give up, the use of alcohol. The moral atrophy argument did not move him. " When all temptations are removed which law can remove, there will still be room enough, nay, much more room, for the play of our moral energies."[1]

Green's services to English Liberalism were very great. His actual programme, as we have outlined it, can be seen to be not very different, save in respect to the temperance question, from that which was gradually forcing itself on all English parties. But the differences between the Tory temperament and the Liberal temperament are very real ones. The Tory, however much he may sympathize with democracy, is at bottom a patriarch. He will not give up the richness of social gradation he sees in the past. The Liberal, on the other hand, however much he may inveigh against Socialism, is at bottom an egalitarian. He is always a little indifferent, or hostile, to the past. Compare Disraeli's sense of the immanence of the seventeenth century in the nineteenth with Green's statement that in the Civil War " neither our conservatism nor our liberalism, neither our oligarchic nor our ' levelling ' zeal, can find much to claim as its own in a struggle which was for a hierarchy under royal licence on the one side, and for a freedom founded in grace on the other."[2]

Now a weakness of mid-nineteenth-century Liberalism, in so far as it stemmed from Benthamism, was that it lacked a metaphysical superstructure flexible enough to permit it to adapt itself to changing conditions. Not even Mill, as we have seen, could supply his followers with a faith, with an imaginative interpretation of the facts of common life. Green did just that. Idealism may seem to the sceptic so willing to adapt itself to the varying exigencies of daily life that he is inclined to dismiss it as a cheat, a mere disguise. But that is a shallow view. Green's idealism, applied to the drinker facing a public house closed by the Government, may not get much beyond forcing a man to be free. But empiricism here can but analyse the difficulty; it cannot

---

[1] *Works*, vol. iii., p. 386.
[2] " Lectures on the English Revolution," *Ibid.*, p. 278.

I*

solve it. Men do solve it, for purposes of getting along, by accommodating their desires to their imagination. By an act of faith, in most hardly distinguishable from habit, they submit to a common weal with which they identify themselves. Faith lives upon sacrifice and limitation. The trouble with Benthamism was that it did not provide for sacrifice and limitation. It roundly asserted the identity of the interests of the individual and the interests of the group. Green, more than any other Englishman, succeeded in reconciling the Benthamite temper with the necessities of a faith. His influence at Oxford was very great indeed. He not only, through such men as Bosanquet, perpetuated his influence among leaders of thought. He worked upon the imagination of hundreds of young men who were to do the work of English politics, and enlisted them for the new Liberalism. In the opinion of a doctrinaire like Spencer, indeed, he gave up all that was good in Liberalism. But if we hold the test of individual liberty to be even more a matter of faith than a matter of fact, if we hold that our senses can only so far be free as our imagination is disciplined, if we hold that even a pragmatic balance between liberty and authority must pay its tribute to mysticism, we must regard Green as one of the saviours of Liberalism.

4. SPENCER[1]

Who now reads Spencer? It is difficult for us to realize how great a stir he made in the world. The *Synthetic Philosophy* penetrated to many a bookshelf which held

---

[1] For Spencer's political thought the essentials are contained in *Social Statics* (it is important to compare, especially for omissions, the original edition of 1851 and that of 1897), *The Man versus the State* (1884), and the *Principles of Ethics* (1879-1893), especially the fourth part, entitled "Justice." The *Principles of Sociology* (1877-1885) is an imposing, but not very necessary, book. The *Education* (1861) and the miscellany published as *Facts and Comments* (1902) throw some further light on his political thought. See Spencer, H., *An Autobiography* (2 vols., 1904); Robertson, J. M., *Modern Humanists* (1895) and *Modern Humanists Reconsidered* (1927); Ritchie, D. G., *Darwinism and Politics* (1889) and *The Principles of State Interference* (1891); Macpherson, H., *Herbert Spencer : the Man and his Work* (1904).

nothing else quite so heavy. It lay beside the works of Buckle and Mill on the shelf of every Englishman of a radical turn of mind. It was read, discussed, fought over. And now it is a drug on the second-hand market, and hardly stirs the interest of the German or American aspirant to the doctorate in philosophy. We are more indifferent to this modern *summa* than to the *summa* of Thomas Aquinas. The completeness of Spencer's downfall is almost sufficient to disarm the critic, and it certainly should predispose him to mercy. But Spencer himself was never merciful, not merciful intellectually at least. He seems never to have harboured any kind of doubt. In a century surely not predisposed to scepticism, few thinkers surpass him in cock-sureness and intolerance. He was the intimate confidant of a strange and rather unsatisfactory God, whom he called the principle of Evolution. His God has betrayed him. We have evolved beyond Spencer.

Spencer was born and bred in religious dissent, and proudly traced his love of rebellion to ancestors who held allegiance to " regulations upheld as superior to regulations made by men."[1]   An education which he asserts to have been both scientific and haphazard early convinced him that those superior regulations were the regulations of Nature as embodied in the scientific principle of cause and effect.[2] Be that as it may, Spencer's social antecedents made him to the full representative of Arnold's " dissidence of dissent." He was acutely class-conscious, and disliked all that is associated with the English gentry—its classical education, its loyalties, its sports, its religion, its art and literature. He wholly lacked a sense of humour, not so much out of moral earnestness as out of incapacity to realize the existence of anything outside himself. Mozley of Oriel having referred lightly to Spencer's works as occupying several yards of shelf, Spencer solemnly estimates that several must mean three at least, and asserts that his works occupy but twenty-one inches, or less than one-fifth of three yards.[3] He had no feeling whatever for

---

[1] *Autobiography* (1904), vol. i., p. 12.
[2] *Ibid.*, vol. i., p. 101.   [3] *Ibid.*, vol. i., p. 49.

the arts, especially when they took the form of social graces. Even his love of music was a form of solitary indulgence. He insisted on the necessity for strict objectivity in the thinker, whether his subject was chemistry or sociology. But he repeatedly makes use of the subjective trick of using eulogistic terms for what he likes, and dyslogistic terms for what he dislikes. In the evolutionary process, he wrote, " as law differentiates from personal commands, and as morality differentiates from religious injunctions, so politeness differentiates from ceremonial observance. To which I may add, so does rational usage differentiate from fashion."[1] Similarly he distinguished between " reverential imitation " (which is primitive and bad) and " competitive imitation " (which is modern and good).[2] He denied to the State any right to interfere with the freedom of play of supply and demand, and carried his allegiance to *laissez-faire* so far as to attack sanitary legislation. But he was subject to insomnia, and we find him asserting the right of the State to prevent by law the unnecessary blowing of locomotive whistles.[3]

A complete analysis of Spencer's system would be an intolerable infliction upon the reader. We shall confine ourselves to the essentials of his political thought, and leave the Unknowable and other first principles in the vague background where they belong. Spencer did indeed aspire to the unification of all knowledge through the principle of evolution. Like Comte, he set himself to apply the methods of physical science to the whole field of human activity, and like Comte considered that in sociology he had at last founded a science of society. Causation as the scientist understands it is our master, and operates in politics as it operates in physics and chemistry. This, of course, is an idea already familiar enough to the eighteenth century. But Spencer considers that in the notion of organic growth his own century has made a necessary emendation to the work of the earlier century. Society is indeed the product of natural laws;

---

[1] *Principles of Sociology*, section 432.
[2] *Ibid.*, section 423.
[3] *Principles of Ethics*, section 296.

these laws, however, are not the laws of mechanics, but the laws of biology, of organic growth.

Now the basic law of organic growth is the Darwinian notion of the survival of the fittest. " Of man, as of all inferior creatures, the law by conformity to which the species is preserved, is that among adults the individuals best adapted to the conditions of their existence shall prosper most, and that individuals least adapted to the conditions of their existence shall prosper least."[1] Thus, in free competition, the best tends to survive and the worst to die out. Even before Darwin, Spencer had made a rough and literary anticipation of this doctrine. In the chapter on " The Evanescence of Evil " in *Social Statics* (1851) he asserted that " faculties in excess " tend to disuse, and that " faculties deficient " tend to use and development, thus working towards an equilibrium, and the eventual disappearance of imperfection.[2] That is, progress is a necessary concomitant of our existence.

All this may be true of the life of the individual organism, but is it true of the group ? Is there not an uncrossed gap between the individual and the group ? Spencer answers that there most certainly is not. A group also is an organism, to which almost all the elaborate detail in which biologists have worked out the principle of the survival of the fittest can be applied. A given society—a State—has its youth, its prime, its old age, and death. It can be analysed into sub-sidiary organs just as one analyses the individual organism. The workers, the men who farm the soil, work the mines and fisheries, factories, and workshops, are the alimentary organs of a society. The wholesalers, retailers, bankers, railway and steamship men correspond to the vascular system of an organism. The professional men—doctors, lawyers, engineers, rulers, priests—the thinkers, in short, perform the functions of the brain and the nervous system.[3] Generalizations on the evolutionary growth of the individual hold true

---

[1] *Principles of Ethics*, section 257.
[2] *Social Statics* (original edition), p. 64.
[3] *Principles of Sociology*, part ii., chaps. vii-ix.

of the society. For instance, " complication of structure accompanies increase of mass " in the society as in the individual.[1] Man is larger and more complicated than the polyp, the British Empire than Athens. Or again, over-organization arrests growth in social organisms as in individual organisms, because too much nutrition is taken to purely regulative organs. The lop-sided bureaucracy of the late Roman Empire quite literally drained blood from productive individuals.[2]

If we look at the whole course of man's *social* development, we can see that the process, naturally enough an evolution from lower to higher, from worse to better, may be summarized as the emergence of militant societies from a primitive anarchy, and of industrial societies from militant societies. The first need of primitive man was discipline, and that discipline had to be external. The savage has first of all to learn to live with other men, to work, to accumulate savings, to create a group capable of maintaining itself against other groups and against a hostile environment. He must obey, and he can obey only through fear. Therefore the first step in civilization is taken by the militant society. Absolute monarchy, an authoritative religion, and a binding set of customs are the necessary characteristics of such a society. Aided by a relatively favourable environment, the best-disciplined, the most militant, society will tend to prevail over other societies. But evolution has a further work to do. The militant society is bound to be deficient in intellect, and hence in inventiveness. Law and religion alike suppress individual differences as dangerous to the cohesive force of the State. But it is only through exceptionally gifted individuals that the species is improved. Now in certain good environments—those of the Mediterranean, and Europe in general—militant societies have arisen and overcome the first crude difficulties of the struggle for life. They have thus been able to permit an increase in the division of labour, a greater attention to the arts of trade. But commerce, as distinct from war, encourages individuality and

---

[1] *Principles of Sociology*, section 446, and 228.   [2] *Ibid.*, section 447.

inventiveness. It thrives on freedom, pines away on regulation. Gradually there arose societies of the industrial type,
destined to prevail over and extinguish the militant type.
We are still, however, far from having attained the perfection
of industrial society. In the modern world, militancy is still
not outgrown, and we are at present in the midst of a transitional stage from the lower type to the higher. England,
with her colonies, and the United States, come much nearer
to the finished type of the industrial society than their less
fortunate neighbours. France has been weighed down with
her militant past, and Prussia seems to be even less industrial
in her temper.

We may, for the present, neglect some of the difficulties
involved in Spencer's general political philosophy, and see
what attitude he takes towards the questions of his day. The
most obvious conclusion to which he was driven is that,
since struggle between individuals is the plainest fact of
evolution, society must do nothing to prevent that struggle.
Now one prime difference between militant and industrial
societies is that in the former men are restrained by external
discipline, in the latter by internal discipline. But you cannot develop internal, or self-, discipline, unless you ensure
that every man shall feel the immediate consequences of his
own acts.[1] The struggle for life in an industrial society
develops the moral and intellectual faculties even more than
the physical. (In fact, Spencer goes a long way towards the
pessimistic doctrine of decadence, and inclines to believe
that physical energy, and especially fertility, is in highly
developed societies sacrificed to intellectual development.[2]
He was himself a celibate.) It follows that society must not
protect the weak against the strong. " The ultimate result
of shielding men from folly is to fill the world with fools."[3]
Liberty is thus an essential of the good society. And by
liberty we must understand a State where " every man has
freedom to do all that he wills, provided he infringes not the

---

[1] *Social Statics* (Revised edition, 1893), p. 106.
[2] *Principles of Sociology*, section 39.
[3] *Autobiography*, vol. ii., p. 5.

equal freedom of any other man."[1] This simple and by no means original formula still leaves unsolved the problem as to when an act of one individual infringes the freedom of another to act. Spencer characteristically dodges the problem. About all the State can do is prevent crimes of violence. It is impossible to draw a clear, consistent line between liberty and authority. You say the State should maintain the poor. What is *maintenance* ? A cabin, a two-room cottage ? Potatoes, or a joint ? Fustian or broadcloth ? No, it is too difficult to draw the line. Therefore do not attempt to draw it. Let Nature take her course, and weed out the poor in her kindly way. " Pervading all Nature we may see at work a stern discipline which is a little cruel that it may be very kind."[2]

The sole function of the State in economic life is the rigid enforcement of contracts—a function corresponding to the repression of crimes of violence. " If it be held that an Act of Parliament can make murder proper, or can give rectitude to robbery; it may be consistently held that it can sanctify a breach of contract; but not otherwise."[3] The English State is foolishly trying to do much more than this. The Liberals, who should be committed to the removal of all restraints, are now even worse than the Tories.[4] We have had Factory Acts and Sanitation Acts in direct violation of economic—that is, of natural—law. Spencer's devotion to the abstract principle of *laissez-faire* goes far beyond that of the Manchester men. He objects to laws against unlicensed physicians, against the freedom of the trade in drugs, against the free issue of paper money. He does not even regard State monopoly of coinage as defensible.[5] Anything the Government does is badly done. Spencer announces triumphantly that in America the private express companies have a money-order system which is replacing that of the post office. Postal arrangements, too, should be left to private initiative.[6]

---

[1] *Social Statics*, p. 55.   [2] *Ibid.*, p. 149.
[3] " Railway Morals and Railway Policy," *Essays* (1858), p. 95.
[4] *The Man versus the State* (together with *Social Statics*, 1893), p. 288.
[5] *Social Statics*, pp. 200 ff.   [6] *Principles of Ethics*, section 378.

In fact, government is not essential, but incidental. It does but mark a stage in evolution.[1] We shall have it to put up with for a while. Now the best form of government at present is clearly democracy. A democratic government will be a cheap one; it will be hostile to ceremonial and other false distinctions; it will be jealous of individual liberty. Spencer was not wholly blind to the fact that in his own time democracy was bringing about the very kind of collectivism he detested. He recognized that the " tyranny of the majority " might be as real as older tyrannies.[2] He thinks the supremacy of Parliament as dangerous as the supremacy of the Crown. The way out is first to educate men to resist, or even to ignore, the State, and secondly, as a transitional measure to construct your representative body so that it is based rather on interests, on natural economic groups, than on territorial divisions.[3] Such a representative body will not fail to regard the protection of private property (less a *right* because it is a *necessity*) against the encroachments of the State.[4]

Within a given State, then, we must work towards absolute individual freedom. But any State is surrounded by other States. It is itself an organism competing with other organisms. Must we not apply Darwinian theories to relations between States ? Shall we not say that here, too, the strong prevail rightly over the weak ? Certainly, replies Spencer. That is just what has happened in the past. But he saw well enough that if you emphasize this struggle between States you are soon tempted to sacrifice the individual organism to the social organism. Darwinism in international relations ends inevitably in the doctrine popularly in vogue in pre-war Germany. The strong State is the militant State, the State where the individual submits to a strict external discipline. Spencer's instincts were too strong for such logic, and he very definitely side-steps the issue. Time will give the victory to the industrial State, to the State that waxes great in wealth and intelligence. To defend

[1] *Social Statics*, p. 13.
[2] *Principles of Ethics*, section 344 ; *The Man versus the State*, p. 411.
[3] *Principles of Ethics*, section 351.   [4] *Social Statics*, p. 133.

itself against predatory neighbours, it will be sufficient for such a State to maintain a small but efficient fighting force, and to use that force only to defend itself against attack on its own territory. As other nations progress in industry international law will supplant war, and we shall have a world federation.

Spencer could not, however, entirely throw over traditional ethical notions in favour of absolute struggle. On the contrary, he values highly the sentiment of sympathy, the Christian ethics of love and forbearance. But the place for them is in the family, and in private life. There is an absolute and fundamental distinction between the ethics of the family and the ethics of society. The family exists to protect the young and the weak. Society exists to reward the strong. The family, then, will do what society must never do: it will artificially support and train the child, it will protect the woman. But we must never attempt to transfer, by analogy, these family ethics to society. " The only justification for the analogy between parent and child and government and people is the childishness of the people who entertain the analogy."[1] (A dangerous bit of petulance on Spencer's part, for it cuts much of the ground from beneath his feet.) Women Spencer regarded as insufficiently intelligent, as too uncritically emotional, to carry on the struggle for life in society. He would not admit them to public life, or give them the vote.[2] Polygamy is the natural accompaniment of militant society, monogamy of industrial society. Monogamy as practised in the British Isles is the fine flower of evolution. " Further evolution along lines thus far followed may be expected to extend the monogamic relation by extinguishing promiscuity, and by suppressing such crimes as bigamy and adultery."[3] Freedom here takes its usual course. Grant freedom of divorce, and the causes of divorce, and therefore divorce itself, become inevitably rarer, and finally disappear.

Even outside the family, there is a place for Christian

---

[1] *Principles of Ethics*, section 362.   [2] *Ibid.*, section 336.
[3] *Principles of Sociology*, section 329.

virtues. We must not, indeed, employ the machinery of the
State to aid the weak. But man cannot live by the ethics of
the jungle. Wise charity is good for the donor as well as for
the recipient. Accident may for a time down even the strong.
Moreover, mutual forbearance is a necessary condition of
that internal discipline which must supplant external
discipline. Therefore we must practise altruism: negative
altruism, or the voluntary restraint of one's self from interference with others, as in not practising late hours on a
musical instrument in a crowded city; and positive altruism
or beneficence, the aiding of our deserving brothers in their
misfortune.[1] Spencer has his softer moments. He writes of
maternal affection, " the glistening eye, the warm kiss, the
fondling caress." It is true that he uses this eloquence to
show that a State system of education is unnecessary.[2]

Education, of course, is the capping of Spencer's practical programme. It must be voluntary, and uncursed with
bureaucratic control. Parents, once they are made aware—
presumably by reading Spencer—of the necessity of educating their children, will be glad to pay for that education.
But to make education attractive it must be made to conform
to the practical common sense of the age. The curriculum
must be wholly reformed. We must abandon what are known
as the classics. The Greeks represent a pretty low stage in
evolution (one thinks of Pericles, and then of Herbert
Spencer, clothes and all!), and the Romans were hardly
better.[3] Classical education is but an outmoded, or soon to
be outmoded, form of personal ornamentation, a form
singularly useless to-day. " Men who would blush if caught
saying Iphigénia instead of Iphigenía . . . show not the
slightest shame in confessing they do not know where the
Eustachian tubes are, what are the actions of the spinal cord,
what is the normal rate of pulsation, or how the lungs are
inflated."[4] But this is an age that is transcending mere
ornament. Already men's clothes are not uncomfortable,
and even women, always less willing pupils of evolution, are,

---

[1] *Principles of Ethics*, section 389. [2] *Social Statics*, p. 160.
[3] *Principles of Ethics*, section 268. [4] *Education*, chap. i., p. 43.

in spite of " the still occasional use of paint," becoming a bit more rational in dress.[1]

Our new education then, will be based on physical science. A man trained to *think* as the chemist or the biologist thinks can turn himself with success to business, to art, to literature. Not even the modern languages—though they must be acquired later as tools—can form the bases of education. The study of language " tends . . . further to increase the already undue respect for authority. Such and such are the meanings of these words, says the teacher, or the dictionary." By science, however, the individual is led to formulate questions and answer them himself.[2] Nor would scientific education stifle, but rather free, the poetic impulse. Science *is* poetry, " the grand epic written by the finger of God."[3]

Science, then, will be the staple of the curriculum. We must above all teach open-mindedness, a willingness to evolve truth from opposing errors.[4] Physical education will be an important factor. " To be a nation of good animals is the first condition to national prosperity."[5] A study of hygiene is the natural accompaniment of physical education. Throughout we shall seek to make study interesting, to enlist the voluntary co-operation of the child. Ethics will take care of themselves, if only each child undergoes the full natural consequences of his acts.[6] Finally, our teachers must be psychologists. The greatest need of the present is the scientific training of teachers. We want a technique.[7] That technique is certainly no longer lacking. Spencer's neglected science of education has become one of the most pretentious of sciences.

We must now return to the abstract framework of Spencer's political philosophy, and point out certain difficulties that confront him, and for which he hardly offers a

---

[1] *Education,* chap. i., p. 24.   [2] *Ibid.*

[3] *Ibid.,* p. 83, The *Education* was written in the 'fifties, when Spencer had not yet abandoned God for the Unknowable.

[4] *Ibid.,* chap. ii. Spencer here leans inconsistently enough to the Hegelian view of truth as the reconciliation of opposites.

[5] *Ibid.,* chap. iv., p. 222.   [6] *Ibid.,* chap. iii.   [7] *Ibid.,* chap. i., p. 26 ff.

satisfactory solution. In the first place, there is the theory of
the State as an organism. As we have seen, Spencer carries
the analogy between the living society and the living individual very far. But he stops short at a point which makes his
whole analogy a mere metaphor. He denies that a society
has any being, any will, apart from the individuals who compose it. Or, as he puts it, " as, then, there is no social
sensorium, the welfare of the aggregate considered apart
from that of the units is not an end to be sought. The
society exists for the benefit of its members; not its members
for the benefit of the society."[1] Again, " society having as an
aggregate no sentiency, its preservation is a desideratum
only as subserving individual sentiencies."[2] But if the organic
theory is only a metaphor, it can hardly pretend to be a
theory. All the toil and trouble of evolution has but produced a figure of speech. The fact is that, like Bentham,
Spencer was a determined nominalist. He could never
bring himself to admit that the individual is merged by his
emotions, his intellect, and his imagination with a group
possessing a life of its own. He could not admit that human
beings, building imaginatively on their sense-experience, are
capable of escaping from the solipsism of that experience into
an experience of an intelligible and common external world.
He therefore faces the same difficulty that confronted
Bentham—the problem of the identity of interests. He
solves it, verbally, by the comforting assurance that " public
interests and private ones are essentially in unison."[3]

He can do this, of course, only by appealing to the kind
of idealistic abstraction, of faith, which he strove to repudiate. Spencer's Evolution is, with almost pathetic literalness, a
deus ex machina come to solve this human tangle. Evolution
decided against the unnecessary blowing of locomotive
whistles much as Kingsley's God decided against corsets.
For, assuming that public and private interests are identical,
how can the individual be sure that he is acting according to
his own interests ? The answer, says Spencer, is that if he is

---

[1] *Principles of Sociology*, section 222.   [2] *Principles of Ethics*, section 347.
[3] *Social Statics*, p. 272.

successful, if he obeys the law of adaptation, he has followed his own interests. Evil is " the non-adaptation of constitution to conditions."[1] But what are these conditions, adaptation to which constitutes good ? Why, simply the conditions of life in society. The primitive man was a predatory creature, an anarchist, and to survive he had to exterminate his enemies. Hero-worship, the love of a person in authority, provided the transition to group life, and bore fruit in the kind of social adaptation which has produced our ethics.[2] Spencer has completed his argument in a circle. Evolution has produced Christian ethics. He wistfully confesses, in the preface to the completed *Ethics*, that the evolutionary philosophy has not been able to produce anything startlingly new in ethical principles.[3] Where, as with those who translated Weissmann's theories into ethics, he detected a repudiation of those right humanitarian feelings he valued so highly, he does not hesitate to throw natural selection overboard.[4]

For the mere word evolution does not turn measurement of fact into measurement of value. The remark has been made again and again, but it must be repeated. The very use of the words " higher " and " lower " imply a standard of value not purely mathematical. Spencer certainly was continually using them in that sense. Was not a prize-fighter, or even an Archbishop of Canterbury, as much a product of evolution as Spencer himself ? Why decrease the supply of prize-fighters and archbishops and increase the supply of Spencers ? Spencer, had he faced the question, could only have replied that he valued philosophers— evolutionary philosophers—more highly than he did prize-fighters and archbishops. The process of evolution he regarded, *sub specie æternitatis*, as inevitable, but in the present

---

[1] *Social Statics*, p. 28.   [2] *Ibid.*, p. 233.

[3] *Principles of Ethics*, vol. ii., preface. " The Doctrine of Evolution has not furnished guidance to the extent I had hoped. Most of the conclusions, drawn empirically, are such as right feelings, enlightened by cultivated intelligence, have already sufficed to establish."

[4] " The Inadequacy of Natural Selection," *Contemporary Review*, February, March 1893.

THE PROSPEROUS VICTORIANS

he hardly regarded it as automatic. Retrogression was as possible as progression. Unsuccessful adaptation might, inexplicably enough, turn out to be successful. England had fought a Crimean War, and was in danger of going backwards from an industrial to a militant society. She was passing Factory Acts and Sanitation Acts, protecting the weak against the strong.

But though England might falter, Herbert Spencer would not. To the end of his life, he defended his own free will under the assuring label of scientific determinism. He sought, as most men seek, but with far greater energy and assurance than most men are capable of, to impose his system of values, his faith, on others. That system was hardly unique. It was, as we have seen, typical enough of a nonconformist, middle-class Englishman of the time, turned a bit markedly towards anti-clericalism and physical science. Nor was his trick of decking out his preferences in words with eulogistic overtones, his dislikes in words with dyslogistic ones, at all peculiar to him. It is the common proceeding of the statesman, the salesman, and, one fears, of the artist and the philosopher. It is a proceeding which adds to the interest and variety, as well as to the stability, of human life. It is the necessary foundation of our faiths, the cement of illusion which really does make public interests private interests. It is not, however, or should not be, the common proceeding of the scientist. But no one now supposes Spencer to have been a scientist. He was a salesman of ideas, and we no longer like his goods.

5. BRADLAUGH[1]

Our Victorians so far have been altogether too respectable.

---

[1] Bradlaugh's most characteristic writing will be found in the files of his *National Reformer*, a secularist and radical weekly. His collected *Speeches* (1890) are useful, and certain of his numerous pamphlets, especially *The Impeachment of the House of Brunswick* (1873), *The Land, the People, and the Coming Struggle* (n.d.) and his pamphlets on Socialism, issued in a steady stream in the 'eighties. See Bonner, H. B., *Charles Bradlaugh, His Life and Work* (1894); Robertson, J. M., *Charles Bradlaugh* (1920); Birrell, A., *In the name of the Bodleian, and other essays* (1905).

We have not studied the ideas of a real man of the people, a real popular agitator, since Cobbett. The Chartists, it is true, might have afforded us such men in abundance. But it is impossible to write of Chartism, even as an intellectual movement, by the method of men. No single man, not even Bronterre O'Brien or William Lovell, is sufficiently typical of the movement. " The Political Ideas of the Chartist Movement " deserves to be written, but such a chapter would not fit into our scheme. Bradlaugh, however, is sufficiently apart to stand by himself. He is a valuable corrective to such sedate and scholarly gentlemen as Bagehot and Acton. In Bradlaugh we may study those disreputable elements in Victorian England which the text-book pattern of the age is apt to neglect. That he was in no sense a great thinker, in no sense a seminal mind, need not disturb us. We are attempting, not a history of political ideas in the grand manner, but a series of studies in political opinion. Bradlaugh does represent an important part of English public opinion, one which the currency of such ideas as Bagehot's on the deferential nature of Englishmen has served largely to conceal.

Bradlaugh's life is a tempting one for the new biographer. This teetotaller was born in Bacchus Walk, Hoxton, of humble parentage, and brought up in the surroundings of starved respectability familiar in the works of George Gissing. His father, a solicitor's clerk on two guineas a week, could—and apparently did—write out the Lord's Prayer " in the size and form of a sixpence."[1] Young Bradlaugh went to work at the age of twelve as office boy at five shillings a week. He early showed a fondness for argument—a fondness rather for lawyer-like disputation than for philosophical dialectic—and was indiscreet enough to exercise it in the only field circumstances allowed him to, religion. Sunday-school study of the Bible raised quite natural doubts in him. His parish clergyman, a martinet of the old school, was far too stupid to turn the boy's questionings into other and less dangerous fields. He tried to

---

[1] Bonner, H. B., *Charles Bradlaugh, His Life and Work* (1894), vol. i., p. 3.

put him down, got him dismissed from his position, and even prevailed on the father to deny his unregenerate son admission to the family home. The result was to confirm the son in his unregeneracy, and to drive him into the pulpit of atheism. Young Bradlaugh lived precariously for years, befriended by the family of Richard Carlile and by other "secularists" like G. J. Holyoake, contrived to acquire a good working knowledge of the law, worked quietly as a clerk under his own name, and lectured and wrote on atheism and republicanism as "Iconoclast." In the end, he turned wholly to the business of agitation through lecturing and journalism. His enemies reproached him with getting rich in this trade, a reproach which never failed to stir him, for he did somehow contrive to live by it. But it was not a profitable trade. Bradlaugh had gifts that, in nineteenth-century England, where caste lines were never strong enough to make impossible the career open to talents, would have enabled him to enrich himself as a good Christian solicitor. Instead, he lectured on the authenticity of the Bible, the causes of the French Revolution, the sins of the House of Brunswick (Hanover), at 3d. admission, and passed his life in a struggle with poverty. He amassed an excellent library, but that was all.

Bradlaugh gloried in the epithet "atheist," and thought Holyoake's "secularist" and Huxley's "agnostic" weak concessions to Christian respectability. Yet he was no romantic Promethean, and his atheism was hardly more than what is commonly called scientific materialism. "He did not deny that there was 'a God,' because to deny that which was unknown was as absurd as to affirm it. As an atheist he denied the God of the Bible, of the Koran, of the Vedas, but he could not deny that of which he had no knowledge."[1] But he did believe in an order of Nature. "To an atheist there are no other causes—there can be no other causes—than may be included in the word 'nature.' 'Supernatural' to the Atheist is a word of self-contradiction. An Atheist may and must concede that there are many things which he cannot now explain, but he does not in this also admit that no

---

[1] From a speech of Bradlaugh's, quoted in Bonner, *op. cit.*, vol. i., p. 87.

explanation would be possible if his knowledge were more complete."[1]

Atheism, then, is no mere negative challenge. "We have no creed, but we have much faith; faith in the possibility of human progress; faith in digging after truth."[2] Organized Christianity must refuse to admit the possibility of human betterment here on earth. It is committed to an other-worldliness which prevents men from getting to work at putting this world in order. "According to religionists, this world's bitter misery is a dark and certain preface, 'just published,' to a volume of eternal happiness, which for two thousand years has been advertised as in the press and ready for publication, but which after all may never appear."[3] Bradlaugh's atheism is thus but the necessary preface to his politics. "You first challenge the imaginary revelation in which the alleged divine endorsement is recorded, you show how the books and their evidence grew in the hands of the Church, how they have used the ignorance of mankind, and made it a weapon and shield of their policy; you strip the king of the certificate of divine revelation, and teach that manliness is higher than kingliness in its own right, and show that society has alone the power out of its own sovereignty to make its own rulers independent of Church and God— this is the province of our scepticism."[4] Montaigne would have been a trifle surprised at this sort of scepticism; but we have before insisted that the nineteenth century was above all an age of faith.

Bradlaugh always insisted that even in his purely theological disputes he was fighting for the poor of England. Infidelity—even professed infidelity—was not uncommon among the educated, though many of them were too weak to acknowledge their unbelief. But religion was regarded as a necessary anodyne for the poor. The boasted right of free speech was not the right of every Englishman. "You have not won free speech yet. You have not won the right for the

---

[1] *National Reformer*, 28th March 1886.　　[2] *Speeches* (1890), p. 205.
[3] *Poverty : Its Effects on the Political Condition of the People* (n.d.), p. 5. This, incidentally, is an excellent example of Bradlaugh's popular style.
[4] *National Reformer*, 27th March 1870.

poor man to be an Atheist yet."[1]   Atheism must therefore unite itself with radicalism.   " The politics of the Free-thought body are essentially Radical, and here the co-opera-tion of the large working-men's associations may be per-manently secured.   Already some of the largest mining organizations work with us on most friendly terms for political ends."[2]

Bradlaugh's politics are founded upon his republicanism. The Crown is the indispensable buttress of the Church and the aristocracy.   Before Englishmen can work out a more just social scheme, they must abolish the monarchy.   We tend, even to-day, to think all Englishmen devoted monar-chists.   It is true that the republican movement was never very strong in the nineteenth century, but for a time in the 'seventies it did attain some sort of organization.   There was held at Birmingham in May 1873 a conference of British republicans numbering fifty-four accredited delegates from as many republican clubs scattered from Aberdeen to Ply-mouth, from Norwich to Cardiff.[3]   The *National Reformer* is full of republican enthusiasm, not to be contained in prose.

> " Has England forgotten Cromwell's teaching ?
> Is Hampden's poured-out blood all in vain ?
> Shall the land which saw a king's impeaching
> Now be bound by a Brunswick chain ?
> Our sires veil their faces in shame
> For the sons who disgrace their name,
> Who bow to a crownèd thing,
> To a puppet they call a king.
> To arms! Republicans!
> Strike now for Liberty!
> March on : march on: Republicans!
> We march to victory."[4]

The right to deal with the Throne is, by the Act of Settle-

---

[1] *National Reformer*, 10th April 1870.   [2] *Ibid.*, 19th September 1875.
[3] For Bradlaugh's part in this movement, see Bonner, *op. cit.*, vol. i., p. 353.
[4] " The English Marseillaise," by " Ajax," *National Reformer*, 26th September 1875.

ment, invested in the English people through their Parliament. Therefore all Parliament need do is coolly and simply to deny the throne to Albert Edward, or to anyone else, and the thing is done.[1]

This end is not to be achieved by revolution. No lasting republic can be set up in England by pike aid.[2] Violence always defeats itself. But Englishmen have already the beginnings of a republic. Household suffrage is almost universal suffrage. If the workers will listen to reason—instead of to Disraeli, for instance—and elect to Parliament members of their own class pledged to carry through a republican platform, we may put an end to the monarchy without violence. Meanwhile, we may agree on certain radical measures which will help to put the coming republic on a sound basis.

Bradlaugh put forward, on first presenting himself (unsuccessfully) to the electors of Northampton in 1868, a political programme which sums up pretty well the ideas to which he held constantly. First, there must be a system of compulsory education—compulsory through the primary grades—administered under the supervision of the national government and supported by local taxation. Second, the law of real property must be modified in the direction of equality of inheritance and easy transferability. The abolition of primogeniture must be carried out at once. Third, pensions to noblemen, of which a greater number than the public realizes have survived the attacks of Benthamism, must be withdrawn[3] and all public departments subjected to a rigorous system of accounting. Fourth, taxation must be consistently revised so as to fall progressively upon wealth, and to take a part of the unearned increment of land. Fifth, the legal relations between labour and capital must be improved by providing special courts of arbitration in labour disputes. Sixth, Church and State must be finally separated by the disestablishment of the Church of England. Seventh, after suitable consultation of experts like Hare and

---

[1] *Impeachment of the House of Brunswick* (1875), p. 6.

[2] Quoted in Bonner, *op. cit.*, vol. i., p. 255.

[3] Bradlaugh lists these pensions in a pamphlet, *Perpetual Pensions* (n.d.).

Mill, a scheme of minority representation must be adopted. Eighth, all disabilities for publishing speculative opinions must be abolished. There must be no law of blasphemy. Ninth, the House of Lords must be reformed. Bradlaugh thinks the best plan is to grant all future peerages for life only. Tenth, the monopoly on public affairs of the old ruling classes, both Whig and Tory, must be broken by the establishment of a new national party to govern by ability alone.[1] To this programme Bradlaugh later added, and helped realize, a bureau of labour statistics to investigate into prices, rates of profits and wages, marketing conditions and the like, and thus to permit a fairer settlement of industrial disputes.[2]

We shall comment later on the economic conservatism of this programme. For the present, it is sufficient to remark that Bradlaugh's republic was not in conception very different from the republic of Robespierre. Bradlaugh belongs to that now old-fashioned school of politics stemming from the revolutions of the eighteenth century. His republic was based on the ideology of liberty, equality, fraternity, " that true liberty, which infringes not the freedom of my brother; that equality which recognizes no noblemen but the men of noble thoughts and noble deeds; that fraternity which links the weak arm-in-arm with the strong, and, teaching humankind that union is strength, compels them to fraternize, and links them together in that true brotherhood for which we strive."[3] He belonged to that London group of radical Englishmen and exiled foreigners which, with all its diversity, represented pretty well the republican tradition in Europe—Simon Bernard, Herzen, Bakunin, Allsop, Talandier, Holyoake, Gustave Jourdain, Félix Pyat.[4] He was, indeed, like Paine before him, honoured by nomination to a French Assembly. Fortunately, he declined the opportunity to take an active part in French politics in 1871.[5]

---

[1] Bonner, *op. cit.*, vol. i., pp. 264-265.
[2] *National Reformer*, 18th June 1876.
[3] *London Investigator*, 1st November 1858.
[4] See the description of the scene at the funeral of Bernard in Bonner, *op. cit.*, vol. i., p. 204.   [5] *Ibid.*, vol. i., p. 321.

Now this republican tradition, from the days of the Jacobins on, has got itself embodied in a ritual, has acquired a symbolism and even a faith, which has enabled it to attain corporate form, and which has, in the Third French Republic, acquired a surprising stability. It never, in England, succeeded in supplanting the hierarchical society so beloved by Liberals like Bagehot as well as by Tories like Disraeli. But there are traces of it in the pages of the *National Reformer*. Bradlaugh, on a trip to the North, describes a miners' meeting which seems almost like a French civic festival. The men from the different collieries entered Durham in a procession, with music and banners. The South Tanfield colliery bore a banner inscribed with the life-size likeness of Charles Bradlaugh, trampling on a broken sceptre, with a crown at his feet. On one side of the St. Helen's and Tindale banner were likenesses of Henry Hunt, Ernest Jones, Feargus O'Connor and Thomas Paine. The reverse of the Nettlesworth banner showed Liberty, a female figure, striking off the fetters from a kneeling man, and the inscription " I am persuaded that an hour of virtuous liberty is worth an eternity of bondage." The West Stanley lodge bore a banner showing a man with a pig's head—or a rat's head, for the drawing was a trifle weak—wearing clerical garments like those of the Bishop of Durham, and inscribed " £15,000 per year."[1]

Such people were not to be moved by Tory democracy. Bradlaugh himself detested Disraeli, and insisted that no alliance was possible between English working men and the old aristocracy. The battle is " between Tory obstructiveness and the advancing masses; between vested interests and human happiness; between pensioned and salaried lordlings and landowners' off-shoots on the one hand, and the brown-handed bread-winner on the other."[2] The ultimate issue of the battle is certain to be victory for the people.

The issue is perhaps still uncertain to-day; but at any rate the people have ceased to feel that Bradlaugh's republic

---

[1] *National Reformer*, 23rd August 1874.
[2] Quoted in Bonner, *op. cit.*, vol. i., p. 228.

THE PROSPEROUS VICTORIANS

is worth struggling for. After the 'seventies, though his Northampton constituency remained true to him, Bradlaugh's following fell off. His later years were spent in constant opposition to the Socialist tendencies of the English Labour movement. His social and economic doctrines had begun to seem old-fashioned. He marks the end of an era in English radicalism.

In endless debates with Hyndman, Bax, and other Socialist leaders, including his own devoutest disciple, Mrs. Annie Besant, Bradlaugh reiterated the stock arguments of economic Liberalism against Socialism. The doctrine of the class war is fratricidal and un-English. " The cry of vengeance raised [against the *bourgeoisie*] was criminal, it was also a blunder; for if nothing was to be done until the middle class was exterminated, then hope was impossible; it never could be exterminated. There should be no question of war in any political movement between the working and the middle classes."[1] Socialists are in too much of a hurry; they want to do by violence what, if it can be done at all, can only be done slowly. But it cannot be done at all. The Socialists, whatever their divisions, are agreed on the abolition of private property, on the control of production by the State. But " all labour under State control means the utter stagnation of special industrial effort; . . . the stoppage of the most efficient incentive to inventive initiative." In the Socialistic State there would be no savings, no capital. There would be no check-up on industrial efficiency, and no discouragement to individual waste. Such a State would be inevitably despotic, would be obliged to put a stop to all freedom of speech, and would therefore end in mental stagnation.[2] No one would do the unpleasant work; a Socialist State would fall from a simple inability to get its bottles washed.[3]

Socialism, then, is not a solution for the difficulties of the

---

[1] From a speech of Bradlaugh's, quoted in Bonner, *op. cit.*, vol. i., p. 327.
[2] " Socialism : Its Fallacies and Dangers," *North American Review* (1887) p. 18.
[3] *Will Socialism benefit the English people ? Written debate with E. Belfort Bax*, p. 16.

English working classes. It aims at a dead-level uniformity which would put an end to progress. It would erect a tyrannical State to do inefficiently what can best be done by individual initiative. The English workman, therefore, will ask of the State only that it prevent unfair competition, that it encourage by law the diffusion of wealth which is the natural result of economic freedom. Bradlaugh voted for the Truck Act, for truck shops are a form of unfair competition. But he voted against the Eight Hours Law, which he considered to be paternalism.[1] His whole programme is based on the belief that the career open to talents is in itself a solution of social difficulties.

For if the State will only remain decently neutral, and not protect vested interests like the Church, the landed aristocracy, and the great capitalists, men will themselves attain a rough, but never deadening equality. First, as to the industrial workers. The State must, of course, provide for them a system of compulsory education, and it must maintain factory and sanitary inspection. But at bottom the workmen must help themselves. This they can do under present conditions, if they will but save. Bradlaugh holds those optimistic doctrines as to the possibility of making each workman a capitalist held to-day only by American economists like Professor Carver. To the workmen he says " You can earn it, the Rothschilds' wealth, the Overstones' wealth, the Barings' wealth—you, the millions, if you are only loyal to yourselves and to one another, may put all this into your own Savings Banks, and your own friendly societies, and your own trade unions, within a dozen years. You accumulate it for others: you can do it for yourselves."[2] The State, indeed, will, by progressive taxation, including inheritance taxes, prevent the extremes of individual accumulation.[3] But the main check on inequality will be the voluntary organization of the workers. Trade unions will cancel the bargaining weakness of the individual labourer. But strikes are not a desirable weapon. They are wasteful, and they pro-

---

[1] Bonner, *op. cit.*, vol. ii., p. 190.
[2] *Ibid.*, vol. ii., p. 189.   [3] *Debate with E. Belfort Bax*, p. 17.

mote an ill feeling which, on the part of the labourer, may end in an embittered espousal of Socialism. " A strike meant starvation, meant misery, meant demoralization; it meant the wan wife and the pining children. . . . He did not mean to say there never were occasions on which strikes were justifiable, but he meant to say that strikes were like wars— they did more mischief than they did good. . . . He held the doctrine, that a bad arbitration was better than a good strike."[1]

Second, as to the agricultural labourers. Here, too, we must avoid the extremes of collective exploitation and of great individual owners. The thing to work for is an independent class of small proprietors. Bradlaugh, like his Jacobin predecessors, is for expropriation—though in a very mild form—but not for collectivism. Like them, he challenges not the principle of private property, but what he regarded as its abuse. Primogeniture, the Game Laws, and all such buttresses of the great landlords must be removed at once by State action—a thing perfectly within the reach of a Parliament elected by universal suffrage. Then the State will take possession of all uncultivated land, indemnifying the owners in Government bonds at the rate of twenty years' purchase, and then lease it in small parcels on long-term leases to tenants willing to work it. Eventually these tenants will buy the land from their profits.[2] For the agricultural as for the industrial worker, salvation lies ultimately in himself. " Especially should the legislature be careful not to profess to do that for the worker, which it is reasonably possible for him to do for himself without the aid of the law. A duty enforced by others is seldom so well performed as a duty affirmed by the doer."[3]

An indispensable condition for this self-help, however, is the possibility of voluntary limitation of their numbers on the part of the lower classes. Malthus's position is in itself impregnable. But Malthus's remedy is an impossible one.

---

[1] Speech to Durham miners, reported in *National Reformer*, 16th July 1876.

[2] *The Land, the People, and the Coming Struggle*, pp. 12-14.

[3] Quoted in Bonner, *op. cit.*, vol. ii., p. 191.

K2

What he calls moral restraint cannot, human nature being what it is, operate effectively to reduce the birth rate. Wicked Christian asceticism and middle-class prudery have combined with the selfish interests of the exploiters of labour, short-sighted capitalists who think to profit from a cheap labour market, to prevent by law the communication to the poor of a knowledge of the methods of artificially limiting births. The rich possess and employ such knowledge. It is unjust—nay, suicidal, to withhold it from the poor. Bradlaugh was one of the pioneers of the neo-Malthusian movement. His secularist publishing-house reprinted a pamphlet, *The Fruits of Philosophy*, by a Bostonian physician named Knowlton. *The Fruits of Philosophy* is a pretty maudlin dissertation on true love in a style not wholly out of fashion with present-day exponents of birth control, but it does in the last few pages impart specific, if rather crude, information on contraceptive methods. Bradlaugh and Mrs. Besant worked together to disseminate the pamphlet, and were tried and convicted for publishing indecent literature. On appeal Cockburn quashed the indictment on the purely technical ground that the indecent passages had not been set forth in full, but the pamphlet was of course suppressed. The trial, however, as Cockburn himself remarked, had given the whole movement a publicity it would not otherwise have obtained so easily, and the ultimate victory lay with Bradlaugh. It is curious to note that medical students were among the most determined hecklers at meetings on the population question in the 'seventies.[1]

Bradlaugh was always in difficulties with the authorities and with the great mass of the respectable. It seems strange now that anyone should want to suppress an atheist. But though Victorian England never seriously attempted to prevent the diffusion of Socialist doctrines which, as Bradlaugh saw, were fundamentally antagonistic to the whole fabric of Victorian civilization, it did try to prevent Bradlaugh's harmless fulminations against the Deity. Local

[1] Bonner, *op. cit.*, vol. ii., pp. 27-55.

Churchmen organized mobs to shout him down; they exercised pressure on hotel-keepers to refuse him lodging; they threatened to take away the licences of halls where he spoke; they put a brass band to play in a field next to the spot where he was trying to give an open-air address. The Devonport chief of police having arbitrarily imprisoned Bradlaugh for trying to deliver a public address, Bradlaugh sued him and was awarded a farthing's damages. Lord Chief Justice Erle upheld the decision, saying that " if the plaintiff wanted to use his liberty for the purpose of disseminating opinions which were in reality of that pernicious description [i.e. atheistic], and the defendant prevented him from doing that which might be a very pernicious act to those who heard him . . . might be a matter he might afterwards deeply regret, it might be that the jury thought the act of imprisonment of the plaintiff under such circumstances was in reality not an injury for which a large money compensation ought to be paid, but on the contrary was an act which in its real substantial result was beneficial to the plaintiff, and so the nominal wrong would be abundantly compensated by the small sum given."[1]

Bradlaugh's election to Parliament from Northampton, and his subsequent refusal to take the Parliamentary Oath in the name of a God he could not accept, caused his rejection as a person incapable of taking his seat. The ensuing struggle is strangely parallel to the case of Wilkes a century before, and ended as that one did, in the vindication of the right of a constituency to send to Parliament the man it has chosen. The whole episode seems now a bit absurd, quite out of place in nineteenth-century England. But it does give point to speculations like those of Bagehot on the irrational inertia of society, on the reluctance of men to admit innovation in matters of faith. The extraordinary thing about the Bradlaugh case is the ineptness of his conservative opponents. They made him a martyr, which is always a mistake. But they did worse. They treated as an enemy a man who was really their ally. Bradlaugh's political and economic philosophy

---

[1] Bonner, *op. cit.*, vol. i., p. 187.

was, as we have seen, essentially conformist. Only his trappings were radical—a republicanism, which, moreover, he was not unwilling to put on the shelf, and an atheism which really was a firm belief in Victorian progress. One is drawn to the belief that most men care more for the trappings than they do for the essentials, and even to the shocking heresy that they cherish their beliefs more highly than they do their interests.

6. MORRIS[1]

Most socialistic thought in the later nineteenth century lies beyond our province. Fabianism, as well as the beginnings of the practical organization of the Labour Party, must be regarded as a part of the intellectual history of the twentieth century. We cannot, however, omit socialist thought entirely. William Morris, though his influence is not wholly dead, is definitely a child of his age. Modern Socialism, if it is still occupied with the problem of the incentive to labour, is no longer anything like so sure as Morris that its chief concern is to make the world safe for Art. *News from Nowhere* is for us rather a symptom than a programme. In Morris we may discern one of the ailings of Victorian society.

Morris is one of the " misguided superiors," born into comfortable middle-class surroundings and educated as an English gentleman. His socialism was not the product of his own economic failure—on the contrary, he was a shrewd and capable business man who could turn even pre-Raphaelite decorative art into commercial profit. Nor was he psychologically at odds with his environment from anything like an

---

[1] Of Morris's writings, those of immediate interest for the historian of political thought are contained in *News from Nowhere* (1891), *A Dream of John Ball* (1888), *Hopes and Fears for Art* (1882), and *Signs of Change* (1888). These, together with additional material, chiefly unpublished lectures on Socialist questions, are collected in vols. xvi, xxii, and xxiii of Miss May Morris's edition of the *Works* (24 vols., 1910-1915). The letters in the *Life* by J. W. Mackail (1899) are indispensable. See also Clutton-Brock, A., *William Morris : his Work and Influence* (1914) ; Phelan, A. A., *The Social Philosophy of William Morris* (1927).

inferiority complex. In the main it is true that he rebelled from the ways of English life because he felt these ways to be ugly. But there are other elements in his socialism. He hated the pedestrian routine of modern industrial life with all the hatred of romantic individualism. He used to say of Bellamy's *Looking Backward* that " if they brigaded *him* into a regiment of workers, he would just lie on his back and kick."[1] He took a certain Bohemian pleasure in defying mere convention. He was touched with that peculiarly English eccentricity which, in the upper classes, is usually disciplined into cleverness and Toryism. Modern English cooking he thought was in a barbarous state, largely through the influence of women, and concluded that " there are two things about which women know absolutely nothing, dress and cookery."[2] He had a high sense of duty, which made him personally uncomfortable over the existence of poverty as a social institution, although, as Rossetti remarked, he would never give a penny to a beggar.[3] But the charitably disposed of this world, like Rossetti himself, do not make good reformers. Morris was a true moralist, more affected by institutions that seemed to perpetuate injustice than by individual instances of injustice. Finally, he loved to tamper with things, to make things better. He might have said of himself what he said of a character in one of his romances. " Even though he half saw it he began to dream about it, as his way was about everything, to make it something different from what it was."[4] Surely society, too, could be made something different from what it was ?

Morris came late to Socialism. His middle age was devoted almost wholly to his work as an artist, and his politics went no farther than voting for liberal candidates. The Bulgarian atrocities first stirred him to action. " I know what the Tory trading stock-jobbing scoundrel that one calls an Englishman to-day would do about it [Turkey];

---

[1] *Works* (ed. by May Morris, 24 vols., 1910-15), vol. xvi., p. xxviii.
[2] Quoted in Mackail, J. W., *The Life of William Morris* (2 vols., 1899), vol. i., p. 224.
[3] *Ibid.*, vol. ii., p. 94. [4] *Ibid.*, vol. i., p. 20.

he would shut his eyes hard over it, get his widows and orphans to lend it money, and sell it vast quantities of bad cotton."[1] His first political activity was to join in 1877 the Eastern Question Association, of which he became treasurer. More and more he came to feel that he had a work to do in politics. " It does sometimes seem to me," he wrote in 1882, " a strange thing that a man should be driven to work with energy and even with pleasure and enthusiasm at work which he knows will serve no end; . . . am I doing nothing but make-believe, then, like Louis XVI.'s lock-making ? "[2] Good furniture was not enough. His conversion to Socialism was a matter of half a dozen years. A reading of Mill's posthumous essay on Fourier convinced him that individualist economics were wrong, that Fourier was right against Mill.[3] He told himself that if he were poor instead of rich, he would be a blank rebel. Factory labour would be an endless misery to him. Was it not then a misery to those who were obliged to undergo it ? No Liberal or Radical political programme got to the heart of the difficulty. Any real change must be social, and social change can only be achieved by giving the poor a new religion. Organized socialism gave promise of being such a religion.[4] Morris therefore espoused it, preached for it, wrote hymns for it, always perhaps a little too self-consciously for a man who has undergone complete conversion.

For though Morris accepted Marx, and even tried to read him, though he clothed the economic interpretation of history in the quaint words of his John Ball, though he talked bitterly of the class war, he was never a good sectarian socialist. His dislike of English society was too much æsthetic and moral, too little mystical, to allow him to lose himself in a common cause. We must first of all see what it was in English society that he disliked.

England is ugly, and gets uglier daily. " Even if a tree is

---

[1] Quoted in Clutton-Brock, A., *William Morris : His Work and his Influence* (1914), p. 139.

[2] *Ibid.*, p. 145.

[3] " How I became a Socialist," *Works*, vol. xxiii., p. 278.

[4] Mackail, *op. cit.*, vol. ii., p. 107.

cut down or blown down, a worse one, if any, is planted in its stead."[1] Whatever of loveliness exists is a heritage from the Middle Ages—the countryside, the village churches, a few lay Gothic buildings here and there. The Renaissance began the corruption which the machine age has finished. Everything man touches, from cotton cloth to poetry, he continues to make ugly. Now a society is no better than its art. In the Middle Ages—though they were very far from being a Utopia—civil order had got reconciled to a sturdy, innate self-respect in the individual. Private wars, murder, robbery there were in the Middle Ages, but no degrading wage slavery, no social snobbery, no flimsy goods, no vulgarity. " Their arms and buckles and belts and the finishings and hems of their garments were all what we should now call beautiful, rough as the men were; nor in their speech was any of that drawling snarl or thick vulgarity which one is used to hear from labourers in civilization; not that they talked like gentlemen either, but full and round and bold, and they were merry and good-tempered enough."[2]

The Renaissance and Reformation corrupted society and politics as they corrupted Art. They confiscated land from the Church and turned it over to a new and rapacious nobility. They set up the civil government as the supreme power, with its chief function the protection of private property. The Reformation revived in a noxious form the ascetic principles of Christianity which in the Middle Ages had found a harmless outlet in monasticism, and consecrated this asceticism as part of the ethics of capitalism. Morris excluded Milton from his emendation of Sir John Lubbock's hundred books, adding that " the union in his [Milton's] works of cold classicism with Puritanism (the two things which I hate most in the world) repels me so that I *cannot* read him."[3] Finally the industrial revolution brought with it middle-class democracy, factory work, wage slavery, and cheap goods.

---

[1] *Works*, vol. xxiii., p. 171.
[2] " A Dream of John Ball," *Works*, vol. xvi., p. 219.
[3] *Works*, vol. xxii., p. xv.

These changes may almost be summed up in their worst aspect. Work has been made unpleasant. Now *Nature* has made work necessary for man, but, just as she has made the act necessary for carrying on the race pleasant, so she clearly meant that work should be pleasant.[1] Man has perverted work by divorcing it from its end, the satisfaction of creating something new, something personal, something beautiful. Worse, he has set up the doctrine that work implies suffering, that it is therefore a moral good. " It has become an article of the creed of modern morality that all labour is good in itself—a convenient belief to those who live on the labour of others."[2] Theorists therefore feel obliged to search for an incentive to labour, to defend competition, even starvation, on the ground that only by such means can men be made to do the necessary work of the world; whereas the true incentive to labour lies open to common sense, in pleasure in the work itself.[3] The energies that in the Middle Ages constructed the throne of a Philip Augustus or a Richard Cœur de Lion no more lovingly and more beautifully than a peasant girl's wedding-chest must remain a mystery to our Manchester theorists. We shall not go far until we bring them back again.

Now our ugly society glories in the fact that it is a competitive society. But " the condition of competition between man and man is bestial only, and that of association human."[4] Competition has undermined the moral virtues of which beauty is the flower. The cult of beauty as preached by our modern poets is a mere ivory tower, the amusement of an aristocratic group, and therefore destined to failure as art. All great art stems from the people, rests on a sound moral basis. As the evils of competition are moral, so must the cure for those evils be moral. Now the root of the trouble is this, that under the so-called career open to talents, all men hope that they, or at least their children, may enter the ranks of the exploiters. " In the days to come," John Ball is told, " poor men shall be able to become lords and masters and

---

[1] *Works*, vol. xxiii., p. 98. [2] *Ibid.*
[3] Mackail, *op. cit.*, vol. ii., p. 244. [4] *Works*, vol. xxiii., p. 172.

do-nothings; . . . and it shall be even for that cause that their eyes shall be blinded to the robbing of themselves by others, because they shall hope in their souls that they may each live to rob others: and this shall be the very safeguard of all rule and law. . . ."[1]

Such a competitive society, though it preach freedom of opportunity, must soon take on the form of a caste society. Modern England is divided into rich and poor with a rigorousness the Middle Ages could not have understood. "The difference between lord and commoner, noble and burgher, was purely arbitrary; but how does it fare now with the distinction between class and class ? Is it not now the sad fact that the difference is no longer arbitrary, but real ? Down to a certain class, that of the educated gentle-man, as he is called, there is indeed equality of manners and bearing . . . but below that class there is, as it were, the stroke of a knife, and gentlemen and non-gentlemen divide the world."[2] Millions are condemned by the mere dropping of their aitches to remain social inferiors all their lives.

In this society, men of learning, artists, lawyers and the like, men who should serve the whole community by serving knowledge and beauty, have become mere spongers on the rich, infected like them with a desire for noisy ostentation. The citizen of the ideal State of *News from Nowhere*, looking back at nineteenth-century universities, says " They (and especially Oxford) were the breeding-places of a peculiar class of parasites, who called themselves cultivated people; they were indeed cynical enough, as the so-called educated classes of the day generally were; but they affected an exaggeration of cynicism in order that they might be thought knowing and worldly-wise. The rich middle classes . . . treated them with the kind of contemptuous toleration with which a mediæval baron treated his jester."[3]

Finally, this competitive society has entirely lost sight of the fact that the end of production is the making available of good, useful, beautiful things. Competition is literally war,

---

[1] *Works*, vol. xvi., p. 283.   [2] *Ibid.*, vol. xxiii., p. 153.
[3] *Ibid.*, vol. xvi., p. 70.

K*

and goods produced are valued for their use as instruments of conquest. Cotton cloth is but the powder and bullets of the great manufacturer. In this struggle the consumer is helpless. " The goods are forced on him by their cheapness, and with them a certain kind of life which that energetic, that aggressive cheapness determines for him."[1] Adulteration follows inevitably, and, fashion aiding, flimsy and pretentious goods drive out the sound as bad coins drive out good ones. Taste is so corrupted that not even expensive products, not even the luxuries of the rich, escape the contamination. And these fruits of the machine, these achievements of large-scale production, are not really cheap. In the first place, they are as we have seen adulterated, sleazy, badly made. In the second place, their real cost is immensely increased by our ridiculous system of marketing. " Competitive salesmanship, or, to use a less dignified word, the puffery of wares, has now got to such a pitch that there are many things which cost far more to sell than they do to make."[2] In the third place, the lauded interplay of supply and demand is so inadequate, so much at the mercy of the war between capitalists for markets, that periodically " the thing is overdone, and the market is glutted, and all that fury of manufacture has to sink into cold ashes."[3] Labourers starve in idleness where recently they had overworked and overspent. In the long run, the vagaries of the cycle of trade cancel out what benefits labour might gain from machine production.

Now one proposed way out of the muddle of English life may be condemned offhand. This is the shallow solution of the Radical party which derives from eighteenth-century individualism. Let the competitive system go on, these Radicals say. Let us have increased democracy in politics, universal suffrage, and so on. Let us protect the small man against the great monopolist. Let us encourage the workman to save, to invest his savings, and set himself up as a capitalist. Let us encourage the agricultural labourer to acquire a small holding, and set himself up as a small pro-

[1] *Works*, vol. xxiii., p. 8. [2] *Ibid.*, p. 103. [3] *Ibid.*, p. 8.

prietor. We shall thus attain a State of rough and happy equality. But this is no solution at all. In the first place, as Marx has pointed out, the inevitable tendency of the times is towards the concentration of capital. But even if you do try and encourage the workman, by profit-sharing and other such schemes, to save a little, you will but succeed in getting a few to lift themselves out of their class, and become worse human material than they now are. The present lower middle class are almost the worst in the community. They ape the bad habits of their betters, and they despise those below them. " Though they live in a kind of swinish comfort, . . . they are ill housed, ill educated, crushed by grovelling superstitions, lacking reasonable pleasures, entirely devoid of any sense of beauty."[1] Similarly peasant proprietorship can but raise a new middle class at the expense of the disinherited, a middle class stuffier and more conservative than the old. The old revolutionary shibboleths can no longer be our guides. " It is not Absolutism and Democracy as the French Revolution understood those two words, that are the enemies now; the issue is deeper than it was; the two forces are now Mastership and Fellowship."[2] Some democrats may call this outworn revolutionary nonsense " practical," because it seems like doing something, because it has the force of habit. But the really practical thing nowadays is steady propaganda for a new principle.[3]

That principle is socialism, revolutionary socialism. There can be no " rose-water cure " for the evils of modern society.[4] Intense, religious propaganda on the part of the small band of socialists must eventually win over the labouring classes, persuade them that the career open to talents is really but a bludgeon held over them by their masters, and lead them on to victory through sheer force of numbers. Morris is not, at least on paper, frightened by the idea of catastrophe. The romantic lover of the simple passionate life of Norse legend feels that our present artificialities, our overburdened, over-intellectual world,

[1] *Works*, vol. xxiii., p. 184.
[2] *Ibid.*, p. 122. [3] *Ibid.*, p. 32.
[4] *Ibid.*, vol. i., p. 366.

must go down as the corrupt Roman world went down. "How often it consoles me to think of barbarism once more flooding the world, and real feelings and passions, however rudimentary, taking the place of our wretched hypocrisies."[1]

Morris, as we have said, accepted the Marxian structure of ideas for the framework of his new republic. John Ball listens—we trust with some amazement—to the Marxian theory of surplus value. The free man of the future "shall sell himself, that is the labour that is in him, to the master that suffers him to work, and that master shall give to him from out the wares he maketh enough to keep him alive, and to beget children and nourish them till they be old enough to be sold like himself, and the residue shall the rich man keep to himself."[2] Chattel slavery of the ancient world has developed through serfdom of the Middle Ages to our present system of slavery through the contract between capitalist and worker. This is an evolutionary process which cannot stop. The rich are getting richer, and the poor poorer. The system will finally break up from over-tension, and evolution will lead through revolution to socialism.[3]

But Morris's Marxism sat lightly upon him. Heckled once at a Glasgow meeting he burst out: "I am asked if I believe in Marx's theory of value. To speak quite frankly, I do not know what Marx's theory of value is, and I'm damned if I want to know."[4] Morris's socialism is old-fashioned and Utopian, though at the heart of it is a problem any society, socialist or individualist, must face—the problem of the incentive to labour. For Morris, art, in its widest sense, is the only possible incentive to useful work. He admits that English workmen do not now care for art. "They do not miss it, or ask for it, and it is impossible as things are that they should either miss or ask for it."[5] Here, indeed, and not in any Marxian dialectic, is the true justifica-

[1] Mackail, op. cit., vol. ii., p. 144.   [2] Works, vol. xvi., p. 272.
[3] Mackail, op. cit., vol. ii., p. 106.
[4] Glasier, J. B., William Morris and the Early Days of the Socialist Movement (1921), p. 32.
[5] Works, vol. xxii., p. 63.

tion for revolutionary socialism. We must destroy the corrupting machine, we must bring back the old handicrafts by the action of a determined minority. Once the worker is transferred to a suitable environment, he can again go to work with pleasure.

Morris, at home in his comfortable house in Hammersmith, hears a crowd of noisy ruffians go by, and begins to get angry, " till I remember, as I hope I mostly do, that it was my good luck only of being born respectable and rich, that has put me on this side of the window among delightful books and lovely works of art, and not on the other side, in the empty street, the drink-steeped liquor-shops, the foul and degraded lodgings. *I know by my own feelings and desires* what these men want, what would have saved them from this lowest depth of savagery: employment which would foster their self-respect and win the praise and sympathy of their fellows, and dwellings which they could come to with pleasure, surroundings which would soothe and elevate them; reasonable labour, reasonable rest. There is only one thing that can give them this—art."[1] But competition, the capitalist system, will not allow the workman to be an artist. " The poor devil of the fourteenth century, his work was of so little value that he was allowed to waste it by the hour in pleasing himself—and others; but our highly-strung mechanic, his minutes are too rich with the burden of perpetual profit for him to be allowed to waste one of them on art; the present system will not allow him—cannot allow him—to produce works of art."[2]

Under such conditions, men will naturally not work unless the club of starvation is held over their heads. Their work, which should free them, enslaves them further. A socialist society must break this vicious circle by abolishing a money economy, and by restoring the worker to his work. Characteristically Morris thought highly of the work of Fourier, and considered him far more important in the history of socialism than St. Simon or Proudhon.[3] Like

---

[1] Mackail, *op. cit.*, vol. ii., p. 21.   The italics are mine.
[2] *Works*, vol. xxiii., p. 90.   [3] *Ibid.*, p. 73.

Fourier, he insisted that variety of work is essential. The monotonous repetition involved in machine work is the most inhuman thing about it. Machines, indeed, we need not entirely abolish. But they must cease to be our masters. " If the necessary reasonable work be of a mechanical kind, I must be helped to do it by a machine, not to cheapen my labour, but so that . . . I may be able to think of other things while I am tending the machine."[1] Steady labour at one task is impossible to the artist. Pleasantly varied tasks, interspersed with periods of rest, are essential. Above all, the worker must see his work through, must produce something finished, something his own, something in which he can take an artist's pride.

On the governmental machinery of the socialist State, Morris is very vague. He inclines to the easy way out involved in the formula that government will not be necessary in a State where industrial conditions make for contentment. He inclines definitely to communism—in the old-fashioned sense of the word—as opposed to State socialism. He holds " that individual men cannot shuffle off the business of life on to the shoulders of an abstraction called the State, but must deal with it in conscious association with each other: that variety of life is as much an aim of true Communism as equality of condition, and that nothing but an union of these two will bring about real freedom."[2] Like Owen, whom he greatly admired, he believed that Nature would ensure diversity even in a society which deliberately sought to control her. He looked forward to a considerable degree of communal life—great halls for the common meals, open-air markets where all would mingle freely, common apartment houses. The separate house of to-day does but nourish an insolent pride of ownership, sets the individual off from the group, prevents a true feeling of social solidarity.[3] In the Utopia of *News from Nowhere* there is no government, but only " arrangements."[4] Government means law courts, police, the army and the navy, and there will be no need of

---

[1] *Works*, vol. xxiii., p. 20. [2] Mackail, *op. cit.*, vol. ii., p. 244.
[3] *Works*, vol. xxiii., p. 23. [4] *Ibid.*, vol. xvi., p. 79.

these. There are no criminals " since there is no rich class
to breed enemies against the state by means of the injustice
of the state."[1] Crimes of violence are produced by private
property, property in things and property in women, and by
family tyranny. In the new society, there will be no such
property. Crimes of passion may occur until men have
completely adjusted themselves to the freedom of the sexes,
but they will be sufficiently corrected by the remorse of the
criminal.

Morris, then, like so many other excellent men, is an
anarchist at heart. He is never drawn in the least towards
the Platonic idea of benevolent despotism. " Fancy a
Carlylean aristocracy of talent, the country under the
benevolent rule of Senior Wranglers and LL.D.'s."[2]
Similarly, he dodged completely the problem of the nation-
State, and its relation to individual freedom. " Modern
nationalities," he maintained, " are mere artificial devices
for the commercial war that we seek to put an end to, and
will disappear with it."[3] Nationality is a mere mechanical
product of capitalist propaganda; men are stimulated into
feeling themselves Englishmen or Frenchmen as they are
stimulated by capitalist salesmanship into feeling a desire for
goods of a certain trade-mark. Socialism will deal with this
as it deals with other capitalist shams.

The socialist agitation into which Morris bravely, and
rather repugnantly, entered was hardly calculated to confirm
him in optimism. Indeed, *News from Nowhere* is even more
than most Utopias the idyllic refuge of a disheartened man.
It was not merely that the radical workmen were indifferent
to art and socialism. The socialists themselves were very
far from practising the solidarity they preached. Morris
describes a meeting in Cleveland Hall in 1887 to protest
against the war menace of Boulangism: " The foreign
speakers were mostly of the ' orthodox Anarchists '; but a Collectivist also spoke, and one at least of the Autonomy section,
who have some quarrel which I can't understand with the

---

[1] *Works*, vol. xvi., p. 80.   [2] Glasier, *op. cit.*, p. 101.
[3] Mackail, *op. cit.*, vol. ii., p. 245.

Cleveland Hall people: a Federation man spoke though he
was not a delegate; also Macdonald of the Socialist Union:
the Fabians declined to send on the grounds of the war-
scare being premature: but probably in reality because they
did not want to be mixed up too much with the Anarchists:
the Krapotkine-Wilson people also refused on the grounds
that bourgeois peace *is* war, which no doubt was a genuine
reason on their part and is true enough."[1] Morris strove
valiantly to further the cause, writing, lecturing, addressing
pathetic meetings like the one described in *The Pilgrim
of Hope*:

> " Dull and dirty the room. Just over the chairman's chair
>   Was a bust, a Quaker's face with nose cocked up in the
>   air;
> There were common prints on the wall of the heads of
>   the party fray,
> And Mazzini dark and lean amidst them gone astray.
> Some thirty men we were, of a kind that I knew full well,
> Listless, rubbed down to the type of our easy-going
>   hell."[2]

But he saw himself pushed out by more energetic and less
art-loving men like Hyndman, saw himself obliged to give
up his journal, the *Commonweal,* saw socialist divisions
increasing. He must have had ironic doubts about the
movement he had hymned.

> " Why then, and for what are we waiting ? There are
>   three words to speak;
> WE WILL IT, and what is the foeman but the dream-
>   strong wakened and weak ? "[3]

Morris is vague beyond most social thinkers. We have
seen that he paid little attention to the actual machinery of
government. Yet he had, like all thinkers, a pattern which
he sought to realize on this earth, a set of values acceptance
of which by his fellows would solve the antithesis of order
and disorder, authority and liberty. Art was for him what

---

[1] Mackail, *op. cit.*, vol. ii., p. 174.   [2] *Works*, vol. xxiv., p. 382.
[3] "The Day is Coming," *Works*, vol. ix., p. 181.

God, Providence, Destiny, Right, or the Law of Nature was for Carlyle what Science was for Spencer, what the Catholic Church was for Newman, a convenient absolute to sum up these regulative values. Now art is a peculiarly untrustworthy absolute. Few men would now find a Morris chair beautiful. The London of *News from Nowhere*, even though the Houses of Parliament have become a dung-market, would not for most of us be a very attractive place. The art of living is not a pre-Raphaelite art. In so far as Morris merely maintains that English society must become more and more collectivist, and that it must be held together as a society by a sort of moral solidarity—or moral sovereignty, if the latter word be stripped of its Austinian rigidity—he was undoubtedly right. But he was wrong in the specific content he assigned to that moral sovereignty.

Again, Morris is perhaps wrong about machine labour. It is almost impossible for men who make a living, or who do but amuse themselves, with the pen not to regard mechanical labour with something of the pathetic fallacy. It is a fact that some men love machines as Morris loved figured wall-papers and fine printing. It may even be a fact that the range of human inequality is so great as to include men who are not irked by tasks involving what to highly strung men would be intolerably monotonous repetition. Such a conclusion may seem a snobbishly superior one, one that can be used to justify the worst tyrannies of the factory system. But to hold it temporarily, to test it by experimentation, is at least a useful corrective to the sentimental assimilation of all men to the creative artist which is one of the unquestioned axioms of the school of Ruskin and Morris.

Yet we cannot wholly dismiss Morris as an artist at odds with his environment. *News from Nowhere* has its arresting passages. Morris and his guide Dick, in " Kensington Forest," come across a band of road-menders, a dozen strong young men " looking much like a boating party at Oxford would have looked in the days I remembered, and not more troubled with their work." It seems that the gangs would compete in getting the work done quickly and well. Dick's friends would chaff him with " Well rowed, stroke!

Put your back into it, bow." Morris thought this not much of a joke, but Dick replied that " everything seems like a joke when we have a pleasant spell of work on."[1] One is tempted at first to dismiss the incident as a quaint and rather ineffective bit of sentimentalism, as simply another attack from a different quarter on the muddied oafs and flannelled fools of modern sport. But it is true that an eight-oared crew puts forth in a race an amount of desperate energy that would dig a great many ditches. To a non-oarsman, at least, that expenditure of energy, in itself, can hardly seem to involve less of the elements to which common language assigns unpleasantness—labour, travail, suffering—than would ditch-digging. By some miracle, the pain of rowing is transcended, and that certainly by no hope of monetary reward. To put the problem of labour as one of turning labour into a sport by rather childish stimulation of the competitive spirit and the team spirit is no doubt putting it in falsely simple terms. But we can hardly avoid Morris's conclusion, that the best of human energies are put forth for their own sake, and that a society that assumes monetary wealth and the fear of starvation to be the best incentives to labour simply will not draw out these human energies at their maximum.

7. MAINE[2]

There is nothing in the personality of Sir Henry Maine to confuse the student of his ideas. A brilliant scholar, with a gift for the kind of generalization he distrusted in others, a faithful civil servant, a valued contributor to the *Saturday*

---

[1] *Works*, vol. xvi., p. 47.

[2] Maine's most characteristic contribution to political thought in the narrower sense is his Tory *Popular Government* (1885). His studies in historical jurisprudence, which can be interpreted in other than Tory senses, have perhaps been more influential. These are *Ancient Law* (1861), *Village Communities* (1871), *The Early History of Institutions* (1875), *Dissertations on Early Law and Customs* (1883). See Grant Duff, Sir M. E., *Sir Henry Maine* (1892); Evans, H. O., *Theories and Criticisms of Sir Henry Maine* (1904); Vinogradoff, Sir P., *The Teaching of Sir Henry Maine* (1904); Morley, J., " Maine on Popular Government," *Studies in Literature* (1891).

Review, he led a sober, useful life which has never tempted the biographers. By temperament a philosophical conservative, he was touched with the liberalism hardly any thinker in an age of progress could avoid. But there is no trace of unrest or rebellion in his life or in his work. He had " as little of the *frondeur* in him as any man I have ever known,"[1] wrote his friend Grant Duff. We may, then, proceed straight to the study of Maine's work.

The author of *Ancient Law* prided himself above all as being the founder in England of the historical, or as he later preferred to call it, the comparative, method of studying human society. Now history is not, for Maine, poetry, drama, " philosophy teaching by example," but a science, and must, like other sciences, arrive at " continuous sequence, inflexible order, and eternal law."[2] The most useful task to which the historian can apply himself is the study of primitive societies. He must, to borrow a useful analogy from the practice of the biologists, set himself to work on " political embryology."[3] The clue to the present lies in the distant past. Now most modern political thought has been falsified by the uncritical acceptance of generalizations like the " Law of Nature " and the " Social Contract," which are completely unhistorical, and which imply an erroneous notion of the origins of our civilization.[4] The objective study of primitive societies, and especially of those primitive Aryan societies from which Englishmen and Hindus alike stem, shows that the patriarchal theory is the only tenable explanation of the origin of our society.

If you go far enough back in the history of Germanic, of Celtic, of Roman, of Hindu peoples (it is this use of the past of peoples geographically separate that raises the historical method into the comparative method) you will find that they all are based on the patriarchal family. This family might be defined as " sexual jealousy indulged through Power."[5]

---

[1] Grant Duff, Sir M. E., *Sir Henry Maine* (1892), p. 23.
[2] *Village Communities and Miscellanies* (1880), pp. 265-266.
[3] *Dissertations on Early Laws and Customs*, p. 247.
[4] *Ancient Law.*, p. 77, ff.
[5] *Early Law and Customs*, p. 209.

The trouble, indeed, with those who, like McLennan, see in sexual promiscuity the origins of social life is that they fail to recognize that sexual jealousy is one of the abiding facts of human nature. The patriarchal family has left numerous traces in the law of more highly developed societies, of which the most obvious is, perhaps, the Roman *paterfamilias*. The family consists of the father, or the patriarch, and his immediate descendants, with their womenfolk. Land and flocks are held in common by the family, and individual private property is unknown. The family, in fact, is a little society, governed despotically by the oldest male member. Gradually it evolves a religion of its own, based on ancestor-worship, an ethics, and a whole set of customary practices. Religion, ethics, and custom come to limit the power of the patriarch, and to fix the status of the individual in the group. There arises, then, the notion of law as opposed to the mere caprice of the ruler. But this notion of law is not at all our modern notion of legislation. The law is discovered, not invented. It does not provide for a change in social relations. It does but sanction an existing arrangement.

The transition between the family group and the larger unit of the tribe begins very early, and is probably coincident with the transition from nomadism to settled agriculture. It is made possible by a procedure common to primitive peoples, and not wholly strange to us, that of legal fictions. The tribe, and later the State, is assimilated to the family. The fiction of *adoption* makes it possible to extend the bounds of the family. Worship of a supposed common ancestor makes it possible to evolve the *gens* and similar groups from the simple family. Meanwhile economic forces are tending to disrupt the tenure of property in common. The family community first becomes the village community, traces of which are clear in modern India, in Ireland, and in the feudal institutions of the conquerors of the Roman Empire. Though the details of this form of economy vary with soils, crops, and similar factors, the land is considered the common property of the community. Given families do possess separate allotments for tillage purposes, but these allotments, originally at least, seem to have been made with the definite purpose of securing equality between families. Capital, which from its etymology was clearly at first in cattle, is not subject to this equal division. It tends to accumulate in the hands of the chief and his immediate followers—a process especially clear in Ireland—and to lead to a division between rich and poor. Successful foreign conquest further aids this tendency to supplant primitive equality with economic classes. The growth of trade, the rise of towns and cities, comes to complete this economic process. Meanwhile, the law undergoes a parallel development. The legal fiction of adoption is followed by other legal devices in the law of testamentary succession, of marriage, of contract, which serve to facilitate the breaking-up of property in common and the growth of property in severalty. The whole process may be summed up, in a phrase which Maine made famous, as the change from status to contract.[1]

But the development from status to contract is not an inevitable one. It may be arrested at any point by a great number of forces. Indeed, only in Western Europe has the development been complete. Only in " progressive " societies has contract fully supplanted status. " The natural condition of mankind (if that word ' natural ' is used) is not the progressive condition. It is a condition not of changeableness but of unchangeableness. The immobility of society is the rule; its mobility is the exception."[2] Men do not easily accustom themselves to innovation, to the effort of doing what they and their fathers have never done. " What is easy to a man is that which has come to him through a long-inherited experience, like walking or using his fingers; what is difficult to him is that in which such experience gives him little guidance or none at all, like riding or skating."[3] Democracy, Maine clearly implies, is like skating, monarchy or aristocracy like walking. We have again the argument from analogy, designed as an appeal to the sister science of biology.

Social immobility is moreover furthered by the imitative

---

[1] *Ancient Law.*, chap. v.
[2] *Popular Government*, p. 170.   [3] *Ibid.*, p. 171.

faculty which man has always possessed. This faculty may indeed be enlisted, through the device of legal fictions, to accustom men to accept a change by pretending that it is really no change at all. We can see in India how fiction, sometimes of the most audacious kind, has transmuted " even broken hordes, mere miscellanies of men . . . into definite social forms, which afterwards might seem as if they had all sprung together from roots deep in the Past."[1] But on the whole this imitative faculty has been an obstacle to change. It leads to the establishment and hardening of fixed social customs. It turns against the innovator the disapproval of the group. It tends to preserve status and limit contract.

Now a man who makes a contract is making, within limits, of course, a voluntary adjustment between himself and the outside world. He is making something of himself. Maine distrusted the revolutionary connotations of the words, and does not himself put the matter this way. But he really does mean by contract what others have meant by individualism or liberty. The man who submits to external conditions, who regulates his conduct by obedience to custom, has not risen beyond status. The man who consults something in him mysteriously his own is the man capable of contract. Freedom of contract can hardly mean more than freedom to pursue one's own interests. History taught Maine what reason had taught Bentham.

Contract has won out over status—or, to use commoner terms, even though Maine did not like them, individualism has won out over collectivism—only in progressive societies. Much has gone into making that victory possible—the growth of commerce, the development of law, and especially of Roman law, the emergence of science and its triumphant warfare with superstition. The Greeks were the first progressive people. " Except the blind forces of Nature, nothing moves in this world which is not Greek in its origin "[2] —a phrase which has been the delight of defenders of classical education ever since Maine coined it. But the most fundamental thing in the whole process is the element of private

---

[1] *Early Law and Customs*, p. 285.   [2] *Village Communities*, p. 238.

property. Maine writes scornfully of " that utter barbarism in which private property is unknown."[1] Property in severalty is historically later than property in common. All our notions of evolution therefore show us that the former kind of property is better than the latter. It is true that " it is not the business of the scientific historical enquirer to assert good or evil of any particular institution. He deals with its existence and development, not with its expediency." But in his very next breath Maine, apparently willing enough to abandon the *rôle* of scientific historian, asserts that " nobody is at liberty to attack several property, and to say at the same time that he values civilization."[2] Civilization and several property have developed together, and are inseparably connected. History may not be philosophy teaching by example, but she does not refuse to teach truths convenient for an English gentleman with a dislike for socialism.

It is not difficult to criticize Maine's use of the historical method. In the first place, his knowledge of detail was often inadequate. Modern historical research has accumulated an immense mass of facts in almost every field of history. So great indeed is this mass that historians are commonly quite overwhelmed by it, and are unable to make any generalizations whatever. It is tempting to see in the cautious professional research historian of to-day a kind of mental weakling, and to regret the fine courage with which Maine threw out generalizations. Yet the conquests of thought are always conquests over fact, and we ought not to yield to a snobbishly artistic contempt for the grubber among facts. Such grubbers have often a humility before the complexity of life which is nearer the critical spirit than is the pride of the theorist. Now Maine simply did not have facts enough. He found traces of his village communities in India, and characteristically concluded that such communities had prevailed all over India at an earlier period. Baden-Powell, who spent much of his life in a study of the land systems of India, found severalty villages through most of

[1] *Early History of Institutions*, p. 128. [2] *Village Communities*, p. 230.

the peninsula, joint villages only in the North and North-West. Even these villages, he concluded, did not give unfailing support to the status-contract theory. He found the greatest variety of stages in village organization, and refused to label any stage as " typical." Maine had reached his conclusions from inadequate evidence.[1] So, too, modern research has found the Roman law far less simple than Maine found it, and it can by no means accept his assurance that European feudalism is almost wholly Roman in origin.

Maine was led to neglect inconvenient facts, or to abandon research after he had amassed a set of convenient facts, by his fondness for ringing generalizations. Of these, the theory of a common " Aryan " origin of his progressive peoples—and some unprogressive ones, like the Hindus—has gone down before the attacks of ethnologists. The very word Aryan is now under suspicion. Again, Maine's theory of sexual relations among primitive peoples—at least among " Aryan " peoples—has not stood up. He was shocked by the writings of McLennan and Lubbock, which asserted that " assemblages of men followed practices which are not found to occur universally even in animal nature."[2] He could not admit the possibility that men had ever practised sexual promiscuity. He could not get the patriarchal family out of such conditions, and he had to have the patriarchal family. Now modern anthropology simply refuses to accept any formula for primitive sexual relations, for the primitive family, or for primitive property. Anthropological research, like historical research, has reached a point where it is forced to be sceptical of generalizations. But if the patriarchal family and primitive communism both go, Maine's famous formula goes also. Divested of the historical inevitability which seemed to Maine to make it respectable and not at all anarchic, the theory of growth from status to contract becomes a mere assertion that modern man is more individualistic than primitive man.

---

[1] Baden-Powell, B. H., *The Land Systems of British India* (3 vols., 1892).
[2] *Village Communities*, p. 18.

The fact that the historical method led to a conclusion as stale as this should lead us to suspect that the method was not as novel as Maine liked to think. He was always insistent on the opposition between the historical method and the *a priori*, or " natural law " method of studying man or society. " Whenever (religious objections apart) any mind is seen to resist or contemn that mode of investigation [the historical method], it will generally be found under the influence of a prejudice or vicious bias traceable to a conscious or unconscious reliance on a non-historic, natural condition of society or the individual."[1] Rousseau is in the modern world the chief protagonist of the theory of the state of Nature. Maine is hardly outdone by Mr. Irving Babbit in finding Rousseau at the bottom of everything he dislikes.[2] Natural law has indeed its origin in the Roman *jus gentium*. But the Roman lawyers at first only reluctantly sought a common rule to facilitate their relations with foreigners. The *jus gentium* became the law of Nature only under Stoic notions of moral equity; and the Stoics interpreted Nature as a restraint upon the passions. The eighteenth century, and especially Rousseau, retained the notion that men are equal before Nature, and added the notion that their desires are good. Therefore democracy appeared as the only justifiable form of government, as a natural society opposed to our present unnatural society.[3]

That is, a man under the influence of these theories would be led to obey only when he had what he wanted. If he had not what he wanted, he would not accept his status in society. But if he consulted the historical method, he would realize that he was a creature of infinitely slow growth, that generations of his fathers had gone into his making, and into the making of his social environment, that he must therefore accept his status as determined by society. Yet as we have seen, Maine's formula for progressive societies by no means counsels this obedience to authority. Maine's difficulty is at

---

[1] *Ancient Law*, p. 187.   [2] *Ibid.*, p. 84 ff.
[3] *Popular Government*, p. vii.

bottom the same as Spencer's. For the historical, or if the term is preferred, the genetic, sciences do not in themselves, any more than do the mathematical or physical sciences, provide a scale of values by which men can guide their conduct. The historian, if he but search far enough, can find almost anything in the past. Unless he is willing to adopt a consistent monism, and apply the idealists' formula to the past, in the form of " whatever has been, has been right," he will be obliged to judge the past as Acton judged it, in accordance with standards which are his own, which do not derive automatically from the historical process itself. The historical method taught Marx the inevitability of socialism, and it taught Maine the impossibility of socialism. Each man must have held that the other was misusing the historical method. We, if we are but willing to accept a pluralistic universe, may say that each found in history what he wanted to find, and that the same opportunity is open to us all. This may seem to some a meaningless surrender to a chaotic subjectivity. It does not, however, imply that there is no such thing as an historical fact in the common-sense use of the word; it does not entitle one to deny that such a person as Oliver Cromwell ever existed. But it does recognize that there is a difference between stating that Oliver Cromwell had a wart on his face, and stating that his policy was wise, or good, or necessary, or in accord with the inevitable evolution of English political life. Since men do differ over such statements as the latter, modesty would at least counsel us to conclude that they may so differ. Or, to put the matter on the plane of the sort of generalizations with which Maine dealt, we may say that he was perfectly justified in maintaining that the experience of the race showed the institution of property in severalty to be a good thing. But he was not justified in maintaining that no sensible man could hold that property in common was a good thing. Above all, he was not justified in identifying private property with so grandiloquent a word as " civilization," nor in holding that the past showed a unilateral development from a primitive communism to modern individualism, nor in holding that anything outside his own desires, any " law

of evolution," taught him that the civilization of England
was higher, or better, than that of China.[1]

At most, an attention to the past of the race, even to a
man as full of theories as Maine, does but encourage a
certain conservatism of temperament. The simple plans of
men have so often been cheated in the past by the complexity of their environment that the student of the past is
led to distrust men's plans. Maine was rash enough in
speculating about primitive societies, but his political thought
is timid when it deals with contemporary questions. Morley
said of *Popular Government* that "the tone is that of the
political valetudinarian, watching with uneasy eye the ways
of rude health."[2] The remark is that of a political opponent,
himself enjoying a rude health that was to receive a bitter
shock in 1914, but it is not wholly unjust. *Popular Government* is a somewhat querulous book.

Maine makes to the defenders of democracy a reproach,
which however justified, sounds strange in the man who discovered the law of change from status to contract. " Democracy is receiving the same unqualified eulogy which was
once poured on Monarchy, and though in its modern shape
it is the product of a whole series of accidents, it is regarded
by some as propelled in a continuous progress by an irresistible force."[3] Poor George Bancroft, who was standing for
" some " in Maine's mind at the moment, did indeed
deserve the criticism. But would it be wholly unfair to say
that the author of *Ancient Law* had his notions, too, of
irresistible development in politics ?

Modern democracy is for Maine the child of Rousseau. It
might be well to add that it is also the child of the *cahiers*, of
the industrial revolution, of a desire for human equality at
least as old as Athens. In fairness to Maine, we must admit
that he elsewhere pointed to the neglect of the *cahiers*, to
" that preference for general explanations of phenomena

---

[1] Maine admits that " our assumption of the absolute immobility of the
Chinese and other societies is in part the expression of our ignorance." Still,
he holds that outside Europe societies are in a " prolonged state of infancy "
rather than in a " different maturity." *Early History of Institutions*, p. 226.
[2] *Studies in Literature*, p. 110.   [3] *Popular Government*, p. 82.

which has always been a heavy drawback on French genius."[1]
But he himself had a fondness for such general explanations,
and he indulged it in *Popular Government*. Rousseau's
notions—and ours—of popular government are but
" another set of deductions from the assumption of a State
of Nature."[2] Man is assumed to have within him good
instincts which are suppressed or misdirected by his
present social environment. These instincts are at their
purest in the common people, less corrupted by convention,
by tradition, than the holders of power, the minority of kings,
nobles, priests, and lawyers. Give power to the common
people, let your government be a mere agent whose acts are
determined by a consultation of the popular voice through
universal suffrage, and you will liberate these good instincts.
A democratic government is a natural government and good;
all others are artificial and bad.

Rousseau is only too right in thinking that the common
man is nearer to Nature. The common man is indeed almost
a savage. " Like the savage, the Englishman, Frenchman,
or American makes war; like the savage, he hunts; like
the savage, he dances; like the savage, he indulges in
endless deliberation; " (compare this with Bagehot's view
that primitive man does not deliberate, but indulges in over-
hasty action) " like the savage, he sets an extravagant value
on rhetoric; like the savage, he is a man of party, with a
newspaper for a totem, instead of a mark on his forehead or
arm; and, like a savage, he is apt to make of his totem his God."[3]
This is the petulance of the cultivated man before the simplicities of popular taste. Maine has the true conservative
distrust of his fellows. Common men do not like the things
he likes. This fact he puts in the form dear to conservatives
from Plato on. Men do not know " what is good for them."
" It is inconceivable that any legislator should deliberately
propose or pass a measure intended to diminish the happiness of the majority of the citizens. But when this multitudinous majority is called to the Government for the purpose
of promoting its own happiness, it now becomes evident that,

---

[1] *Early Law and Customs*, p. 292.
[2] *Popular Government*, p. vii. [3] *Ibid.*, p. 144.

independently of the enormous difficulty of obtaining any
conclusion from a multitude of men, there is no security that
this multitude will know what its own happiness is, or how
it can be promoted."[1]

In fact, democracy in practice becomes inevitably government by parties, or rather by the alternation of parties. And
since these parties must each strive to enlist the greatest
number of voters, they must make their appeal on grounds
of sentiment and prejudice. They must fit themselves to the
lowest common denominator, the inferior man. " Some men
are Tories or Whigs by conviction; but thousands upon
thousands of electors vote simply for yellow, blue, or purple,
caught at most by the appeals of some popular orator."[2]
True differences between parties tend to be sunk in these
stereotypes, and the party struggle becomes a mere step to
personal power for the leaders, a mere indulgence of primitive combativeness for the followers. Parties in a democracy
tend to become very like one another, and each party grows
more and more homogeneous. Again, a democracy is always
seeking, in the name of a sentimental doctrine of equality, to
put an end to " the strenuous and never-ending struggle for
existence, the beneficent private war which makes one man
strive to climb on the shoulders of another and remain there
through the law of the survival of the fittest."[3] Yet, though
Malthus has been re-enforced by Darwin, though the survival of the fittest has become the central law of biological
science, " it is evidently disliked by the multitude, and thrust
into the background by those whom the multitude permits
to lead it."[4] Democracy is hostile to the progress of which it
claims to be the fruit. It is true that American democracy
has not put an end to this struggle, that in no country is
there so great an inequality of private fortune and domestic
luxury. But the Americans, thanks to Hamilton, have
erected their Constitution as a check upon democracy.[5]
" The Americans of the United States . . . are a nation because
they once obeyed a king."[6]

Now democracy is in theory the rule of the majority.

[1] *Popular Government*, p. 166.   [2] *Ibid.*, p. 32.   [3] *Ibid.*, p. 50.
[4] *Ibid.*, p. 37.   [5] *Ibid.*, p. 51.   [6] *Ibid.*, p. 28.

Since it aims at levelling, since it gives free rein to the censoriousness of common men, it does indeed show a jealousy of individual distinction, it does encourage indirectly, and it does enforce, especially in social life, the tyranny of the majority.[1] But in actual practice popular governments are peculiarly open to the tyranny of minorities, of crank minorities, not of the enlightened few. Democracy must promise immediate blessedness. What wonder if groups of men, inspired by that blind and hasty faith which is one of the weaknesses of human nature, should strive to exact fulfilment of the promise, and become sectaries of civil life, irreconcilables who would force their standards on the majority ? Maine makes an unfortunate choice for an example of the irreconcilables when he points to the Russian nihilists and their disregard for the Tzarist majority, for the Russia of 1880 was hardly a democratic society.[2] He insists that the tyranny of the crank minority is typical of popular governments, that the process of legislation is in such governments fatally easy. " A number of persons, often a small minority, obtain the ear of the governing part of the community, and persuade it to force the entire community to conform itself to their ideas."[3]

Moreover, democracies are helpless before modern nationalism. " There is no more effective way of attacking them than by admitting the right of the majority to govern, but denying that the majority so entitled is the particular majority which claims the right."[4] The doctrine of self-government applied to national groups contains within itself a fatal tendency to a *reductio ad absurdum*. Let the Irish govern themselves. But who are the Irish ? Has Ulster any less right to self-determination than the rest of Ireland ? Nationalism really aims at a diversity inconsistent with democratic egalitarianism.

Finally, democracies are self-destructive, and must end, as Aristotle long ago saw, in dictatorship. Already even England is in the first stage of this process. The House of

---

[1] *Popular Government*, p. 22.   [2] *Ibid.*, p. 26.   [3] *Ibid.*, p. 170.
[4] *Ibid.*, p. 28.

Lords is being shorn of its power. " We are drifting towards a type of government associated with terrible events—a single Assembly, armed with full powers over the Constitution, which it may exercise at pleasure."[1] Moreover, the House of Commons itself is too large to govern. Its weakness, and the modern trust in professional administrators, " will probably lead to a constitutional revolution, the House of Commons abandoning the greatest part of its legislative authority to a Cabinet of Executive Ministers."[2] Once arrived at this stage, that of dictatorship is not far off. Perhaps we are now as inconscient of the failings of democracy as were the French nobility in the eighteenth century of the failings of aristocracy. Maine could dimly distinguish in the 'eighties what some men think they can now discern clearly, the figure of an English Mussolini.[3]

Maine on democracy is what is popularly known as a destructive critic. He was engaged in pointing out what he regarded as the dangers of popular government, and not in suggesting how to avoid those dangers. But by implication at least we may discern his own programme. He puts great trust in the English Constitution, in the famous mixed government which gives a definite place to Crown, lords and commons, and thereby prevents any one element in English society from imposing its will on the rest. He trusts that the gifts of common sense and moderation, of reluctance to snatch at Utopian political good worked out by pure reason, which have hitherto been English characteristics, will continue. But chiefly he trusts that Englishmen will not surrender themselves and their possessions to the modern State. Maine may almost be said to mark a turning-point in English conservatism, as Green marks a turning-point in English liberalism. Just as Green is a liberal who, in spite of certain qualifications, trusts the State, the common thing, to improve and thereby to liberate the individual, so Maine is a conservative who distrusts the State.

Maine's famous attack on the Austinian doctrine of sovereignty is really a defence of the individual, bolstered by

---

[1] *Popular Government*, p. 126.   [2] *Ibid.*, p. 95.   [3] *Ibid.*, p. 5.

his natural contractual relations with other individuals, by his ethical inheritance, by his group loyalties, against the exactions of the modern Leviathan State. Austin's sovereignty is arrived at by a process of abstraction, legitimate enough as an intellectual device in certain sciences, but not in jurisprudence. " We reject in the process of abstraction by which the conception of Sovereignty is reached . . . the entire history of each community."[1] There is much more in sovereignty than force, more in laws which are the commands of sovereigns than regulated force. " The vast mass of influences, which we may call for shortness moral, perpetually shapes, limits or forbids the actual direction of the forces of society by its Sovereign."[2] These influences we can analyse and understand only by the use of the historical method. This method will lead us in contemporary politics to abandon the utilitarian idea of sovereignty, and to accept what later writers were to call pluralism. It will in particular lead us to question one of the simplifications which has most aided in popularizing the omnipotent modern State—the notion of rigid national differences. Nationality is but one of the products—one of the accidents—of history, and is perpetually modified by changing institutions. You cannot explain the present condition of Ireland by a glib reference to the Irish " character."[3] Above all, race theories founded on linguistic similarities are unscientific, and dangerous allies of unscrupulous power. Pan-Germanism, pan-Slavism, are modern inventions, abstractions quite at odds with the facts of history. The theory is at its worst when " men, and particularly Frenchmen, speak of the Latin race."[4] The modern State is already sufficiently a creature of abstraction without adding to its prestige the abstraction of nationality.

Our best resort to-day is to let Nature—not, of course, the Nature of Rousseau—take its course, to trust in the whole nexus of human relationship which has been built up, and which is now building up, under freedom of contract. " Legislation has nearly confessed its inability to keep pace with the activity of man in discovery, in invention, and in the

---

[1] *Early History of Institutions*, p. 360.   [2] *Ibid.*, p. 359.
[3] *Ibid.*, pp. 96-97.   [4] *Village Communities*, pp. 209-210.

manipulation of accumulated wealth. . . . The law even of the least-advanced communities tends more and more to become a mere surface-stratum, having under it an ever-changing assemblage of contractual rules with which it rarely interferes except to compel compliance with a few fundamental principles, or unless called in to punish the violation of good faith."[1] Speaking before the council in India on a Bill proposing jail penalties for frauds in contract, Maine said, " Knowing, as they all did, that all the modern progress of society seemed to be intimately connected with the completest freedom of contract, and *in some way almost mysteriously dependent on it*, he should shrink from tampering with so powerful an instrument of civilization."[2]

Maine's conclusions thus strangely resemble those of that dangerous radical, Herbert Spencer. His Toryism almost rejects the State, a conclusion that would have profoundly shocked Burke. Nor can we say that Maine's devotion to history does much, in the long run, to soften his individualism. In spite of his insistence on the complexities of social relationships, in spite of his implied pluralism, in spite of his distrust of the common man, he remains true to his formula, and would allow the helpless and ignorant individual somehow to save himself by contract. The historical method did not give his conclusions scientific validity— certainly not if universal acceptance be a test of scientific validity. He thought that with the abolition of feudal dues the French Revolution ceased to be a social movement, and that during the Terror " nothing remained for its authors except to tear one another to pieces."[3] Now M. Mathiez, who has devoted a lifetime to a painfully exact research into the French Revolution, and who devoutly insists that history is an exact science, concludes that only during the Terror were social issues really paramount. The study of history may make men wiser, it may even make them more humble, but it does not furnish indisputable formulas capable of solving present political difficulties.

---

[1] *Ancient Law*, pp. 295-296.
[2] *Speeches*, in Grant Duff's *Sir Henry Maine*, p. 90. The italics are mine.
[3] *Early Law and Customs*, p. 299.

L

8. KIDD[1]

Only in a history of opinion could Benjamin Kidd find place. *Social Evolution* was far too ephemeral a book to be ranked as a contribution to political thought. But in its day its success was so great and so immediate that it must clearly have fulfilled a need, the need of the man in the street to have an opinion, an opinion as easy and comfortable as possible. The work of an unknown and self-educated man, *Social Evolution* (1894) sprang at once into prominence, was frequently reprinted for half a dozen years, was discussed in reviews and journals. It was the kind of book that makes the especial delight of American women's clubs, and seems to have been even more successful in America than in England. It must interest us first because it marks one of the most fantastic forms of that attempted alliance between biology and politics we have noted before in other forms. Kidd contrived, to the delight of true believers everywhere, to turn biology to the service of what he at least held to be the Christian religion, to turn against the followers of Buckle and Spencer their dearest weapon. Moreover, *Social Evolution* served for thousands of the uncritical a purpose similar to that served a century before by the work of Malthus. Just as the *Essay on Population* was seized upon eagerly by routine conservatives as the final justification for doing nothing about the social order, so *Social Evolution* was seized upon by such conservatives in the 'nineties. It gave them the comfortable assurance that Nature, as well as God, held socialism to be impossible. It took the sting out of progress by making progress an easy, mystical achievement that did not at all interfere with the inertia of the respectable *bourgeois*. Its solution of the social question was too unreal to last. But we may well conclude our study of nineteenth-

---

[1] Kidd is a man of one book, the *Social Evolution* (1894). He can hardly be said to have added much save words to this in *The Control of the Tropics* (1898); *Western Civilization* (1902) and the unfinished *Science of Power* (1918). See Mackintosh, R., *From Comte to Benjamin Kidd* (1899); Pringle-Patterson, A. Seth, *The Philosophical Radicals and other Essays* (1907).

century political thought in England—a study which has sought to analyse the ideas of the common man as well as those of the philosopher—with a book which has in it nothing of the twentieth century, and certainly nothing at all of eternity.

" Progress is a necessity from which there is simply no escape, and from which there has never been any escape since the beginning of life."[1] Kidd starts with this axiomatic truth. Progress is no invention of the present age. From the beginning, all organisms have been engaged in a ceaseless warfare, and in this warfare the best have survived. Human beings, far from having succeeded in abating this warfare, have but made it more intense by enlisting their higher capacities in it. " The law of life has been always the same from the beginning,—ceaseless and inevitable struggle and competition, ceaseless and inevitable selection and rejection, ceaseless and inevitable progress."[2]

It is true that there is an alternative to progress— decadence. Here we must have recourse to a biologist who has developed the incomplete theories of Darwin to their fullest extent. Weismann has shown that acquired characteristics cannot be inherited. Survival is determined by accidental, but transmissible, variations in individual organisms. If all the individuals of a given generation compete freely, the less fit individuals will die out before they can propagate unfit young, or at the worst these young will die in infancy. The more fit, however, will attain full maturity, will propagate fit young, and as this process goes on the whole average fitness of the species will be raised. Other accidental variations will further raise the average fitness, and progress will go on inevitably. But if you attempt to interfere with this process by protecting the unfit against competition, you allow fit and unfit to propagate equally. You then get *panmixia*, the mixture of all possible degrees of fitness and unfitness, in which, in the course of time, deterioration must commence. " If all the individuals of

---

[1] *Social Evolution*, chap. ii., p. 37. (I have used the second American edition, 1898.)   [2] *Ibid.*, chap. ii., p. 41.

every generation in any species were allowed to equally propagate their kind, the average of each generation would continually tend to fall below the average of the generation which preceded it, and a process of slow but steady degeneration would ensue."[1]

Equipped then with the latest fashion in biology—with the struggle for life, the non-inheritance of acquired characteristics, and the dilemma of progress or decadence—let us see how all this applies to man in society. Now man is completely a part of the natural world, and all his actions are subject to the law of evolution. The struggle for life among men has a twofold aspect: there is the struggle between groups, or organized societies; and there is the struggle between individual members of the same group. In both struggles the law is the same. A society is an organism, and undergoes birth, life, and death like any other organism. Man's biological triumph is due largely to his capacity for forming such societies. The fittest society is the one that can enlist to the fullest the disciplined energies of its members for war or for economic competition, and can thus prevail over other societies. But these energies can be most fully developed in any society only if the struggle for life between their individual members is complete. Only in this internal competition are inventive gifts, initiative, reason (in its useful sense) developed.

But if we look closely at this problem of the relation between the society as a whole and the individual organisms that make it up, we become aware of an extraordinary fact, a fact which no political theorist has yet fully seized. The uncontrolled struggle between individuals within a given society we have seen to be indispensable if decadence is not to overtake the whole society. But the immediate personal interests of the majority of these individuals are not served by that uncontrolled struggle. The strong are few, the weak are many, and at any given moment the interests of the weak are, of course, to keep themselves alive, to do as well as they possibly can. The individual, using what we must call his

---

[1] *Social Evolution*, chap. ii., p. 39.

reason, could not possibly accept for himself life in a London slum, merely because the interests of the race required it. Therefore reformers like Bentham have assumed that the interests of the individual are identical with the interests of the race, and starting with the assumption that reason is the best guide, have worked out humanitarian reforms which tend to put a stop to full competition. But these men are on the wrong track. The extraordinary fact Kidd had discovered was this: " The interests of the social organism and those of the individuals comprising it at any particular time are actually antagonistic; they can never be reconciled; they are inherently and essentially irreconcilable."[1]

Yet reason obstinately insists that the struggle can be suspended in the interests of the individual, and reason to-day has gone on from Bentham to Marxian socialism. The socialists are quite justified in maintaining that it is to the interests of the many to abolish competition, to reward all alike regardless of their biological merit. Socialism is, indeed, the suicide of society. But why should John Jones worry about that ? It will not mean suicide for him. Society will not suffer until after the Joneses are all dead. Yet men in the past have not followed their reason to the destruction of society, and we need not greatly fear they will do so now. For something deeper than reason has caused men to sacrifice themselves to the good of the race. That something is religion. " A religion is a form of belief, providing an ultra-rational sanction for that large class of conduct in the individual where his interests and the interests of the social organism are antagonistic, and by which the former are rendered subordinate to the latter in the general interests of the evolution which the race is undergoing."[2]

It follows that a " rational religion " is a complete impossibility, a contradiction in terms. Reason can never teach us to sacrifice ourselves to the common good, to sacrifice the present to the future, to obey our gifted superiors and accept subordination. All religions, from primitive animism up, have served to give this ultra-rational support to the social

---

[1] *Social Evolution*, chap. iii., p. 84. [2] *Ibid.*, chap. v., p. 111.

organism. But our especial interest must be in Christianity, obviously the most biologically perfect faith. Let us observe first that a religion must balance the disintegrating self-assertiveness of the individual and the altruistic identification of the individual with the group. It must keep alive both elements, both of which are necessary to progress.[1] Now Christianity from its beginnings to the end of the Middle Ages was forced to combat the individualistic decay of the Roman Empire and the crude barbaric selfishness of the Teutonic invaders by an exaggeration of the principle of self-sacrifice. Reason was completely humbled before authority. Had it not been for the Renaissance and Reformation, the victory of Christianity over human selfishness might have been so complete as to have arrested progress. But the Reformation saved the race. It liberated thought for fruitful use in art and science. This, however, is but an aspect of its work. It really turned into genuinely humanitarian channels those altruistic feelings which mediæval Christianity had turned into a barren asceticism.[2]

Nothing is more curious in Kidd's work than the bit of prestidigitation by which he turns Protestant ethics into Weismannism. He would seem committed by his assumptions as to the survival of the fittest to a fine gory struggle, to " Nature red in tooth and claw," to the ruthless suppression of the weak. He would seem obliged to conclude that the humanitarian movement which has characterized modern Europe was an attempt to set aside the necessary condition of evolution. Not at all. He welcomes the " deepening and softening " of human feelings, the growth of altruism as seen in the emancipation of slaves, the abolition of aristocratic privileges, the rise of democracy. He hails the Liberal party as the party of progress,[3] and praises their recent support of measures calculated to improve the living conditions of the working class. For this altruistic movement, sanctioned by our deepest religious feelings, does not abrogate the struggle for life; it actually broadens it, humanizes it, makes it more efficient.[4] Altruism would achieve equality of

---

[1] *Social Evolution*, chap. v., p. 109. [2] *Ibid.*, chap. vii., p. 165.
[3] *Western Civilization*, p. 16. [4] *Social Evolution*, chap. viii., p. 242.

opportunity for all. The career open to talents is but one way of phrasing what Christianity has so long laboured for. We give education to all, we prevent by law the erection of unsanitary lodgings, we protect the workmen by Factory Acts from the short-sighted rapacity of his employer, all in order to lift the plane of competition from the barbaric to the civilized. The school of *laissez-faire* did its work by achieving the political equality which must be the basis of further equality. We must go beyond *laissez-faire*, and achieve *social* equality—or better, " conditions of equal social opportunities " for all.[1]

We shall, then, have in the future a society based, not on the crude economic struggle of *laissez-faire*, which already in America tends to produce a colossal tyranny of trusts,[2] but on the " higher " competitive basis indicated by the law of evolution. Here one might expect Kidd to explain in detail how he draws the hair-line between such legitimate forms of government interference as Factory Acts and such illegitimate forms as State ownership and operation of railways. One might expect him further to define equality of social opportunities. Does this imply an identical education for all up to twenty-one, and thereafter the devil take the hindmost ? Does it mean that society must value a mechanic who has acquired great skill at his trade as much as a surgeon who has acquired great skill at his, and therefore reward them equally ? What are the specific values which regulate the higher competition ? Who are the unfit ? But Kidd is not to be drawn into such a difficult discussion as this. Like all the evolutionists, he assumes that evolution alone knows.

He does, however, round out his work with a grand formula. Organized religion, which gives an ultra-rational sanction for unselfish conduct in the individual, conduct necessary to achieve through faith that identification of individual and social interests which reason fails to make, has hitherto found in Christianity its highest form. Now we cannot, as men like Spencer think, abandon religion for a positive, rational scientific attitude towards the universe.

---

[1] *Social Evolution*, chap. viii., p. 243. [2] *Western Civilization*, p. 437.

But the older Christianity is losing its hold. We must reconcile science and religion by adding to the humanitarian ethics of Christianity a faith in " projected efficiency."[1] Older religions secured from the individual the necessary sacrifice of his immediate interests as dictated through his reasons either by fear, or by the promise of reward in a concrete, if future, State. We must attain a higher mysticism. We must consciously sacrifice ourselves, consciously accept limitations (including, presumably, our immediate annihilation if something or somebody decides we are unfit) in order that the future may be better than the past. " The universal empire towards which our civilization moves . . . represents that empire in which it has become the destiny of our Western Demos, in full consciousness of the nature of the majestic process of cosmic ethics that has engendered him, to project the controlling meaning of the world-process beyond the present."[2]

Kidd's feat in saving religion from the positivists and making it the first servant of evolution endeared him to many good souls. " In an age of apparently increasing Materialism, and with the aid of the very calculus which Materialism had been supposed to supply and support, he rehabilitates Idealism, and tells us that in something barely apprehended by our consciousness, beyond the present horizon and scheme of things, lies the secret, in the long run, even of material success."[3] Anglo-Saxon imperialism was a pretty idealistic thing after all, and the new God, even more surely than the old, must approve the Boer War. But Kidd's readers were no doubt even more impressed by his defence of competition than by his attempts to gloss over competition with satisfying ethical generalities. Kidd won popularity as an out-and-out Weismannian in politics. His readers were willing to pass over mystic passages on the future, on the " deepening and softening " of Western feelings, in favour of such good Tory doctrine as that contained in his attacks on neo-Malthusianism. Progress depends on the tendency of the population " to continually press upon " (Kidd

---

[1] *Western Civilization*, pp. 31-67.   [2] *Ibid.*, p. 481.
[3] *Spectator*, 22nd February 1902.

288

deliberately uses the split infinitive as a rhetorical device) " and tend to outrun the conditions of existence for the time being." Human reason tends to come into conflict with Nature over this requirement. A modern Englishwoman has actually written of " this absurd sacrifice to their children of generation after generation of grown people." There is talk of " new restrictive influences," and an attempt to practise them. But such an attempt would suspend the conditions of selection, and " the conditions of selection being suspended, such a people could not in any case avoid progressive degeneration even if we could imagine them escaping more direct consequences."[1]

Now Kidd does not, any more than the other evolutionists, escape the difficulty that the evolutionary process itself cannot tell us what to call " higher " in the present, and what to call " lower." But there are still other difficulties. In the first place, even as regards individual organisms, biologists do not unanimously accept Weismann's theories. The inheritance of acquired characteristics, though it seems unlikely, is not yet finally disproved. The law of *panmixia* and inevitable retrogression is even less certain. Finally, the mechanism of variation, with all its implications for eugenics, is by no means established. In the second place, the application to the study of social groups of any biological theory based on the study of individual organisms is now seen to be little more than a tempting, but dangerous, use of analogy. There are of course difficulties of the kind Spencer faced when he denied that a society could have a common " sensorium." But there is a further decisive difficulty. However uncertain the transmission of acquired characteristics from the individual organism to its progeny may be, a social organism (if we may for a moment entertain the analogy) can hardly otherwise be defined than as an organism for the direct transmission of its acquired characteristics to its members. Englishmen inherit at least from Alfred the Great, if not from the Germans of Tacitus.

Kidd of course recognizes this fact of social inheritance on every page. But he is not even a consistent Weismannian

---

[1] *Social Evolution*, chap. viii., pp. 222-223.

L*

as regards individual inheritance. He writes of the "mental scale" which makes the white man superior to the Damara, not as an actual biological superiority—he even hints that black men have brains as good as those of white men—but as "the slowly-perfected product of an immense number of generations stretching back into the dim obscurity of the past," and adds that, "we obtain the power which it gives us over uncivilized man, not as a gift direct from nature to ourselves, but as a part of the accumulated stock of knowledge of the civilization to which we belong."[1] But this stock of knowledge enables us, as social animals, to live a life quite different from that of warring atomic individuals, a fact which Kidd himself was quite willing to admit. It permits us to abrogate, as he himself wanted to abrogate, the crude struggle to survive.

Kidd further lays himself open to criticism by his use of the word "reason." As against the Benthamites, he was justified in maintaining that there is often a conflict between the interests of the individual and the interests of the community, and that the individual who follows his "rational self-interest" will frequently act in an anti-social way. He was right, also, in emphasizing the rôle of religion in reconciling the individual to acceptance of a common social discipline which puts limitations on his pursuit of what he thinks desirable for himself. But he was not justified in giving to reason the narrow definition he gave it. The reason of the nominalist may be unable to rise from the individual to the group, may be a sterile denial of such obvious facts as the group-will. But reason was hardly a monopoly of the Age of Reason. As Kant and Coleridge used the term, for instance, it implies the capacity to correct our desires by our values, to bring imagination to the aid of critical analysis, and to arrive at judgments which have, not indeed a scientific objectivity, but a human objectivity, an objectivity which represents a sharing of the objects of our emotions with others. Reason, in this sense, far from driving the individual to anti-social actions, is at one with faith (and habit) in sanctioning submission to what it conceives to be common

[1] *Social Evolution*, chap. ix., pp. 291-292.

good. It is not, indeed, the infallible guide Kidd, like Bentham, was searching for. It proceeds tentatively, modestly, and at its best tolerantly, to put order into the chaotic struggle Kidd so admired. Kidd himself, like so many other extreme individualists, had no appreciation of the value of humility and toleration. He is guilty of the villainous paradox that since Nature demands toleration—that is, freedom for each organism to develop as far as other organisms will let it—we must be intolerant only of intolerance.[1]

Finally, there remains Kidd's ingenious formula of " projected efficiency." Like many of his contemporaries, he was aware that men were abandoning one of the fundamental precepts of historic Christianity. The Christian religion from its beginning down through the Middle Ages was pessimistic and other-worldly in a sense few men to-day can really understand. Historic Christianity denied that men can enjoy happiness on this earth; or, if the word happiness seems too vague, historic Christianity denied that men can ever get what they want on this earth. In particular, it denied that men can satisfy their senses—that they can get pleasant things to touch, to smell, to taste, to see, and to hear. It did indeed promise these things, or their equivalent, but only in heaven. And the surest road to heaven lay through suffering on earth, through the suppression of sense-desire, through the mortification of the flesh. Now mediæval society was not a joyless one. But thousands and thousands of men put up with suffering for the sake of reward in another world. Thousands of men quite literally sacrificed the enjoyment of goods purchasable with money in order to invest that money in a share of eternal happiness. The capital, the surplus over a bare living, of a mediæval town like Chartres went into its cathedral as our modern surplus goes into railways and factories. But hardly anyone now believes in historic Christianity. We do not really believe in heaven or in hell. We do very definitely believe that we can be happy here on earth. We do not seek to

---

[1] *Western Civilization*, p. 397.

mortify, but to indulge, the flesh. We are not pessimists, but optimists. The simplest of us are quite good Benthamites. Now this attitude has its dangers. We cannot all get what we want. Our baulked appetites do not in themselves provide us with a discipline. The discipline of an ascetic Christianity would seem impossible of re-establishment. Kidd, seeing the need of such a discipline, thought he had found it in the formula whereby heaven, instead of being a promise of a tangible future reward for individual acceptance of limitations, of discipline, became simply the metaphysical concept of the future of the race. But a metaphysical heaven is a poor substitute for a concrete one. A cosmic process is no discipline. Our heaven is inescapably on earth, and in the present. Renunciation may still be necessary, and the earthly heaven may have to be won much as the Christian heaven was to be won. But the ideas which will justify and compel that renunciation will presumably have to have more colour than those of Kidd. "Projected efficiency" is quite the dimmest of the gods.

CHAPTER V

CONCLUSION

It is difficult to make the nineteenth century come out neatly as a period, a decent, well-rounded, historical period. You cannot find any pat phrases for it, like the "Age of Reason" or the "Great Awakening." It did things in its own way, but somehow failed to do them with the final grace of a style. Certain museums, like the Metropolitan Museum of New York, have courageously assembled rooms to illustrate the decorative arts of the nineteenth century, and have placed them, probably without deliberate irony, in their proper time-sequence after the eighteenth century. The result is curious. It is not that a *salon* of the 1840's could possibly be mistaken for anything else. The nineteenth century was avidly antiquarian, but so, too, was the sixteenth. The nineteenth century, like the sixteenth, transmuted what it borrowed, so that Ruskin's Venetian Gothic was as different from that of mediæval Venice as Michelangelo's Renaissance from the Rome of the Cæsars. Whistler might use bamboo and green paint liberally, but his Peacock Room belongs in London, or even in Washington, rather than in Japan. Nineteenth-century decorative art failed to achieve the unity of a style. Its ingredients failed to mingle properly, and remained apart in a kind of hash. The hash indeed is different from any one of its elements and indeed from anything else. It is quite recognizable—as hash.

This same diversity, this multiplicity of elements unabsorbed into a common thing, is evident in the other aspects of human activity in the nineteenth century. To be sure, there is apparently always a mysterious element in this world making for diversity; or, perhaps, life always escapes the annihilation which the complete success of the thinker or of the artist would bring. At any rate, not even that neatest of centuries, the eighteenth, is comfortable in the strait-jacket of generalizations, whether they be the generalizations of the critic working in the glib medium of words, or the generalizations of the connoisseur seeking a wordless

293

identity of recognition. Right reason did not ride with John Wesley in pursuit of the devil through the slums of England, the tears shed over *George Barnwell* were not rhetorical tears, and Strawberry Hill is at least a symptom of the Gothic revival, if it is not the disease itself. But the nineteenth century is almost perversely resistant to attempts to define it. In literature, " Victorian " has nothing like the precision of " Elizabethan." Not even the simple opposition of romantic and classic, which serves so well in the latter half of the eighteenth century, is of much use in the nineteenth.

So, too, in political thought no great simplifying categories are readily available. The nineteenth century did make certainly underlying assumptions. Victorian Englishmen were as sure of perpetual progress as men of the second century were of the approaching end of the world. But progress hardly adds anything immediately to mere living. Faith in progress is faith in an order constructed out of human desires for quite definite satisfactions, or it is no faith at all. When we come to consider what kind of order nineteenth-century Englishmen embodied in their political faiths, we find their minds as variously furnished as their houses. The nineteenth century is a warring ground of political doctrines. True, so are most other centuries, say notably the seventeenth. But the conflict of men and ideas in seventeenth-century England, or even the more complex conflict of men and ideas in sixteenth-century France, can without too much apparent distortion be dramatized into a kind of unity. Certain doctrines emerge with the imprint, with the style of a given century. Such are the doctrines of the Divine Right of Kings, of the natural goodness of man, of the separation of powers. Now it is not impossible so to dramatize the politics of nineteenth-century England, not impossible to distinguish, in Newman's sense of the word, certain " notes " of English political thought in the period— indeed we are about to attempt to do so—but the task seems harder, and its conclusions more open to exceptions, than for previous centuries. Perhaps we are too near the nineteenth century to see its true outlines; or perhaps the nineteenth century really was what it thought itself to be, an exceptional age.

Certainly the nineteenth century agreed with Ranke that its task was above all one of reconstruction. The revolutions of the late eighteenth century—the American, the French, and the industrial revolutions—had struck the Western mind with a sense of catastrophe which, one is inclined to believe, far exceeds our present sense of the catastrophic nature of the Russian Revolution. Men as far apart as St. Simon and Maistre set out consciously to rebuild an authority and a faith which all men might accept. Something essential, men felt, had been destroyed, and there was as yet nothing to put in its place. Quite ordinary people could agree with Morris that " we not only are, but we feel also ourselves to be living between the old and the new." The nineteenth century was consciously an age of transition, an age of groping. It was sometimes quite romantically proud of the fact, and invented a phrase, the *mal du siècle*, to consecrate its uncertainties.

Reconstruction meant that after all, there was something to build with. The commonplace that the nineteenth century was a century of history can hardly be questioned. Not that the nineteenth century invented history, or even scientific historical research, which goes back at least as far as Mabillon. But fashionable eighteenth-century thought had seen in the past little but a tissue of errors, a hindrance, in so far as it had got itself enshrined in custom, to men who knew so much more than their fathers had known. If, however, wrote Acton in the true nineteenth-century vein, the past has been a burden, a knowledge of the past is the surest way of lifting that burden. Liberal and conservative alike sought to reinforce their programmes by explaining that the course of history led surely up to them. Men appealed to history as their grandfathers had appealed to Nature. When one compares the views of a Brougham and a Disraeli on the history of the Whigs and the Tories, one doubts whether they thereby anchored themselves more firmly in objective fact. Maine spent his life attacking the law of Nature in the name of the law of history, but the historical method led to much the same conclusions on freedom of contract as those the history-scorning Bentham had reached. No doubt the study of history taught the nineteenth century a certain respect for the immobility of social groups, a certain sense of the difficulties confronting the social reformer, without which its vigorous pursuit of social panaceas would have been disastrous. No doubt, too, that its diligent study of the historic and prehistoric past of the race uncovered facts which no political thinker can do without. But it was a little too sure that history, like Nature, explains itself. Here as elsewhere the nineteenth century could not bring itself to a healthy scepticism. M. Paul Valéry has recently revived his countryman's famous *boutade* that history is a " fable convenue "; and M. Croce has long insisted that, if the true historian makes the past live in the present, he thereby identifies the past with his own living will. The nineteenth century, anxious though it was to preserve the sovereignty of the self-conscious individual, insistent though it was on the fact that living things grow and are not made, was unwilling to make full allowance for the subjectivity it postulated. In history it sought for finality, for complete agreement (up to the present at least). In spite of its abandonment of the eighteenth-century world machine, in spite of its acceptance of a universe subject to growth, it would not entertain the possibility that growth is a miracle, and that therefore there is a limit to our ability to predict and control growth. It discovered the dynamic State; but it was a bit aghast at its own discovery.

We are thus brought to a second great commonplace about the nineteenth century. It was the century of progress. Its world was not static, but dynamic. It brought home to ordinary men the notion of evolution. Again, this notion was not wholly new. Histories of the idea of progress commonly go back to Ionian Greece. But the mediæval man was as certain about his earth as he was about his heaven, and he never thought of either as really changing. And, though men like Condorcet are sure of the fact of human improvement, the kernel of eighteenth-century political thought is a conviction that there is a pattern of the State as unchanging, though in motion, as Newton's universe (which of course is also in motion), and that once thought has ascertained that pattern, men have but to conform their actions to it to attain a perfect bliss. The nineteenth century substituted progress for perfectability. The difference may seem purely verbal, but it is real enough at bottom. For the notion of progress leaves the process of growth open at both ends. By implication, it leaves the past as uncertain as the future. It is true enough, as we have pointed out, that the nineteenth century had not the full courage of its belief in progress. Spencer contrived to know as much about the cosmic process as Thomas Aquinas had known. He takes away with the one heavy hand of ethical conviction what the other hand of evolution had offered. So many nineteenth-century evolutionists did this sort of thing, so many identified their private desires with those of the new deity, that it is small wonder that there has been a reaction against the idea of progress. But progress offered us with the winning modesty of a Bagehot or with the generous, if morally indignant, fervour of a Huxley is too attractive a gift to be refused. The doctrine of progress has too often been merely an uncritical extolling of the virtues of the machine age, of Western civilization, of an approaching *pax Anglo-Saxonica*. It has been the peculiar property of a group of sincere but narrow votaries whose world has been formed above all by the Protestant Reformation and the French Revolution, and whose " liberalism " is profoundly distrustful of many of the irrational graces and corporate loyalties of human life. Progress has been wedded to other abstractions like Liberty, Democracy, and Nationality, as if it were not already abstract enough in itself. But for better or for worse, the idea of progress is now an indispensable part of our intellectual equipment. We may not feel for China or Mexico the contempt of the evolutionist who is sure those nations have not properly evolved. But we cannot escape the fact that our lives are different from the lives of the primitive cave-dwellers from whom we almost certainly descend. We rarely limit ourselves to the modest adjective " different," most of us, in our innermost consciousness, commit ourselves to such evaluating terms as " higher " or "fuller." We may not be the masters of the process of evolution, but we are certainly its children.

Nineteenth-century political thought busied itself with the task of reconstructing a social order which had collapsed with the *ancien régime*. It sought that order in the study of history guided by the idea of progress. It formed an amazing number of solutions. Nothing is more striking in nineteenth-century political thought than its variety. Hardly a man of those we have studied in these pages can be said to be anything like in complete agreement with another. What may be called eternal contrasts of temperament, like the contrast between the liberal's optimistic trust in his fellow men, and the conservative's pessimistic distrust of them, run through the century. Maine, like Coleridge, was in this sense a Tory by temperament; yet their programmes differ greatly. English socialists seem to have little but the label in common. Owen, the Ricardian socialists, Morris, Hyndman, and the Fabians are all agreed that poverty must be abolished, but they are far from agreed as to the steps necessary to abolish it. Indeed, one of the obstacles in the way of writing a history of English political thought in the nineteenth century according to the method of ideas rather than that of men is the fact that there seem to be as many ideas as men. Schools of thought indeed there are, like the historical school; and certain common methodological concepts, like that of society as an organism. But to employ such categories is to list together men who have little in common. Spencer, Bagehot, and Kidd all appealed to biology, but with very different results.

A striking thing about these divergent political philosophies is that they led so few men to scepticism. Nineteenth-century Englishmen did indeed come to lose what they called their faith; but they commonly then set about to wail over their loss. To doubt led not to a fertile Pyrrhonism, not to a scientific willingness to rest content with a working hypothesis; it led to the lost-sheep attitude of a Clough. To identify one's scale of values with the order of the universe is perhaps more than a temptation to the thinker; it may well be a necessity of human thought. But it would seem that the nineteenth century committed itself rather unreservedly to this process. It found its own diversity extremely uncomfortable. "We are not made to dwell among ruins," wrote St. Simon after the French Revolution. We must get to work and rebuild—rebuild our society. But there were so many architects, and each was so sure of his own plan! Men built much and variously—Liverpool and Manchester, New Lanark, North Oxford, Regent Street, Letchworth, and Kelmscott. They were all, however, building New Jerusalems. The nineteenth century, we must repeat, was an age of faiths.

If, however, we ask ourselves whether some generalizations can be made to measure the differences between English political thought in 1800 and in 1900, the answer need not be wholly negative. The purely personal elements present at the beginning of the century certainly exist at its end. Making allowance for the differences in their environment, and above all for the discredit which has fallen on the phraseology of the Age of Reason, there is a similarity between the shallow self-confidence and assertiveness of a Brougham and the same qualities in a Winston Churchill. But the balance has altered. In the first place, as the century went on the struggle between *laissez-faire* and State intervention saw the increasing practical triumphs of intervention. At the end of the century, the bland confidence of the Manchester school in self-help for all has given place to the irritated and unheeded protests of Spencer against the Factory Acts. Not even the discovery of the struggle for life could save economic individualism, and we have seen how Kidd found that social legislation was necessary to the "higher" competition. That the nineteenth century solved the antagonism between liberty and authority is obviously not true. But the end of the century saw the problem cleared of a great deal of abstract economic dogmatism with which it had been cluttered at the beginning of the century.

Again, nineteenth-century England, by the very fact that she was forced to experiment with it, did something to make democracy a fact rather than a bugbear. Here, too, we, as heirs of that century, are faced with a problem by no means solved. Democracy is to-day in some circles almost as suspect, its true political implications almost as much in doubt, as in the days of Burke. But after all, the nineteenth century did virtually establish universal suffrage, it did destroy the power of the House of Lords, it did make serious inroads on the sense of caste in Englishmen. We are to-day faced with the problem of leadership—or, if you prefer, that of aristocracy—but we can no longer find a solution in a God-made landed interest. Disraeli's Tory democracy is no longer a living formula. When towards the end of the century Maine attacked democracy in *Popular Government*, he was obviously on the defensive. His irritation at the assumption of the advocates of democracy that that form of government was somehow clothed in inevitability, though it is an irritation with which it is easy to feel an intellectual sympathy, is in itself a tribute to the strength of democracy.

Party alignments throughout the century are with difficulty reconciled with clear-cut distinctions in political thought. Toryism has always had an interventionist tradition, and through the magic of Disraeli took on for a time the guise of democracy. The Tories in 1867 carried through the most radical political reform of the century. Much social, if not socialistic, legislation has had a Tory origin. On the other hand, Liberalism was at first identified with absolute economic freedom, and even radicalism went no farther than the first French Republic. By the end of the century, however, there is discernible a settling-down of party allegiances in conformity with social programmes. Toryism, in accordance with its old habits, has come to rest in the radicalism of a previous generation. The Conservative party is now the party of the victors in the struggle of the industrial revolution. It has indeed its extreme fringe, a group of earnest men who represent the survival of Christian socialism. But on the whole the Conservative party has come to defend the capitalism which has evolved from Manchester. Its very protectionism is no real desertion of Manchester, but a patterning after the successful protectionism of the hitherto most thriving child of the industrial revolution, the United States. It is the Tory to-day who is most likely to regret "Government interference." Liberalism, however, has

CONCLUSION

followed Mill and Green far towards a socialistic organization of society, and in so far as it has any vitality, has
merged with Labour to work for a social democracy that
aims at the abolition of the kind of inequality the nineteenth
century held to be an indispensable foundation for society.

If as regards actual programmes the difference between
political thought in 1800 and 1900 is to be summed up as a
shift by which radical, democratic, liberal, or popular thought
—a precise adjective is hard to find—turned from individualism to collectivism, while conservative, aristocratic,
anti-popular thought turned from a collectivism determined
by the survival of feudal loyalties to individualism, the
difference between the methodological background of
political thought in 1800 and in 1900 is by no means so
clear. Yet in general it may be said that during the century,
conservative and liberal thinkers alike were led to view
society less and less as a mechanism, and more and more as
an organism. This change is measured by the increased
prestige of biology in the minds of political thinkers. We
have already emphasized sufficiently the alliance between
biology and politics. It was an alliance that hardly taught
modesty to political thinkers, and it is not to-day as firm an
alliance as it once was. For one thing, we have come to feel
that the later nineteenth century, under the influence of
biological leads, had altogether too much distrust of the
human intellect. Psychology, anthropology, and history
combined to teach Bagehot and his contemporaries that
civilized man is the creature of centuries of growth, that his
vital processes are still the vital processes of the savage, that
what we call his reason is the servant, not the master, of his
desires, and that therefore reason is still a pretty useless, or
even dangerous, tool in politics. Now as a corrective to the
eighteenth-century belief in the reasonableness of man, this
anti-intellectualism was of great value. But held as an
ultimate truth it was almost self-destructive. Reason alone
can recognize and remedy unreason, even in politics. Reason
may be the youngest child of evolution, but hardly the
weakest, and certainly not the most ill-favoured. Kidd's
conclusion that reason is impotent, save to destroy, is a

caricature on the thought of the century, but a revealing caricature. Even Bagehot praised stupidity with rather less than half-playfulness. The work of the anti-intellectual social psychologists has been of the greatest use. The part of imitation, the *rôle* of the unconscious, the behaviour of mobs, the apparently inevitable sway of symbols and stereotypes, the gap between a man's professions and his practices —a gap which, since he does not perceive it, does not in the least make him a hypocrite—all this is of permanent value for political thought. But the thinkers who analysed all these irrational workings of the political consciousness of the man in the street were at least attempting to free their own minds from the limitations they were studying in others. At the very worst, they might in charity have admitted the possibility of extending their emancipation to others. On the whole they did not, and took refuge in a defensive anti-intellectualism which had its roots in the eighteenth century they disliked. Rousseau's Nature had a strange survival in the work of the evolutionists.

This alliance with biology further strengthened one of the most important currents in nineteenth-century opinion. The eighteenth century had been all but unanimously on the side of nurture; the nineteenth century, if only to show itself a natural and ungrateful child, was to swing violently over to the side of Nature. In the timeless dispute over the question as to whether heredity or environment plays the greater part in human life, the nineteenth century without hesitation took the side of heredity. The French Revolution had made evident the failure of the environmentalists in their attempt to tamper with Nature. Malthus had proved conclusively—at least to his more hasty readers, which is to say the majority—that the more conditions of human existence were bettered, the more misery was stored up for an over-populated and not too distant future. Carlyle and his followers had insisted that schemes for improving men's social environment could not possibly redeem their souls, and that redemption itself was a mystery beyond the search of the environmentalist. Finally, the work of Darwin, especially when capped by that of Weismann, served to make the intellectual temper of the late nineteenth century as fanatically devoted to heredity as that of the late eighteenth had been to environment. Hundreds of ambitious and quite unscientific genealogies showed that virtue and vice bred true, and by the beginning of the present century the Jukeses and the Kallikaks, the Edwardses and the Coleridges had become almost household words.

Now faith in heredity—which must not be confused with the scientific study of genetics—is socially significant as an attempt to stabilize a given society within the limits of existing inequalities of political and economic status. The rich are the able, just as the poor are the incompetent. Both classes breed true. Any attempt to *alter* the distribution of wealth—let alone any attempt to *equalize* its distribution— must be made in defiance of a law of Nature, and is therefore bound to fail. Heredity served the Victorians as original sin had served the Church, to hold together a society unequally privileged. But Victorian society was never really stabilized, never, indeed, achieved more than a fleeting compromise with the forces of social change. Moreover, one of the dangers of an appeal to a scientific principle, even though the appeal is made wholly in the spirit of religion, lies in the undogmatic character of true science. Biologists themselves have gone far beyond Weismann, have ceased, indeed, to put the problem of heredity in the extremely simple terms used during the last century. Social writers are thus obliged either to follow in the steps of the biologists, and abandon their assurance that they have in direct, blending heredity a complete clue to social processes, or else to admit that their " heredity " is merely another god. A considerable body of minority opinion even in Victorian times continued its faith in environment; socialism, indeed, could hardly afford to desert Owen wholly, even in espousing Marxian determinism. Yet such was the prestige of nature as opposed to nurture that many a hopeful soul, meliorist by temperament, was driven to eugenics for a solution of the conflict between his hopes and what his contemporaries assured him were hard facts.

Biology, then, influenced political thought towards

an exaggerated distrust of the human intellect and an exaggerated trust in the principle of heredity as understood by Weismann. Yet in spite of, or in part even because of, its alliance with the biological sciences, political thought at the end of the century was richer than at the beginning. It had ramified into a number of special studies which are a bit optimistically called the social sciences. Now these sciences are still in the awkward age. They are noisy, impertinent, and dreadfully sure of themselves. They do not know the virtue of the tentative. They attempt to cover their insufficiencies by an appeal to the methods, or rather to the prestige, of the physical sciences. They confuse their hypotheses with the will of God. They attempt to arrive at a finality beyond judgment and taste, though they can succeed only with the aid of both. But nineteenth-century history, jurisprudence, economics, anthropology, psychology, education, and other social studies did go far towards attaining a discipline of their own. They did an enormous amount of specialized spade-work. Thanks to them, political thought has infinitely more material to work with than it had in the eighteenth century.

How wisely it will use that material it is not for us to hazard a guess. We are perhaps as lost in transition as we can now discern the nineteenth century to have been. But we cannot complain that the last century has left us nothing but ruins. On the contrary, it has left us a vast number of projects of construction in all stages of completion—save the final. It threw itself whole-heartedly into a vast number of social experiments, from infant schools to imperial States. In spite of the World War and the Russian Revolution, the nineteenth century did not end with a cataclysm. It has handed on its experiments pretty well intact. Modern political thought need not profess to repudiate the work of the nineteenth century, as that century professed to repudiate the work of the eighteenth. We may take the lesson of evolution as learned, and be content with the problems we have inherited. We may achieve the contentment the nineteenth century did not achieve, if we will but admit that, since change is inevitable, we do not stop change by calling it progress.

BIBLIOGRAPHICAL APPENDIX

A

No standard work does for nineteenth century political thought in England what Leslie Stephen's *History of English Thought in the Eighteenth Century* does for the preceding century. The student will have to piece together a new one of his own from the following :

MURRAY, R. H., *Studies in the English Social and Political Thinkers of the Nineteenth Century*. 2 vols. 1929.

Comprehensive, but very discursive.

DAVIDSON, W. L., *Political Thought in England: The Utilitarians from Bentham to J. S. Mill*. 1915.

BARKER, E., *Political Thought in England from Spencer to the Present Day*.

These two volumes in the Home University Library are, of course, very brief; the latter is surprisingly compact and successful.

SOMERVELL, D. C., *English Thought in the Nineteenth Century*. 1929.

An interesting book, aiming, as the author explains, to study thought in the form of opinion rather than in that of philosophy.

HEARNSHAW, F. J. C. (Editor), *The Social and Political Ideas of some Representative Thinkers of the Age of Reaction and Reconstruction*. 1815-1865. 1932.

A symposium, and therefore rather uneven. The second half of the century will presumably be treated in a subsequent volume.

GRAHAM, W., *English Political Philosophy*. 1914.

BIBLIOGRAPHICAL APPENDIX

B

THE following books are suggested to round out those already mentioned in bibliographical notes in the text. I have grouped them according to certain schools of thought; that is to say, I have by that very grouping sketched an outline of a history of English political thought in the nineteenth century according to the method of ideas. But any such classification is purely tentative and partially arbitrary.

I. CONSERVATISM, PHILOSOPHICAL, AND ECCLESIASTICAL

In addition to Coleridge, Disraeli, Newman: Wordsworth, W., *Tract on the Convention of Cintra* (1809) repr. in *Prose Works*, ed. Grosart (1876); Southey, R., *Colloquies on the Progress and Prospects of Society* (1829); Whibley, C., *Lord John Manners and his friends* (1925); Ward, Wilfred, *W. G. Ward and the Oxford Movement* (1889), *W. G. Ward and the Catholic Revival* (1893). But the books on the Oxford Movement are almost countless. There is a very full bibliography in Brilioth, Y., *The Anglican Revival* (1925).

II. UTILITARIANISM

In addition to Bentham, Brougham, and J. S. Mill: Fawcett, Mrs. H., *Life of the Right Honourable Sir William Molesworth* (1901); Grote, Mrs. H., *The personal Life of George Grote* (1873); Mill, James, *A Fragment on Mackintosh* (1835), *Commerce defended* (1818); Bain, A., *James Mill* (1882); Wallas, G., *Life of Francis Place* (3rd ed. 1919); Austin, J., *Lectures on Jurisprudence*, 2 vols. (4th ed. 1873); Brown, W. Jethro, *The Austinian Theory of Law* (1906); Sidgwick, H., *The Elements of Politics* (1891), *Miscellaneous essays and addresses* (1904).

III. POLITICAL RADICALS, FREE-THINKERS, CHARTISTS

In addition to Cobbett and Bradlaugh: Campbell, Theophila, *The battle of the Press, as told in the story of the Life of Richard Carlile* (1899); Holyoake, G. J., *Sixty Years of an Agitator's Life* (1909); McCabe, J., *Life and Letters of George Jacob Holyoake*, 2 vols. (1908); Linton, W. J., *The English Republic*, ed. K. Parkes (1891), *Memories* (1895); Lovett, Wm., *Life and Struggles*, ed. and with an introduction by R. H. Tawney, 2 vols. (1920). There is no work on the theoretical aspects of Chartism, though much can be got from Hovell, M., *The Chartist Movement* (1918), esp. Chap. III and from West, J., *A History of the Chartist Movement* (1920). Since most of these radicals were touched with anti-clericalism, they can be found in Robertson, J. M., *A History of Free Thought in the Nineteenth Century* (1924). But the whole history of the theoretical basis of this continental type of radicalism remains to be written.

IV. SOCIALISM, UTOPIAN, RICARDIAN, AND CHRISTIAN

In addition to Owen and Kingsley: Hodgskin, T., *Labour Defended against the Claims of Capital* (1825), *The Natural and Artificial Rights of Property Contrasted* (1832); Halévy, E., *Thomas Hodgkin* (Paris, 1903); Thompson, Wm., *Inquiry into the Principles of the Distribution of Wealth most conducive to Human Happiness* (1824); Bray, J. F., *Labour's Wrongs and Labour's Remedy* (1839). But there are many writers, mostly obscure, who may be classified as socialists, from Spence and Ogilvie to James (Bronterre) O'Brien. For them see Beer, M., *The History of British Socialism*, 2 vols. (1923). For Christian Socialism, see Maurice, F. D., *Learning and Working* (1855); Maurice, F., *Life of J. F. D. Maurice, chiefly told in his own letters* (1884); Ludlow, J. M., *Christian Socialism and its Opponents;* Headlam, S. D., and others, *Socialism and Religion* (in Fabian Socialist Series, No. 1, 1908). For both earlier and later phases of the movement, see Woodworth, A. V., *Christian Socialism in England* (1903), with bibliography.

V. VICTORIAN LIBERALISM

In addition to Cobden, Bagehot, Acton, Green: Gladstone, W. E., *Gleanings of Past Years*, 7 vols. (1879), *Speeches*, ed. A. T. Bassett (1916); Morley, J., *Life of Gladstone*, 2 vols. (1911); Bright, J., *Speeches*, ed. J. E. Thorold Rogers, 2 vols. (1868); Morley, J., *Recollections*, 2 vols. (1917), *Critical Miscellanies*, 4 vols. (1886-1908), *On Compromise* (2nd ed. 1877); Harrison, F., *The Meaning of History* (1894), *Order and Progress* (1875), *National and Social Problems* (1908).

VI. EVOLUTIONISTS

In addition to Spencer and Kidd: Huxley, T. H., *Lay Sermons* (1870), *Social Diseases and Worse Remedies* (1891), *Method and Results* (1893); Buckle, H. T., *History of Civilization in England*, 2 vols. (1857-61); Robertson, J. M., *Buckle and his Critics* (1895); Ritchie, D. G., *Darwinism and Politics* (3rd ed. 1891).

VII. HISTORIANS AND LAWYERS

In addition to Maine and Acton: Bryce, J., *The American Commonwealth*, 2 vols. (rev. ed. 1911), *Modern Democracies*,

APPENDIX

2 vols. (1921), *Studies in History and Jurisprudence,* 2 vols. (1901); Seeley, J. R., *The Expansion of England* (2nd ed. repr. 1921), *Introduction to Political Science* (1896); Dicey, S. V., *Introduction to the Study of the Law of the Constitution* (8th ed. 1926), *Lectures on the Relation between Law and Public Opinion in England during the Nineteenth Century* (2nd. ed. 1914); Stephen, J. F., *Liberty, Equality, Fraternity* (1874), *Horæ Sabatticæ* (3 series, repr. 1892); Lecky, W. E. H., *Democracy and Liberty,* 2 vols. (new ed. 1899); Freeman, E. A., *Comparative Politics* (1874).

VIII. THE BEAUTIFUL AND THE GOOD
In addition to Morris and Newman: Ruskin, J., *The Crown of Wild Olive* (1866), " *Unto this last* "; *four essays in political economy* (74th thousand, 1906), *Fors clavigera; Letters to the Workmen and Labourers of Great Britain,* 8 vols. (1871-1884); Hobson, J. H., *John Ruskin, Social Reformer* (1898); Arnold, M., *Culture and Anarchy,* ed. J. D. Wilson (1932), *Mixed Essays* (1880); Elias, O., *Matthew Arnold's politische Grundanschauungen* (Leipsig, 1931) with bibliography.

IX. THE PLURALISTS
In addition to Acton: Maitland, F. W., *Collected Papers* (1911); Gierke, O., *Political Theories of the Middle Ages,* transl. and with an Introduction by F. W. Maitland (repr. 1927); Fisher, H. A. L., *F. W. Maitland* (1910); Figgis, J. N., *The Divine Right of Kings* (2nd ed. 1914), *Churches in the Modern State* (2nd ed. 1914), *Studies of Political Thought from Gerson to Grotius* (2nd ed. 1916). The later figures in the school belong clearly to the twentieth century.

X. THE IDEALISTS
In addition to Green: Bradley, F. H., *Ethical Studies* (2nd ed. rev. 1927); Bosanquet, B., *The Philosophical Theory of the State* (3rd ed. 1920), *Social and International Ideas* (1917); Jones, H., *The Working Faith of a Social Reformer* (1910).

XI. SOCIALISTS—CHIEFLY MARXIAN
Hyndman, H. M., *The Economics of Socialism* (1896), *The Historical Basis of Socialism in England* (1883); Bax, E. B., *The Ethics of Socialism* (1889), *Outspoken Essays* (1897). But the later development of socialism in England is beyond the province of this study. The student may make a start with the second volume of Beer's previously cited work and with Pease, E. R., *The History of the Fabian Society* (2nd ed. 1925).

INDEX

ACTON : background, 199 ; definition of liberty, 199 ; Federalism, 209 ; moral law, 201 ; on American Civil War, 205 ; on dangers of democracy, 205 ; on English Constitution, 207 ; on nationalism, 206 ; Papal infallibility, 211 ; pluralist, 209 ; rights of minorities, 208 ; rôle of historian, 201

Adams, J., 210

Alton Locke, 117

Anti-Corn Law League, 104

Arnold, M., 111, 221, 227

Ashley, 146

BABBITT, I., 50, 273

Bagehot, 180, 246, 301 ; anti-intellectualism, 195 ; conservative elements, 188 ; *English Constitution*, 193; essayist, 180 ; *laissez-faire*, 197 ; on Anglo-Saxon superiority, 182 ; on equality, 194 ; on freedom of discussion, 186 ; on inadequacies of bureaucracy, 196 ; on middle class, 184 ; on ruling class, 187 ; *Physics and Politics*, 181, 189 ; theory of unconscious imitation, 190 ; typical Victorian Liberal, 185

Bax, 247

Bellamy, 253

Bentham, 60, 61, 86, 90, 92, 100, 285, 291 ; atomism, 16, 29 ; codification of laws, 20 ; egalitarianism, 18 ; eighteenth-century characteristics, 15; ethical values, 24 ; French revolutionary doctrines, 21 ; hedonistic calculus, 17 ; identity of interests problem,17, 29 ; political programme, 23 ; psychological roots, 15 ; weakness of his psychology, 27

Besant, Annie, 247

Biography, place in political thought, 9

Bosanquet, 226

Bossuet, 49

Bradlaugh : atheism, 241 ; background, 240 ; economic individualist, 248 ; his circle of foreigners. 245 ; neo-Malthusian, 250 ; Northampton election, 251 ; opposes socialism, 247 ;

political programme, 244 ; positive creed, 242 ; republicanism, 243

Bright, John, 187, 213

Brougham, 61, 70, 92, 295 ; eighteenth-century characteristics, 33 ; Erastian on Church, 37 ; flatters middle class, 34 ; *laissez-faire* economics, 38 ; law reform, 37 ; new Whig, 41 ; on colonies, 38 ; parliamentary reform, 35 ; political career, 31 ; *Political Philosophy*, 39 ; poor relief, 36 ; popular education, 36 ; popularizer of Bentham, 32 ; shallowness, 40

Buckle, 5, 227, 282

Burke, 63, 76, 130, 207, 281

Byron, 92

CANNING, 137

Carlile, Richard, 241

Carlyle, 86, 88, 89, 90, 129, 159, 213 ; addiction to argument from analogy, 168 ; against *laissez-faire*, 172 ; as preacher, 165 ; background, 167 ; conservatism, 167 ; definition of liberty, 172 ; does not have programme, 165 ; imperialism, 176 ; inconsistency, 169 ; on Anglo-Saxon superiority, 175 ; on bureaucracy, 173 ; on work, 170 ; struggle for life, 171

Champion, 3

Chartism, 88, 144, 240

Chesterton, 62

Christian Socialism, 88, 117

Cobbett, 83, 167, 178 ; as interventionist, 70 ; conservative of the flesh, 62, 75 ; consistency, 63 ; domesticity, 65 ; eighteenth-century elements, 68 ; failure of his understanding, 72 ; gifted journalist, 64 ; morals, 66 ; not a thinker, 61 ; on women, 65 ; paper money, 71 ; seems to accept *laissez-faire*, 69 ; Tory pamphleteer, 63

Cobden, 88, 213 ; admires America, 112 ; as ordinary liberal, 103 ; dislikes classical education, 111 ; English foreign policy, 108 ; ethical justification for Free Trade, 105 ; his master

INDEX

ideas, 104; Philistine, 111; social reformer, 113; utilitarian, 111.

Coleridge, 89, 93, 135, 213, 290; concept of Clerisy, 80; condemns industrialism, 83; condemns *laissez-faire*, 84; *Constitution of the Church and State*, 77; idealist in philosophy, 84; influence, 76; on Proprietage and Nationality, 78; State a moral unit, 82; Tory democrat, 82; use of word "reason," 78; youthful Jacobinism, 76

Communism, 56

Comte, 72, 228

Conservatism, kinds of, 75

Corn Laws, 33, 104, 138, 144

Crimean War, 109

Critic, his place in history of political thought, 8

Darwin, 277

Dicey, 87

Dickens, 185

Disraeli, 2, 70, 86, 88, 166, 180, 244, 295, 300; against bureaucracy, 142; artist, 132; distrusts rationalism, 133; imperialism, 145; obligations of landed aristocracy, 143; on Church of England, 141; on Peel, 137; on Whigs, 136; Tory Democrat, 138; use of history, 134

Döllinger, 211

Eldon, 73

Evolution, theory of, in politics, 6, 159, 171, 189, 229, 283, 302

Eyre case, 187

Faguet, 2

Figgis, 1

Fourier, 5, 56, 261

Free Trade, 88

Godwin, 131

Grammar of Assent, 164

Grammont, 184

Green, T. H., 90, 301; at Oxford, 213; attitude towards landed gentry, 223; definition of liberty, 215; indifference to history, 225; on ideal and real, 217; on temperance legislation, 224; relation between individual and group, 218; relation between metaphysics and politics, 212; State intervention, 219; universal suffrage, 221

Halévy, 17

Harrington, 210

Harrison, F., 127

Hegel, 93, 215

Hobbes, 191

Holyoake, G. J., 241

Huskisson, 137

Huxley, 193, 241, 297

Hyndman, 247, 264

Ideas, place of, in politics, 3, 101, 161

Johnson, S., 67

Jowett, 214

Kant, 290

Kidd: Compromise on *laissez-faire*, 287; criticism of his use of biology, 289; imperialism, 288; on *rôle* of Christianity in society, 286; on *rôle* of reason in society, 285; "projected efficiency," 291; sudden success, 282

Kingsley, 76, 88, 90, 149, 200, 237; *Alton Locke*, 117; attitude towards Nature, 120; Christian Socialism, 121; conservatism, 127; eupeptic Carlyle, 129; muscular Christianity, 119; Nordic supremacy, 128; on Manchester School, 122; on Rights of Man, 124; Regius Professor of History, 128; typical Victorian, 116

La Mennais, 154

Lawrence, D. H., 99

Locke, 44, 68, 80

Lovell, William, 240

Machiavelli, 204

Maine, 192, 295; against socialism, 271; attacks Austinian Sovereignty, 280; criticism of party government, 277; defects of method, 271; from status to contract, 269; gives new turn to Toryism, 279; historical method, 267; legal fictions, 268; on family in primitive societies, 268; on national-

INDEX

INDEX